the complete photo guide to

window
treatments

the complete photo guide to
window
treatments

Do-It-Yourself
Draperies, Curtains,
Valances, Swags,
and Shades

edited by Linda Neubauer

**Creative Publishing
international**

Minneapolis, MN

Creative Publishing international

Copyright 2007
Creative Publishing international
400 First Avenue North
Suite 300
Minneapolis, Minnesota 55401
1-800-328-3895
www.creativepub.com
All rights reserved

President/CEO: Ken Fund
Vice President Sales & Marketing: Peter Ackroyd
Executive Managing Editor: Barbara Harold
Senior Editor: Linda Neubauer
Photo Stylists: Joanne Wawra, Teresa Henn
Creative Director: Michele Lanci-Altomare
Senior Design Manager: Brad Springer
Photographers: Steve Galvin, Andrea Rugg, Peter Caley
Production Manager: Laura Hokkanen
Photo Researcher: Kathleen Stoehr
Illustrator: Deborah Pierce
Cover Design: Chad DeBoard
Page Design and Layout: Lois Stanfield
Sample Sewer: Teresa Henn

Library of Congress Cataloging-in-Publication Data
The complete photo guide to window treatments : do-it-yourself
draperies, curtains, valances, swags, and shades.
     p. cm.
Includes index.
  ISBN-13: 978-1-58923-294-5 (soft cover)
  ISBN-10: 1-58923-294-1 (soft cover)
  1. Draperies. 2. Draperies--Pictorial works. I. Creative Publishing
International. II. Title.
  TT390.C63 2007
  646.2'1--dc22   2006034243

Printed in China
10 9 8 7 6 5 4

Contents

Choosing a Style

WINDOW TREATMENTS HAVE tremendous impact on your home's décor. Considering how much space window treatments take up, their color and pattern have as much or more influence over the decorating scheme of the room as the furnishings, wall décor, and artwork. The ambiance of the room is reflected in the style of the window treatment, from casual fabric roller shades to formal pinch-pleated draperies, and lots of choices in between.

In the overall decorating budget, window treatments often cost more than the furniture, especially when the treatments are custom designed for you. You can reduce those costs by half if you make them yourself. You don't need professional sewing skills to get professional results. Even though some styles require long expanses of fabric, most window treatments are easily made with just straight seams and hems. Even complex looking pleated draperies are easy to make, following the directions and photos in this book.

The choices for DIY fabric window treatments include top treatments, curtains and draperies, and shades. Any of the designs in this book can be used alone, especially if a simple, casual look is what you want. Some shade styles—clouds, balloons, and hobbled—do very well on their own. Top treatments by themselves soften the window frame and add color and style. That might be your choice for a laundry room or over the kitchen sink. Most often top treatments are paired with shades, curtains, or draperies, where they not only embellish the look but hide clunky lift mechanisms or other hardware. The more layers there are in a window treatment, the more formal it becomes. Goblet-pleat draperies over sheer curtains might be your choice for a master bedroom. For your living room, you might choose flat Roman shades with rod-pocket side-panel curtains topped off with box-pleated valances.

Form

Like the rest of your home, your window treatments are a reflection of you and your favorite decorating style. There are styles to match any mood and décor—casual, fun, upbeat, contemporary, trendy, classic, formal, traditional—and hundreds of possible fabrics, rods, and trims to make your window treatments unique.

What length should you make your treatment? There are suggestions and examples for each style. In general, sill-length curtains are very casual, suitable for kitchens, bathrooms, and bedrooms. Floor-length, breaking on the floor, or puddling on the floor are all more formal. Use these lengths for the living room, dining room, or master bedroom. If your curtains are intended to open and close, however, avoid the puddles.

Function

Consider what you want your window treatments to do for the room. At the very least, they disguise the hard surfaces and angles of the windows with soft, graceful folds of fabric. Some treatments must block or screen the light that enters the room and provide privacy. These usually need to open and close by sliding back and forth on a rod or raising and lowering. If the treatment is simply decorative, it can hang over the top of the window frame, be drawn back to the side, or hang over the sides of the window frame. If the window is frequently opened and closed, choose a design that gives you easy access to the window.

For most of the treatments in this book, you have the choice of making them lined or unlined. Lining gives curtains, draperies, shades, and top treatments more body and protects the fabric from sun damage. It can also prevent light from shining through the fabric and making seams more visible. Of course, if sheer or semi-sheer curtains are what you have in mind, they should be unlined.

How to Use This Book

HERE ARE INSTRUCTIONS for fifty different styles of window treatments that you might use for your home. Some are classic styles that have stood the test of time and some are more contemporary and trendy. Photographs show each style in a variety of room settings with different fabrics, embellishments, and hardware. You'll see how decorators have approached common window shapes and locations as well as unique arrangements and sizes.

Once you have chosen a style, the step-by-step instructions will tell you how to construct it from beginning to end: measuring, cutting, sewing, and installing. It is a good idea to read all the instructions before you start. The "What you need to know" section will help with the planning; it covers information like what size to make the treatments, what types of fabric are suitable, and how and where to mount the hardware.

Also, before you start, read through "Window Treatment Basics" beginning on page 293. Its insights and tips will help you get professional results. You may not be familiar with some of the special terms used for window treatments, so these are explained in "Terms to Know" beginning on page 300. The terms appear in italics the first time they come up in a project.

Materials

Each project has a materials list of things you'll likely need to buy. The list doesn't tell you how much fabric to buy because that depends on the size of the window, the length of the treatment, and how far out to the sides of the window you want the treatment to go. The materials list assumes you already have on hand basic sewing supplies, such as pins, fabric shears, steel tape measure, carpenter's square for marking straight cutting lines, fabric marking pens or pencils, sewing machine and attachments, thread, iron, and pressing surface.

Cutting directions

Most window treatments are made from large rectangles or long lengths of fabric that are cut straight across the ends, with the length running parallel to the selvages. Often two or more widths of fabric must be sewn together. Cutting directions are set apart in each project to help you find the correct cut length of each piece and the total cut width. You simply multiply the cut length by the number of fabric widths needed to determine how much fabric to buy. Sometimes you have to draw a detailed diagram or make a pattern to find out how much fabric to buy and how to cut it. For those projects, the cutting directions are integrated into the first few steps and you have to complete them before you go shopping.

Take some time to check out all the top treatments, curtain and drapery styles, and shades, and then start planning your own window treatments. What a thrill it will be when you tell everyone you made them yourself!

Top
Treatments

Freeform Scarf Swags

A FREEFORM SCARF is an uninhibited spirit, draping effortlessly across a window frame and softening edges. A full-width, unshaped length of fabric, a freeform scarf can be sewn up in minutes. Depending on the fabric, the swag can be simple or elegant. You can choose to hang the treatment from either a decorative rod or wall-mounted swag holders.

Sheer on sheers (opposite)
This is the freeform scarf at its most elegant. It tops fabric/vane combination shades that look like sheer draperies when open and provide total privacy when closed. The swag's hemmed ends taper in gentle cascades to an elegant length just above the deep baseboard trim. Swags with such ample fullness can be sewn from extra-wide sheer fabric.

Royal treatment (top)
Deep eggplant purple velvet draws the eye upward and provides a striking contrast to the light green walls. The delicate glass-bead trim is simply draped along the lower edge—no need to stitch it on. Without this top treatment, the sheer draperies would have disappeared into the window frame, leaving an unnoticed corner of the room.

Unifying design (right)
Windows of two different heights are unified by a graceful freeform scarf swag. The swag also echoes the vaulted ceiling. It enhances rather than blocks it.

$\mathcal{W}$hat you need to know

You can **design** scarf swags with single or multiple swoops. For a formal look, plan the swag tails to break at or puddle on the floor. The sides of shorter, less formal scarf swags can fall to the same or different lengths, to the bottom of the window or to two-thirds or one-third the window length. Large, loose knots of fabric can be worked in at the upper corners or between swoops.

Lightweight, drapable **fabric** works best for scarf swags. If the fabric has neat narrow selvages, they can be used as the finished edges, eliminating the need to sew or fuse lengthy side hems. Reversible fabrics, such as sheers and many yarn-dyed solid-color fabrics, are recommended for short swags because you will catch glimpses of the wrong side at the inner edges of the tails. If you want to use a patterned fabric, avoid fabric with a one-way design, as the design will be upside down on one side of the window.

A scarf swag can be **mounted** on swag holders of various styles or on a decorative rod. If using swag holders, mount one at each side of the window, just above the window frame and even with the frame sides. If the swag has multiple swoops, mount an additional holder for each swoop. If using a rod, mount it just above the frame with the outer brackets even with the sides. It takes a bit of practice and patience to drape scarf swags the way you want them to look. Fanfolding the entire length of the swag beforehand makes styling easier.

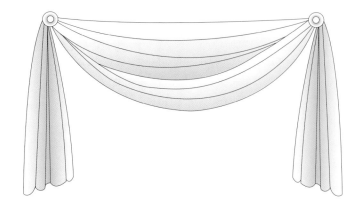

Materials

- Swag holders or decorative rod and brackets
- Tools and hardware for installation
- String
- Lightweight, drapable fabric, length determined in step 4
- Velcro strap or twill tape for bundling fabric and securing to holders or rod
- Safety pins
- Double-sided carpet tape, for securing swag to window frame or rod, optional

Making a single swag

1 Mount the swag holders or decorative rod. Drape a length of string over the rod or holders, following the line you want on the upper edge of the finished swag. (It may stretch straight across the top of the window or dip slightly.) Continue the string to the desired finished lengths at the sides. This will be the finished length on the upper edge of the swag.

2 Drape a second string over the rod or holders, dipping to the lowest points for the centers of the swags and falling to the desired finished lengths

at the sides. This will be the finished length of the lower edge of the swag. Mark both strings where they touch the pole or swag holders.

3 Measure and write down the lengths of the strings for each section. Measure the lengths shown on the diagram: 1 is from the long left point to the holder; 2 is from the long right point to the holder; 3 is the distance across the pole or between holders; and 4 is the length of the swoop between holders.

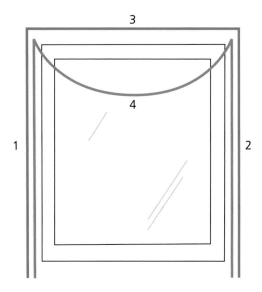

4 You will use the full width of the fabric. To find the *cut length* of the fabric, add measurements 1, 2, and 4 plus 2" (5 cm) for hems. For ends that puddle on the floor, add 15" (38 cm) for each puddle; for ends that just break at the floor, add 4" (10 cm) for each break.

5 If the selvages are neat and inconspicuous, the long edges do not need to be finished. Otherwise, trim off the selvages evenly, and turn under and stitch ½" (1.3 cm) double-fold hems on the long edges. Turn under and stitch ½" (1.3 cm) double-fold hems on the ends of the fabric length.

(continued)

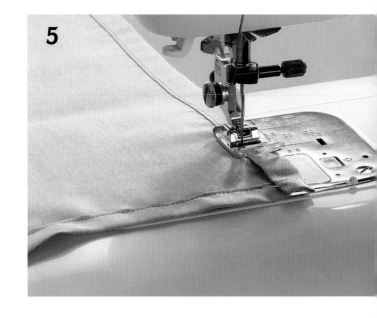

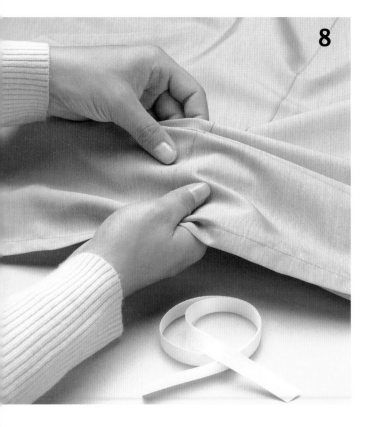

6 Measure from the left end of the fabric a distance equal to measurement 1; mark both selvages with a small safety pin. Repeat from the right end, measuring a distance equal to 2.

7 Subtract measurement 3 from 4; divide the result in half. Mark points on the upper edge of the center section this distance inward from the marks made in step 6. (The distance between points should equal measurement 3.) Draw light diagonal pencil or chalk lines from these points to the pin marks on the lower selvage.

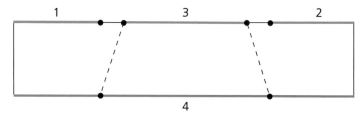

8 Fanfold the swag along the marked lines, keeping the number and depth of folds consistent; secure with a Velcro strap or twill tape.

9 Hang the swag over the rod or holders; tie or safety-pin it in place inconspicuously. If you want a straight upper edge, secure it to the rod or window frame with double-sided carpet tape.

10 Arrange the folds in the swag and down the sides. For ends that puddle on the floor, bundle and tie the swag end, flip it under, and arrange the swag around the bundle.

Making a swag with multiple swoops

1 Mount the hardware and drape two strings. If the swoops are evenly spaced and of equal depth, write down one measurement along the upper edge of the swoops and another measurement as the combined total of all the lower edges. Subtract the upper length from the lower length and divide the difference among the swoops; mark the upper and lower edges. If the swoops are spaced differently or are of different depths (diagram), take separate measurements for each swoop and mark as shown.

2 Mark the diagonal lines as in step 7 opposite. Fanfold and tie as in step 8. Hang and style the swag.

Making a swag with a knot

1 Mount the hardware and drape two strings as for single or multiple swoops. Allow 14" (35.5 cm) for each knot when calculating the total length of the fabric.

2 Determine the differences between the upper and lower edges. Mark light pencil lines across the fabric, leaving 14" (35.5 cm) spaces between lines if the swoops will be separated by a knot.

3 Fanfold along each marked line, keeping the number and depth of folds consistent; secure the folded bundles with Velcro straps or twill tape.

4 Tie the fabric between bundles into a large, loose knot over the rod or swag holder. Pin the bundles together inside the knot. If the treatment has multiple knots, begin in the center and work out toward each side.

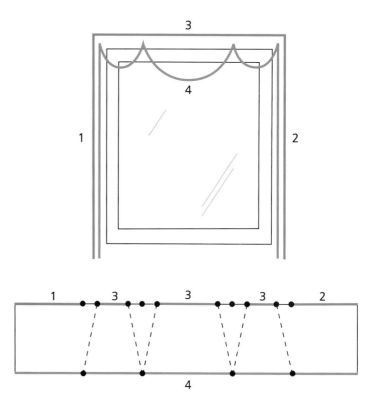

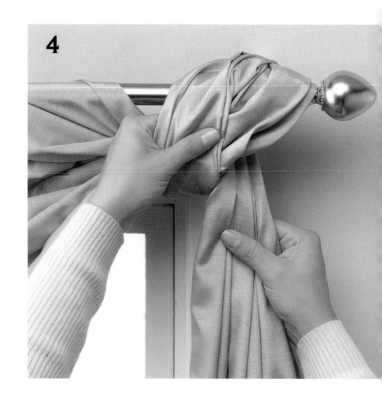

Bias Swags

A BIAS SWAG drapes in smooth, graceful folds. The fabric falls that way because it is cut with the true *bias* running through the center of the swag. Bias swags work particularly well in rooms with high ceilings. The drooping folds draw the eye from the top of the window down and then back up again.

The bias swag can look light and airy when made in semisheer fabric accented in beads that catch the light. For a traditional look, make a bias swag in medium-weight patterned fabric and trim with bullion fringe. A single swag for a small window is a lovely top treatment and easy to make. Even multiple bias swags are easy to construct because you make each swag individually and simply overlap them as you mount them.

Clever stripes (opposite)
The striped fabric in these swags, gently folding at an angle, was obviously cut on the bias. Draped well below the heading over tie tab curtains, the swags hide the gap between the top of the window and the decorative rod. The stripes are echoed in the upholstered cushions of the dining chairs, pulling the overall room design together.

Rich style (above)
The deep folds of these elegant bias swags, accented with long bullion fringe, are the perfect choice for this high-style interior. The majestic swag holders look like the tops of ancient columns.

Rings (left)
Overlapped at the center, these white satin bias swags are attached to a decorator pole with clip-on rings. The rings (which could also be sewn on) are an unexpected touch for a swag treatment.

What you need to know

Design this top treatment as a single swag or overlapping multiple swags. The pattern for the swag is made from one-fourth of a circle. The instructions that follow are based on a circle with a 42" (107 cm) radius and result in a swag that is 36" (91.5 cm) wide and 20" (51 cm) long at the center. Swags sewn this size can be a few inches narrower and longer or wider and shorter by varying the spacing between the rings on the pole. For larger swags, begin with a larger circle.

Make a swag with a soft, airy look, using semisheer decorator **fabric** for the outer fabric and the *lining*. For a more formal, traditional look, the swag can be made from a medium-weight decorator fabric and trimmed with a bullion fringe along the curved edges. Bias swags made from striped or plaid fabric can be very interesting.

To **mount** the swags, attach either clip-on or sew-on rings to the upper edge and slide the rings onto a decorator pole. To keep the rings from shifting, apply a small amount of floral adhesive clay or poster putty to the inside of each ring along the top. Hang swags over a traversing *undertreatment* on a rod with a deep enough *projection* to keep the swags from rubbing against the undertreatment as it moves. If the undertreatment is mounted on a utility rod, mount the pole for the swags high enough to hide the undertreatment's upper edge. Bias swags can also be mounted on the same rod as a stationary undertreatment.

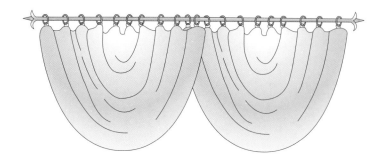

Materials (for one swag)

- Paper for making pattern
- Medium-weight decorator fabric
- Drapery lining
- 2 yd. (1.85 m) bullion fringe, optional
- Clip-on or sew-on drapery rings; 10 rings work well for hanging a single swag on a 36" (91.5 cm) pole
- Decorator pole
- Tools and hardware for installation
- Floral adhesive clay or poster putty

Making a pattern

1 Cut a 42" (107 cm) square of paper; fold it in half diagonally. Using a string and pencil, draw an arc between the square corner and the fold, marking the lower edge of the swag. Cut on the marked line through both layers.

2 Mark the folded edge 5" (12.7 cm) from the upper point. Draw a line from the mark to the opposite edges, perpendicular to the fold. Cut on the marked line.

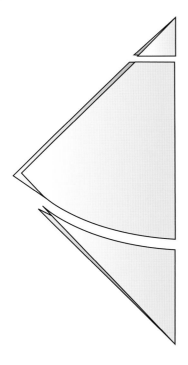

3 Fold under 2" (5 cm) on the long straight edges. At the lower edge, trim the area that is folded under, following the curve. Unfold the pattern.

(continued)

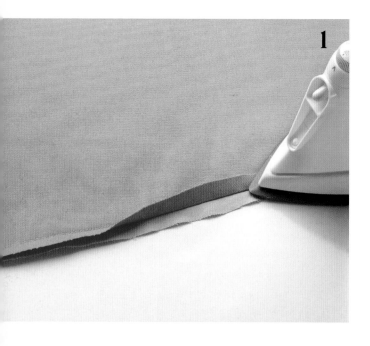

Cutting directions

- Cut one piece of decorator fabric and one piece of *lining*, using the pattern drawn on page 23. Align the straight edges of the pattern to the *lengthwise* and *crosswise grains* of the fabric. If you are cutting more than one swag, cut a single layer at a time for the most efficient use of the fabric.

Making a bias swag

1 Pin the decorator fabric and lining right sides together, along the curved edge. Stitch a $1/2$" (1.3 cm) seam; press the seam allowances open.

2 Turn the swag right side out. Press the curved edge.

3 Press under 1" (2.5 cm) twice on the long straight sides, folding the decorator fabric and lining together. Stitch close to the inner fold. Repeat at the upper edge. Apply fringe to the curved edge if desired.

4 Attach 10 drapery rings to the upper straight edges of the swag, positioning one ring at each end, one at each corner, and the remaining six rings evenly spaced between the ends and corners.

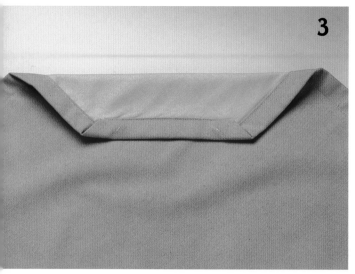

5 Hang the rings on a mounted decorator pole. Arrange the swag to the desired width and length. Arrange the swag into four deep, curving folds, pulling the fabric forward between rings. Pull the fabric between the center two rings forward.

6 Apply floral adhesive clay or poster putty to the inside of the rings, along the top, if necessary to keep the rings from shifting.

Overlapping swags

7 Atttach 18 rings to the upper straight edges of the swags as in step 4, opposite, overlapping the swags by one fold width, so the two center rings are attached to both swags.

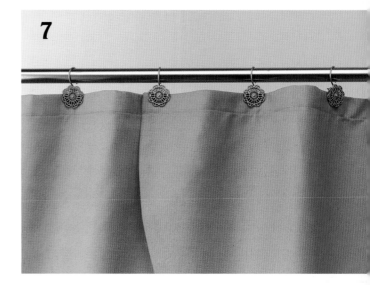

Tapered Scarf Swags

TAPERED SCARF SWAGS look like freeform scarf swags (page 14), but have a more precise drape with smooth, even folds and are lined for extra body. Used alone to punctuate the top of a window or as a complement to draperies or blinds, the versatile tapered scarf swag is suited for many décor styles. Depending on the fabric and hardware chosen, as well as the length of the tails, a tapered scarf can work in rooms as varied as a breakfast nook and a stately living room.

Peaked arch (opposite)
Wide, arched windows can be a tricky situation. This tapered scarf swag with multiple swoops that rise to a peak over a living room window pulls the window together. The dramatic treatment draws attention to the window without impeding the view. Decorative fringe and swag holders complete the look.

Simple elegance (top right)
Cotton jacquard decorator fabric turned infinitely elegant. Wedges cut from the fabric during construction allow effortless draping of the tapered scarf over holders into precise folds.

Casual print (bottom right)
Floral print fabric was draped through scarf rings to form this easy single swoop treatment. Because there are hidden seams at the points where the swag goes through the rings, a directional print like this can run upward on both tails.

What you need to know

Design swags that drape into a single swoop or into multiple swoops. The tails can stop just short of, break at, or puddle on the floor (the last is most formal). Shorter tails that come to the bottom of the window frame or to points two-thirds or one-third the window length have ends that angle up and in toward the window. In this method, the shaping of the swag is achieved by cutting wedges of excess *fullness* from a length of fabric at each point where the swag crosses a swag holder or pole. The swag is then constructed by sewing the angled pieces together and adding a *lining*.

This scarf swag uses the full width of the **fabric** and can be either self-lined or lined in a contrasting fabric. Nearly any decorator fabric can be used, from semisheer to brocade. Even one-way prints are suitable, because the direction of the fabric can be switched at a tail seam.

Holders for **mounting** the swags are available in several styles, including medallions and scarf rings; decorative tieback holders and holdbacks can also be used. A tapered swag with a single swoop can also be draped over a decorative pole. Mount the holders at the upper corners of the window frame and in any other desired locations before beginning the project, and measure for the treatment using twill tape.

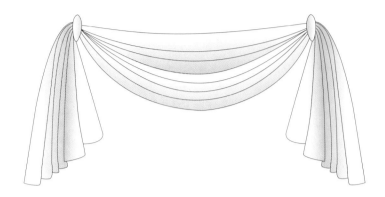

Materials

- Decorative swag holders (one holder at each upper corner of the window for a swag with a single swoop, and one holder for each additional swoop) or decorative pole
- Tools and hardware for installation
- Twill tape
- Decorator fabric for swag, length determined in step 1, page 28 for swag with single swoop or step 1, page 30 for swag with multiple swoops
- Matching or contrasting fabric for lining, length equal to decorator fabric
- Double-sided carpet tape, optional

Measuring for a single swoop

1 Mount the swag holders or decorative pole in the desired locations. Drape a length of twill tape over the holders or pole, extending to the desired length of the sides and stretching straight across the top of the window. This will be the finished length of the top and outer sides of the swag.

2 Drape a second length of twill tape over the holders or pole, extending to the desired

shortest points of the tapered sides and dipping to the lowest point desired at the center of the swoop. This will be the finished length of the bottom and inner sides of the swag. Mark both tapes at the holders or outermost points on the pole.

3 Measure and record the lengths of the tape for each section. Measurement 1 is from the long point to the holder or pole, 2 is from the short point to the holder or pole, 3 is the distance straight across between the holders or along the pole, and 4 is the length of the lower edge of the swoop.

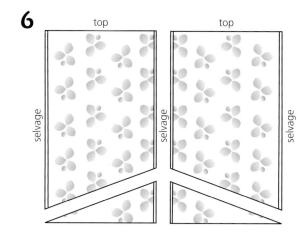

Sewing a single swoop

4 Cut the full width of the fabric, with the length equal to measurement 4 plus two times measurement 1 plus 3" (7.5 cm) for seam allowances. Measure from each end of the fabric a distance equal to 1 plus 1" (2.5 cm). Cut across the fabric perpendicular to the selvages at these points, to separate the end pieces from the center.

5 Turn one end piece completely around, if the fabric has a one-way design, so the upward direction on both ends points to the middle; when hung, the design will face in the correct direction on both ends. Label the top of each end piece.

6 Subtract measurement 2 from measurement 1. Mark a point on the inner edge of one end piece this distance from the lower cut edge. Draw a line from this point to the lower outside corner; cut away the triangular wedge. Repeat for the other end piece, cutting the angle in the opposite direction.

7 Subtract measurement 3 from measurement 4; divide this measurement in half. Mark a point on the top edge of the center piece this distance from one cut end. Draw a line from this point

(continued)

Top Treatments   **29**

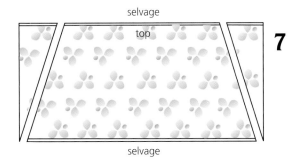

7

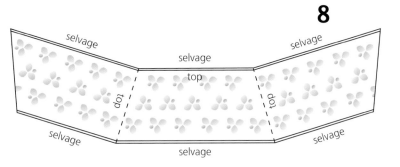

8

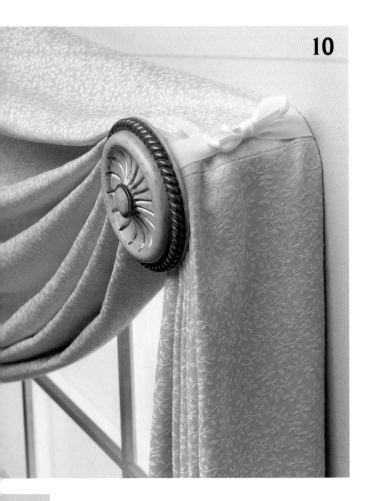

10

to the lower corner; cut away the triangular wedge. Repeat for the opposite cut end of the center piece.

8   Trim off the selvages. Cut the lining, using the swag pieces as patterns; label the tops of the lining pieces. Stitch the swag pieces together using ½" (1.3 cm) seams, easing the edges to fit; repeat for the lining pieces. Press the seam allowances open.

9   Pin the lining to the swag, right sides together. Stitch a ½" (1.3 cm) seam all around, leaving an opening along the center top for turning. Trim the corners diagonally. Press the lining seam allowance toward the lining.

10   Turn the swag right side out; press the seamed edges. Slipstitch the opening closed. Fanfold the swag along the seam lines, keeping the number and depth of folds consistent. Tie the folds with twill tape. Hang the swag through scarf rings or over medallion-style scarf holders or tieback holders. Or hang the swag over a pole, with the center swoop in front. Arrange the folds in the swag and sides. Remove the twill tape. If necessary, secure the fabric to the holder or pole inconspicuously, using double-sided carpet tape.

Measuring for multiple swoops

1   Mount the swag holders or pole in the desired locations. Drape a length of twill tape over the holders or pole, extending to the longest points of the tapered sides and stretching straight across the top of the window or pole. This will be the finished length of the top of the swag.

2   Drape a second length of twill tape over the holders or pole, extending to the shortest points of the tapered sides and dipping to the lowest point desired at the center of each swoop. This

will be the finished length on the bottom of the swag. Mark both tapes at the holders or at the attachment points on the pole.

3 Measure and record the lengths of the tape for each section. Measurement 1 is from the long point to the holder or pole. Measurement 2 is from the short point to the holder or pole. Measurement 3 is the distance straight across between the holders or along the pole. Measurement 4 is the total length of all the swoops between the end holders or end attachment points to the pole.

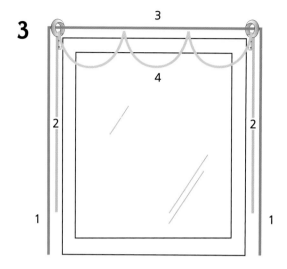

Sewing multiple swoops

4 Cut the full width of the fabric, with the length equal to measurement 4 plus two times measurement 1 plus 1" (2.5 cm) for each swoop plus an additional 2" (5 cm). Measure from each end of the fabric a distance equal to measurement 1 plus 1" (2.5 cm). Cut across the fabric perpendicular to the selvages at these points. Follow steps 5 and 6 on page 25.

5 Measure the length of the center piece; divide this measurement by the number of swoops in the swag. Mark the center piece into lengths of this size; cut the fabric perpendicular to the selvages at these points.

6 Subtract measurement 3 from measurement 4. Divide this measurement by the number of swoops in the swag; then divide this number in half. Mark a point on the top edge of one swoop piece this distance from one cut end. Draw a line from this point to the lower corner; cut away the triangular wedge. Repeat for the opposite cut end of the same piece. Cut identical wedges from each remaining swoop piece. Complete the swag as in steps 8 to 10, opposite.

Tailored Swags

IFFERENT FROM SCARF swags, the tailored version of this popular top treatment is more structured and has a formal pleated look. It is not formed at the window, but rather created with a muslin pattern to fit the window perfectly. This treatment is often designed in lavish layers of multiple, overlapping swags and coupled with floor-length pleated panels at the ends or with jabots (page 38) at the ends and between swags. Though they may appear to be a long sweep of fabric simply draped over a rod or board, in fact each swag and any side pieces are made separately and invisibly attached with staples or hook-and-loop tape. In traditional interiors, the jabots are usually placed behind the swag. Placing the tails in front makes the window appear narrower and taller.

Layers of swags (opposite)
Swags in alternating earth tones create drama but also softness for a master bedroom. The sheer, deep swag hung in back echoes the arched side window.

Traditional arrangement (top)
This opulent swag in rich red is board-mounted over full-length stationary side panels.

Many pieces (left)
Each piece of this treatment was made and attached separately. The lustrous ivory stripe fabric of the top swags was used to line the jabots, unifying the look.

*W*hat you need to know

Design your treatment with one swag or many, depending on the width of the window and your preference. Each swag should be no wider than 40" (102 cm). This size can be adapted to any window size by increasing or decreasing the overlapping of adjoining swags. A swag is usually 15" to 20" (38 to 51 cm) long at the longest point in the center. Shallower swags may be used on narrow windows.

Make the swag pattern from muslin or an old sheet that will drape softly. Drape the muslin and pin it at different positions until you find the look you like. For each swag, you will need 1 yd. (.95 m) of decorator **fabric** and *lining* if the draped tape measurement (step 1) is less than the fabric width; you will need 2 yd. (1.85 m) if the draped measurement is more than the fabric width.

Mount the swags to a cornice, mounting board, or decorative pole placed 4" (10 cm) above the molding if used alone, or about 4" (10 cm) above the drapery rod if used over draperies. The board or pole *return* must be deep enough to clear the underdrapery. In homes with beautiful moldings the swags may be mounted inside the window on a board that fits inside the frame, and there are no returns.

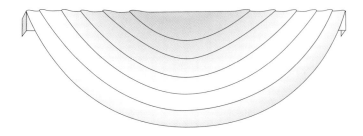

Materials

- Muslin or an old sheet for making pattern
- Decorator fabric
- Lining
- Mounting board, cornice, or decorative pole
- Heavy-duty stapler
- Tools and hardware for installation

Making the pattern

1 Drape a string to simulate the planned shape of the swag. For double swags, drape two strings. If the swag will go under the jabots, it usually

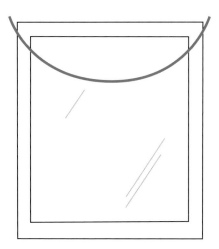

extends to within 2" (5 cm) of the ends of the mounting board.

2 Cut muslin for the swag pattern 36" (91.5 cm) long with the cut width equal to the measurement of the draped string plus 4" (10 cm). Draw a line 1" (2.5 cm) from the upper edge, and mark the desired finished width of the swag centered on the line. Centered on the lower edge, mark the measured length of the string. Connect the marks, forming diagonal guidelines. Divide each guideline equally into one more space than the number of folds; mark. For example, for five folds, divide each line into six spaces.

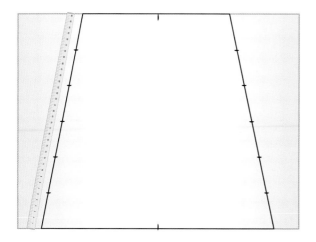

3 Pin the upper edge of the muslin to a padded surface, such as an ironing board, with the marked line along the front edge. Fold the muslin on the first mark of the diagonal line, and raise the fold to the top line, about 5" (12.7 cm) from the end; pin. Repeat on the opposite side.

4 Fold the muslin on the second mark of the diagonal line, and raise the fold to the top line, ½" (1.3 cm) outside the first fold. Repeat on the opposite side. Continue pinning the folds in place along the upper marked line.

(continued)

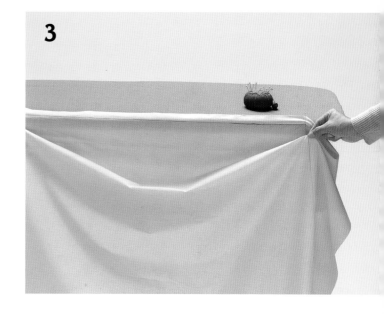

3

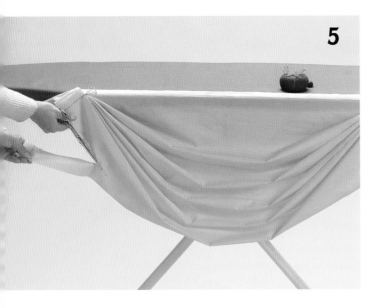

5 Adjust the pins and folds as necessary to achieve the desired appearance. Trim the excess fabric straight across, 1" (2.5 cm) from the upper edges. Trim the outer edge to about 3" (7.5 cm) from the last fold.

6 Unpin the folds. Fold the pattern in half lengthwise to check that the sides match; adjust the cutting lines as necessary. Use the pattern to cut the swag and lining. Add ½" (1.3 cm) seam allowance on the lower edge.

Making a Tailored Swag

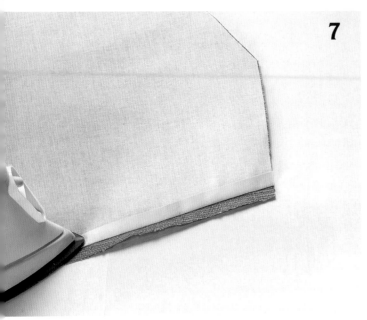

7 Pin the lining to the swag, right sides together, along the lower curved edge. Stitch the curved edge in a ½" (1.3 cm) seam. Press the lining seam allowance toward the lining. Turn the swag right side out; press the stitched edge.

8 Pin the swag front and lining together along the open edges. *Finish* the edges together by serging or zigzag stitching.

9 Fold the swag at the notch points and pin the folds in place along the upper edge, just as they were arranged when you made the pattern. Pin the upper edge of the swag to a padded surface to check the way it drapes. Make minor adjustments as needed. Remove the swag from the padded surface, keeping the folds pinned in place.

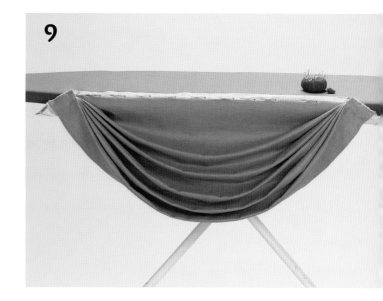

9

10 Stitch across all the folds at the upper edge.

11 Cut the mounting board to the correct length. Secure angle irons to the bottom of the mounting board, near the ends and at 45" (115 cm) intervals, using pan-head screws. Mount the board (page 296), centered above the window frame. Remove the screws that hold the mounting board to the angle irons, leaving the angle irons on the wall.

12 Center the swag on the mounting board with the edge of the swag 1" (2.5 cm) from the front edge of the board. Staple the swag to the board at 6" (15 cm) intervals.

13 Mount the swag by reattaching the board to the angle irons.

Jabots

THE JABOT (also known as a tail or cascade) is a decorative fabric drop that adds interest and beauty to a tailored swag treatment. It can be sleekly pleated or softly gathered, simple or ornately trimmed. Though a jabot sometimes looks like an extension or tail of the swag, it is a separate lined panel of fabric that is attached over or under the board-mounted or pole-mounted swag. Typically, jabots taper to a point, revealing a contrasting lining at the inner edge. A jabot is a vertical element that can visually balance the horizontal swag.

Walls of windows (opposite)
A long treatment of swags and jabots stretches across all these windows, tying them together while letting in lots of sunlight. The short contrasting jabots are made from shaped and pleated cylinders of fabric. Decorative hardware medallions add an elegant touch.

Corner treatment (top)
Tailored board-mounted swags with jabots in pristine white transform the corner of this dining room. Each asymmetrical treatment has the jabot in the corner. Plump Chinese ball knots add emphasis.

Odd numbers (left)
This photo shows part of a single treatment that spans two identical windows (another swag and long jabot complete the right side). In the design of window treatments, odd-numbered combinations (three, five, etc.) are best. Notice how this treatment was designed in combinations of five: five pleats on the shorter and longer jabots, as well as five swag folds. Coordinating tassels were added.

$\mathcal{W}$hat you need to know

Jabots can be **designed** in many styles, though most often they are knife-pleated with pleats turned outward. Jabots on the sides of the window are 9" to 11" (23 to 28 cm) wide and taper upward on the inner edge, revealing the contrasting *lining* on the underside of the pleats. Side jabots are usually mirror images of each other, though they can be different lengths to create asymmetrical effects. The jabot length should be about one-third of the drapery or window length, or should fall to the sill or floor. Its shortest inner point should be lower than the center of the swag. Jabots between swags taper upward from a center long point, which is usually shorter than jabots on the sides of the treatment. Jabots are also made in a variety of shapes resembling neckties or flared fabric cylinders. Some can be fashioned from simple squares, rectangles, or wedges of fabric that are *lined-to-the-edge*. Other jabots, such as the pleated cylinder shown on page 43, are created from a pattern.

Fabric used for the jabots in a treatment should be the same as the fabric used for the swags, if you want to create the illusion that they are one continuous piece. The lining should be a decorator fabric, either the same as the face fabric or a contrasting color.

Jabots are **mounted** to the board or pole either under or over the swag at the outer edges of the window treatment or between multiple swags in a treatment. When the treatment is mounted on a board or cornice, the jabot has *returns* that cover the ends of the cornice or mounting board.

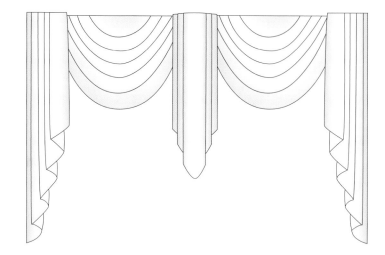

Materials

- Muslin or an old sheet for making pattern
- Decorator fabric
- Drapery lining
- Mounting board
- Heavy-duty stapler
- Tools and hardware for installation

Making side jabots

1 Cut muslin for the jabot pattern three times the finished width plus the return depth plus 1" (2.5 cm) for seam allowances. Cut the length 1½" (3.8 cm) longer than the desired finished length at the return. Mark a point on the lower edge the depth of the return plus ½" (1.3 cm). On the side opposite the return, mark the vertical edge 1½" (3.8 cm) longer than the desired shortest point. Connect the marks in a diagonal line. Cut out the pattern for the jabot.

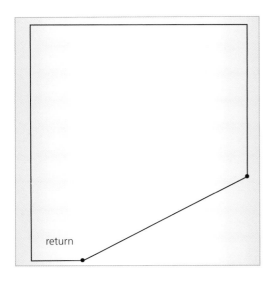

return

2 Place the jabot fabric and lining fabric right sides together. Cut out the jabot, using the pattern. Remove the pattern. Pin the layers together around the outer edge. Repeat for the jabot on the other side of the treatment, but flip the pattern so the jabots are mirror images (taper in opposite directions).

3 Stitch ½" (1.3 cm) seams on the sides and bottom. Trim the corners diagonally. Press the lining seam allowance away from the lining. Turn the jabot right side out and press. Repeat for the other jabot.

4 *Finish* the upper edges together by serging or zigzag stitching. Lay a jabot, lining side up, on a pressing surface. Fold under the long side the depth of the return and press the fold.

5 Turn the jabot right side up. Fold the jabot into evenly spaced pleats and press lightly. Pin the pleats along the upper edge. Stitch ½" (1.3 cm) from the upper edge to hold the pleats in place.

6 Repeat steps 4 and 5 for the other jabot, making sure the pleats are equal in size.

(continued)

5

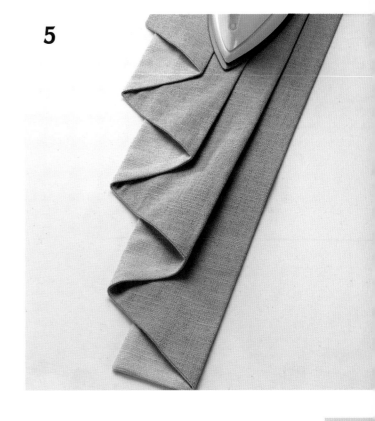

7 Staple the swag to the board (page 37), if the jabots will go over the swag. Place the top of one jabot at the end of the mounting board, with the upper edge 1" (2.5 cm) from the edge of the board and the pressed fold at the corner. Staple the return edge to the board. Position the pleats on the mounting board over the swag. Miter excess fabric at the corner and staple in place. Repeat for the second jabot. Or secure the jabots first and then staple the swag over them.

Making inner jabots

1 Cut muslin for the jabot pattern three times the finished width plus 1" (2.5 cm) for seam allowances. Cut the length 1½" (3.8 cm) longer than the desired finished length at the center. Mark a point at the center of the lower edge. Draw the vertical outer edges 1½" (3.8 cm) longer than the desired shortest points. Connect the marks in diagonal lines. Cut out the pattern for the jabot.

2 Using the pattern, cut one jabot and one lining piece. Place the jabot and lining right sides together. Stitch ½" (1.3 cm) seams on the sides and tapered lowered edge, pivoting at the center point on the bottom. Trim the corners diagonally. Press the lining seam allowance away from the lining. Turn the jabot right side out and press.

3 Finish the upper edges together by serging or zigzag stitching. Working from the center outward, fold the jabot into evenly spaced pleats and press lightly. There will be a box pleat at the center and knife pleats that point toward the outer edges. Pin the pleats along the upper edge. Stitch ½" (1.3 cm) from the upper edge to hold the pleats in place.

4 Staple the swag to the board (page 37). Staple the jabots to the mounting board, centered over the points where the swags meet.

Making cylinder jabots

1 Enlarge the pattern to the desired size and cut it out. For each jabot, cut two mirror-image pieces of the same fabric or of two contrasting fabrics (outer fabric and lining), using the pattern.

2 Align the straight outer edges of one piece, right sides together, and stitch a ½" (1.3 cm) seam, forming a cone. Press the seam allowances open. Repeat for the lining.

3 Pin the outer fabric and lining right sides together along the lower flared edge. Stitch a ¼" (6 mm) seam, pivoting at the point. Turn the jabot right side out and press the lower edge.

4 Align the upper edges of the outer fabric and lining and finish them together by serging or zigzag stitching.

5 Fold the jabot along the fold lines, including the long seam sewn in step 2. Press lightly. Baste across the top to hold the pleats in place. Staple the jabot in place over the swags.

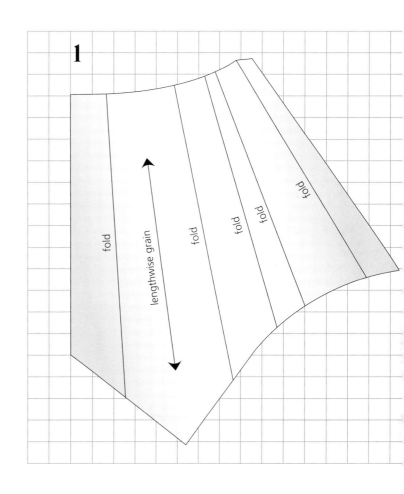

Flip Toppers

LAT FABRIC PANELS that flip over decorative rods are very easy to make, yet so many creative designs are possible. These toppers are simply lined-to-the-edge panels made with two contrasting or coordinating fabrics. The edges are often fringed, beaded, or banded. The panels can come to a point or other shape. For added interest, the topper can be secured with buttons or grommets with ties, though they usually stay in place just by flipping them over the rod.

Asian inspiration (opposite)

Bright botanical prints pop against the black background of this elegant, Asian-inspired treatment. Several individual flip toppers, including long end panels, were hung over a decorative rod at various heights.

Layers (top)

Three thin flip toppers that look like elegant bell pulls accented with gorgeous red and gold tassels are layered over a straight flip topper panel, turning a small library window into a focal point.

Triple bay (right)

Three triangle-point flip toppers mounted on pressure rods accentuate a bay window in this dining room. In each, you see the floral print of the top layer and the plain fabric of the lining. Fringe is silhouetted against the glass.

What you need to know

Because you first create a paper pattern, you can **design** your flip topper with straight, curved, or pointed lower edges—any shape imaginable. Sometimes a printed fabric design will offer inspiration for the topper shape.

Medium-weight to heavyweight decorator **fabrics** can be used for flip toppers; lightweight fabrics can be used for one side if they are opaque. If your topper must be wider than the standard decorator fabric width, look for fabric with a nondirectional print that can be *railroaded* to avoid unsightly vertical seams. A layer of *interlining* is sandwiched between the front and back fabrics to add body, prevent shadowing of printed designs, and give support for any buttonholes or grommets.

Mount a decorator rod just above the window or higher on the wall if you want to create the illusion that the window is higher. If there is an *undertreatment*, the flip topper should stand at least 2" (5 cm) in front of it. The sides of the flip topper should extend slightly beyond the window frame or undertreatment; there are no *returns* on flip toppers. If mounted between kitchen cupboards or inside deep window frames, plain pressure rods can be used.

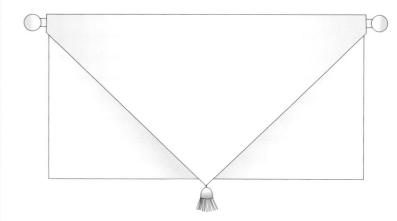

Materials

- Decorative curtain rod
- Tools and hardware for installation
- Wide kraft paper or newsprint for making pattern
- Two coordinating, firmly woven fabrics
- Drapery lining
- Paper-backed fusible adhesive, 3/8" (1 cm) wide
- Buttons or small grommets and ribbons or cording, optional

Making a flip topper

1 Mount the rod just above the window frame, with the finials extending just beyond the sides of the frame. Measure from bracket to bracket to determine the pattern width. Hang a tape measure over the rod to determine the pattern length, as shown in the diagram.

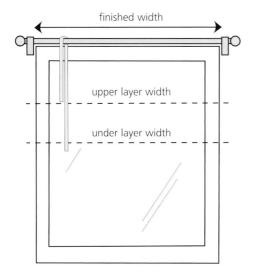

finished width

upper layer width

under layer width

2 Cut a paper pattern; shape the lower edges as desired. Hang the pattern over the rod to check the fit and shape. Draw a line where the pattern crosses the rod. Measure the total pattern length and buy equal amounts of two fabrics and lining. Preshrink all three fabrics if you intend to launder the topper.

(continued)

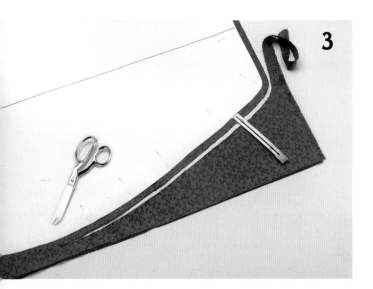

3 Pin the pattern over one of the fabrics. The outer edge of the pattern is the stitching line for the topper. Mark the cutting line on the fabric ½" (1.3 cm) beyond the pattern edge. Cut out the fabric. Remove the pattern.

4 Place the other fabric faceup over the interlining. Place the cut fabric facedown over both layers, aligning all grain lines. Pin the layers together around the edge of the cut fabric. Cut the other layers, leaving the pins in the fabric.

5 Stitch around the edge, using ½" (1.3 cm) seam allowances; leave a 10" (25.5 cm) opening for turning along one straight side. Clip the outer corners diagonally; clip up to, but not through, the stitching at inner corners and on curves.

6 Press the seam allowances open. Press back the seam allowances of the opening ½" (1.3 cm). Fuse a 10" (25.5 cm) strip of fusible adhesive over the seam allowance of the opening, following the manufacturer's directions.

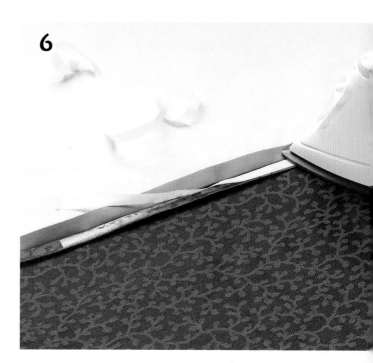

7 Turn the topper right side out through the opening; press. Remove the protective paper backing from the fusible adhesive strip; fuse the opening closed.

8 Fold the topper front down, using the line drawn on the pattern as a guide. If you are using buttons or grommets, mark the placement of any buttonholes or grommets. Sew buttonholes and cut them open. Or insert grommets, following the manufacturer's directions.

9 Refold the topper. Mark the placement for buttons or ties on the lower layer. Sew on buttons or ties. Flip the topper over the rod and secure.

Triangle Valances

THE TRIANGLE VALANCE, which hangs to a point like a kerchief, is casual, pretty, and easy to make. A square of decorator fabric is folded in half diagonally and stitched to make a self-lined triangle. The side points of the triangle are secured to the upper corners of the window, allowing the center to fall to a point in relaxed folds. A crystal, string of beads, or tassel can be dangled from the center point of the triangle.

Mini-triangles (opposite)
A chain of petite triangles adds a whimsical touch to a child's bedroom. Narrow ties in a smaller, coordinating plaid join the triangle corners and secure them to decorative rods with cute bows.

Straight-grain kerchief (right)
This striped triangle valance adds color and patterning to a dressing area.

$\mathcal{W}$hat you need to know

Designing a triangle valance is easy because the size is adjustable. For instance, a valance made from a 45" (115 cm) square will fit a window width of 36" to 45" (91.5 to 115 cm) simply by pulling up more or less fabric at the upper corners. Experiment with muslin or an old sheet. As an easy guide, begin with a square the same width as the window. The wider you make the valance, the longer it will be at the center, so for very wide windows, make a continuous valance of small triangles with overlapping ends.

Any **fabric** will work, though lightweight and medium-weight fabrics that drape softly work the best. Plaids can be dynamic when turned on point this way. If the fabric tends to let light through, *interline* the valance with drapery lining.

In the directions that follow, the valance is **mounted** by pulling the ends through small rings secured to hooks at the upper corners of the window frame. Triangle valances can also be mounted by tying the corners to a decorative rod or pulling them through rings at the ends of the rod.

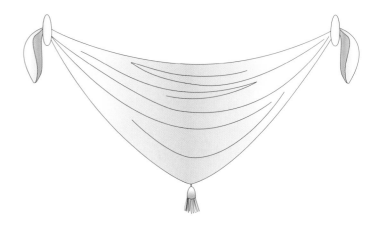

Materials

- Test fabric, such as muslin
- Decorator fabric
- Paper-backed fusible adhesive, $3/8$" (1 cm) wide
- Embellishment for center point, optional
- Metal rings, 1" (2.5 cm) diameter
- Cup hooks or tieback hooks
- Tools and hardware for installation

Making a triangle valance

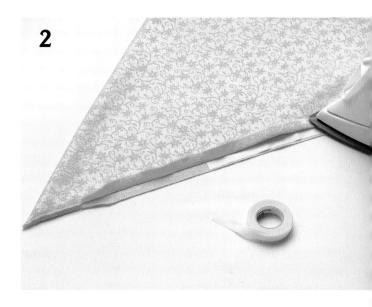

1 Cut a square of decorator fabric, using a carpenter's square to ensure right angles and equal sides. Fold the square in half diagonally, right sides together. Stitch ½" (1.3 cm) from the cut edges, leaving a 6" (15 cm) opening for turning.

2 Taper the seam allowances at the narrow points; trim diagonally across the square corner. Press the seam allowances open. Press back the seam allowances of the opening ½" (1.3 cm). Fuse a 6" (15 cm) strip of fusible adhesive over one seam allowance of the opening, following the manufacturer's directions.

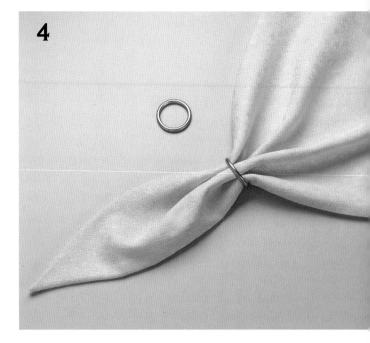

3 Turn the valance right side out through the opening; press the seamed edges. Do not press the bias fold. Remove the protective paper backing from the fusible adhesive strip; fuse the opening closed. Stitch an embellishment to the center point, if desired.

4 Insert the side points of the valance through metal rings. Test the fit by holding the valance up to the window; adjust the amount of fabric pulled through the rings, if necessary. Hand-tack the valance to the rings. Hang the rings on cup hooks or tieback hooks installed at the upper corners of the window frame.

Lined Rectangle Valances

*L*INED RECTANGLE VALANCES are simply a length of fabric lined-to-the-edge with the same or contrasting fabric. Many different looks can be created by changing the dimensions of the rectangle or the way the valance is hung, either clipped to a decorative rod or stapled to a mounting board. The valance can have sleek, straight lines or lots of dips and curves. The simplest version, taught in the steps that follow, is merely draped flat over a mounting board, much like a short tablecloth. Add your choice of trims to make your treatment unique: think about beaded edging, brush fringe, or tassels.

Ripples (opposite)
A long, narrow, self-lined rectangle in subtle earth tones is attached to the rod with rings at evenly spaced intervals, unifying this casual sitting area. The rippled effect is created simply by pulling the fabric forward between rings.

Quick and easy (top)
This purple rectangle valance, lined in pale blue, is accented with beads and tassels and draped from decorative finials. Though quick and easy to make, it pulls together the bathroom color scheme without overpowering the small space.

Mock swag (left)
Styled to look like a soft swag, this board-mounted lined rectangle softens this dormer window. Delicate beaded edging accents the slight curve and box-pleated corners.

*W*hat you need to know

Sketch your **design** and measure the window to plan the dimensions of the valance. In the directions that follow, a simple kerchief valance is stapled to a mounting board so the face and sides hang to the same length. The corners fall to soft rounded points. For this *self-lined* valance, a long rectangle of fabric is folded in half lengthwise and seamed on the sides and top to encase the raw edges. Thus, the same fabric forms the face of the valance as well as the *lining*. *Interlining* gives the valance more body and prevents show-through on patterned fabrics.

The right **fabric** depends on the way you intend to style your valance. Choose medium-weight, drapable fabric for a relaxed look. Choose a firmly woven fabric that is slightly stiff to create more rigid dips and curves. To avoid distracting seams in this valance, select a fabric that can be *railroaded*, such as a solid color or a print that can be turned sideways.

Plan to **mount** the board just above the window frame, 1" (2.5 cm) beyond the frame on the sides. This will allow room to install the board, using angle irons at the ends. If your valance will be hung from a rod, decide whether or not you want the window frame to show and install the rod accordingly.

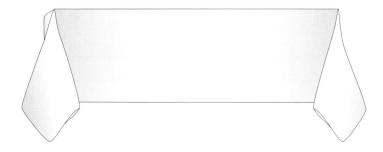

Materials

- Mounting board
- Tools and hardware for installation
- Decorator fabric
- Drapery lining for interlining the valance
- Heavy-duty stapler

Cutting directions

Railroad the fabric to eliminate the need for seams.

- The *cut length* (vertical) of the fabric equals twice the drop length plus twice the mounting board *projection* plus 1" (2.5 cm).

- The *cut width* (horizontal) of the fabric equals the length (end to end) of the mounting board plus twice the drop length of the valance plus 1" (2.5 cm).

- Cut the interlining the same width and exactly half the length of the valance fabric.

Making a lined rectangle valance

1 Cut the board and cover it with fabric. Mount the board (page 296), centered above the window frame. Remove the board, leaving the angle irons on the wall.

2 Place the interlining over the wrong side of the valance panel, aligning the sides and upper edge. Baste within the ½" (1.3 cm) seam allowance.

3 Fold the valance right sides together, aligning the long edges and sides. Stitch ½" (1.3 cm) seams at the ends and the upper edge. Leave an opening along the upper edge for turning the valance right side out.

4 Trim the corners diagonally to within ⅛" (3 mm) of the stitching. With the interlining side down, press the seam allowances open.

5 Turn the valance right side out and press. Stitch the opening closed.

6 Center the valance over the mounting board, aligning the upper edge of the valance to the back of the board. Staple the valance to the mounting board, inserting the staples near the back of the board. Begin in the center and work toward the ends, spacing the staples 4" to 6" (10 to 15 cm) apart.

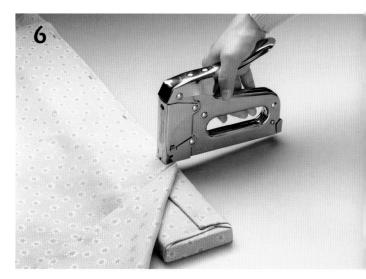

7 Mount the valance on the angle irons, replacing the screws in their original holes. Adjust the front corners of the valance to fall in gently rounded folds.

Butterfly and Stagecoach Valances

THESE VALANCES are made of folds of fabric held up with tabs or straps. They look as if they could be lowered, but they are stationary treatments. A butterfly valance has fanfolded fabric that droops in the center and flares at the sides. A stagecoach valance is rolled up from the bottom around a wooden dowel or PVC pipe and tied in place with straps.

Softly elegant (opposite)
In these gray-green butterfly valances, wide contrasting tabs hold the fanfolded fabric in place, allowing the lower edges to swag gently.

Setting the stage (top right)
This butterfly valance spans a deep-set window over a buffet. The mounting board for the valance projects out from the window frame far enough so that it doesn't interfere when the shade behind it is raised and lowered.

Inside-mount stagecoach (bottom right)
Contrasting lining draws attention to the rolled bottom of this inside-mounted stagecoach valance. Straps tied under the roll are cut from a striped fabric that coordinates with the floral print.

What you need to know

Butterfly and stagecoach valances can be **designed** slightly longer than most valances because of the visual weight at the lower edge. They are usually mounted outside the window frame but can be mounted inside if the casing is deep enough. For the instructions that follow, the butterfly valance is styled with *returns*. The stagecoach valance has no returns and is suitable for an inside mount or as a shallow outside-mounted valance. The straps for the butterfly valance are one continuous length. The stagecoach valance straps are two pieces that tie under the rolled fabric.

Medium-weight decorator **fabric** is suitable for either style of valance. Contrasting fabrics and companion prints are perfect for *lining* the stagecoach and for the straps on either style. *Underlining* gives the valance more body and prevents show-through when patterned fabrics are used.

Mount a stagecoach valance on a 1 × 2 board, whether it will be installed inside or outside the frame. Mount a butterfly valance on a mounting board that will project out from the window frame far enough to clear any existing treatment by 2" to 3" (5 to 7.5 cm). The length of the mounting board should be 2" (5 cm) wider than the window frame or 4" (10 cm) wider than any existing blinds or curtains.

Materials

- Mounting board
- Tools and hardware for installation
- Decorator fabrics for valance and straps
- Plain lining for butterfly valance; decorative lining for stagecoach valance
- Heavy-duty stapler
- 1³/₈" (3.5 cm) wooden dowel or PVC pipe, cut to finished width of valance
- Masking tape

Cutting directions

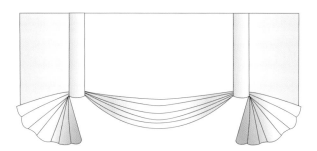

Butterfly valance

- The *cut length* of the fabric and lining is equal to the finished length (at the straps) plus 25" (63.5 cm).

- The *cut width* of the fabric and lining is equal to the finished width plus twice the *projection* of the mounting board plus 1" (2.5 cm). Piece full and partial fabric widths together as needed to obtain the cut width.

- For two straps with a finished width of 1¹/₂" (3.8 cm), cut two pieces 4" (10 cm) wide and twice the finished length plus 4" (10 cm).

Stagecoach valance

- The cut length of the fabric and lining is equal to the finished length plus 14" (35.5 cm).

- The cut width of the fabric and lining is equal to the finished width plus 1" (2.5 cm). Piece full and partial fabric widths together as needed to obtain the cut width.

- For each strap, cut two fabric strips the full width of the fabric, with the cut width equal to the finished strap width plus ½" (1.3 cm).

Making a butterfly valance

1 Cut the board and cover it with fabric. Secure angle irons to the bottom of the mounting board, near the ends and at 45" (115 cm) intervals, using pan-head screws. Mount the board (page 296), centered above the window frame. Remove the screws that hold the mounting board to the angle irons, leaving the angle irons on the wall.

2 Seam fabric widths together, if necessary. Pin the outer fabric and lining right sides together. Stitch a ½" (1.3 cm) seam around the sides and lower edge; leave the upper edge unstitched.

3 Trim the lower corners diagonally. Press the lining seam allowance toward the lining. Turn the valance right side out, and press.

(continued)

3

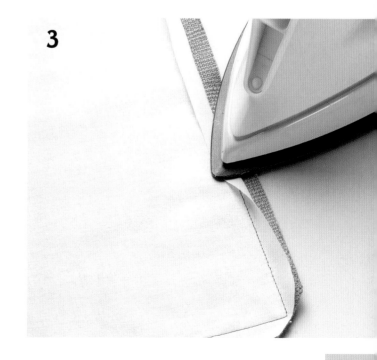

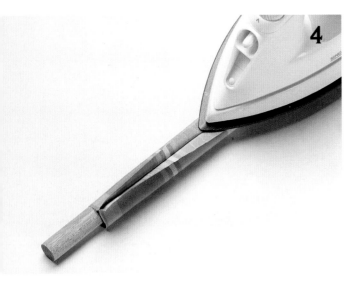

4 Fold one strap piece in half lengthwise, right sides together. Stitch a ½" (1.3 cm) seam along the long edge. Press the seam allowances open with the tip of the iron, taking care not to crease the fabric folds. Turn the strap right side out, centering the seam on the back; press. Repeat for the second strap.

5 Mark the location for the straps, 6" to 10" (15 to 25.5 cm) from each end, depending on the width of the valance. Pin one end of a strap, right side up, to the top of the valance at each mark.

6 Wrap the straps under the bottom of the valance. Pin the loose end of each strap in place on the lining side of the valance, raw edges even.

7 Stitch the outer fabric and lining together along the upper edge of the valance, catching the straps in the stitching. *Finish* the raw edges together, using zigzag stitches or by serging.

8 Mark lines on top of the mounting board 1" (2.5 cm) from the front and sides. Center the valance on the board, with the upper edge of the valance along the marked line. Staple the valance in place at 2" (5 cm) intervals. Apply two staples at each strap.

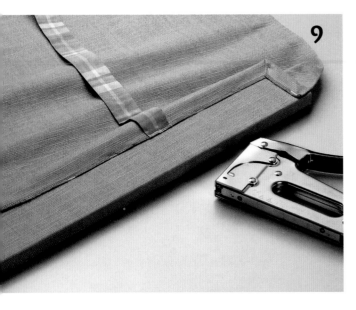

9 Wrap the sides of the valance around the ends of the mounting board, with the upper edges along the marked lines. Miter the corners. Staple the sides in place.

10 Mount the valance by reattaching the board to the angle irons.

11 Fanfold the lower 24" (61 cm) of the valance into five or six pleats, with the bottom fold turned under. Slip the straps under the folds.

12 Pull the folds down into a gentle swag. Adjust the folds near the straps.

Making a stagecoach valance

1 Follow steps 1 to 3 for the butterfly valance. Stitch the outer fabric and lining together along the upper edge of the valance. Finish the raw edges together, using zigzag stitches or by serging.

2 Fold a strap in half lengthwise, right sides together. Stitch the long edge and one short end, using ¼" (6 mm) seam allowances. Trim the corners diagonally. Turn the strap right side out and press, with the long seam on an outer edge. Repeat for all the straps, preparing two straps for each location.

3 Mark the locations for the straps at the top of the valance. Staple the valance to the mounting board, lapping the upper edge of the valance 1½" (3.8 cm) onto the top of the board. Do not place staples at the markings for the straps.

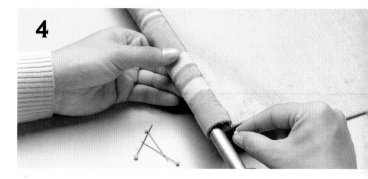

4 Center the dowel or PVC pipe on the right side of the valance at the lower edge; tape it in place. Roll up the valance to the desired finished length, and pin it to keep it from unrolling.

5 Sandwich the valance between two straps at each placement mark. Tie the ends under the rolled pole and adjust the length of the straps from the upper edge. Staple the straps to the board. Trim off any excess length at the top.

6 Mount the valance by reattaching the board to the angle irons. Hand-tack the rolled fabric to the front straps, catching only the back layer of fabric on the straps. Remove the pins that were preventing the fabric from unrolling.

Rod-Pocket Valances

ONE OF THE PRETTIEST toppers is the rod-pocket valance, with fabric gathered along a rod. With a wide heading and lots of fullness, a rod-pocket valance creates a feminine look just right for a little girl's room or powder room. The trend, though, is toward a short or no heading and less fullness. With this approach, the treatment will work in many rooms and décor styles.

No heading (opposite)
With a wide pocket and no heading, this rod-pocket valance looks less feminine.

Satin-stitched hem (top)
Green scalloped satin stitching edges the bottom of this sweet rod-pocket valance.

Turning corners (left)
The rod has been bent to follow the angle of this bathing alcove. The treatment softens the stark look of the privacy shades, and decorative beaded edging adds interest.

What you need to know

The rod pocket is the portion of the valance where the rod or pole is inserted; stitching lines at the top and bottom of the rod pocket keep the rod in place. To find the depth of the rod pocket, measure around the widest part of the rod; add 1/2" (1.3 cm) to this measurement, and divide by 2. The heading of a rod-pocket valance is the optional extension at the top that forms a ruffle when the valance is on the rod. The depth of the heading is the distance from the top of the finished valance to the top stitching line of the rod pocket.

Rod-pocket **designs** vary depending on the rod or pole used, whether or not there is a heading and how deep it is, and the *fullness* of the style. In the directions that follow, the valance is *lined* to add body and prevent light from showing through. For a lightweight, airy feeling, however, the lining can be left out.

Sheer, semisheer, lightweight, and medium-weight **fabrics** can be used. Generally, the lighter the fabric, the more fullness the valance can have, from triple fullness for sheer fabrics to one-and-one-half times fullness for a casual look with medium-weight fabric.

Several types of rods can be used for **mounting** rod-pocket valances, including flat rods in widths of 1", 2 1/2", and 4 1/2" (2.5, 6.5, and 11.5 cm). Wood and metal pole sets with elbows or finials can also be used and are available in several diameters. On a pole with elbows, the sides of the valance return to the wall. When a pole with finials is used, *returns* can be created at the sides of the valance by stitching an opening in the front of the rod pocket for inserting the pole.

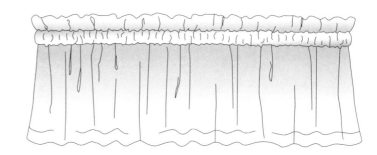

Cutting directions

- The *cut length* of each valance piece is equal to the finished length (from the underside of the rod to the hem) plus twice the rod-pocket depth plus twice the heading height plus 4 1/2" (11.5 cm).

- The *cut width* of the valance is equal to the rod length plus twice the *projection* of the rod, multiplied by the amount of fullness desired, usually two to two-and-one-half times. After calculating the full cut width, divide this number by the fabric width and round to the nearest number of full and half widths to piece together.

- The *lining* should be cut the same width as the decorator fabric but 3" (7.5 cm) shorter.

Making a rod-pocket valance

1 Seam fabric widths together, if necessary, adding any half widths at the sides. If an even number of full widths are needed, divide one in half lengthwise and add a half width to each side of the center full width to avoid a seam in the center of the valance.

```
            heading
            rod pocket
side seam                              side seam
    seam                        seam

            bottom hem
```

2 Press under the lower edge 4" (10 cm) for the hem. Then unfold the pressed edge and turn the cut edge back, aligning it to the pressed fold line. Press the outer fold. Refold the lower edge, forming a 2" (5 cm) double-fold hem. Stitch, using a blindstitch or straight stitch.

3 Follow steps 1 and 2 for the lining, pressing under and stitching a 1" (2.5 cm) double-fold hem in the lining.

4 Pin the valance panel and lining panel wrong sides together, matching the raw edges at the sides and upper edge. Trim any excess at the sides so the panels are the same width. At the bottom, the lining panel will be 1" (2.5 cm) shorter than the valance panel. Press and stitch 1" (2.5 cm) double-fold side hems, handling the decorator fabric and lining as one fabric.

(continued)

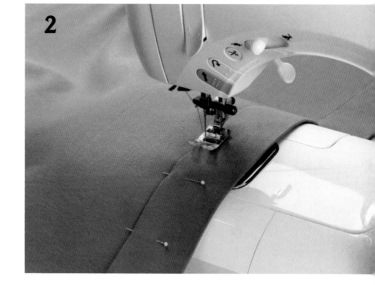

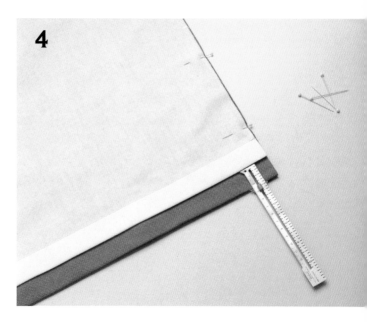

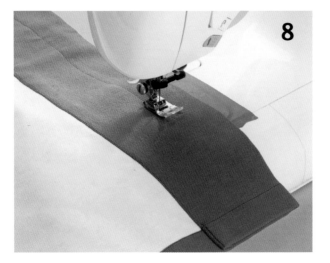

5 Press under ½" (1.3 cm) on the upper edge. Then press under an amount equal to the rod-pocket depth plus the heading depth. If the valance will be mounted on a pole with elbow returns, omit steps 6 and 7.

6 Measure the distance from the wall to the center of the pole. Unfold the upper edge of the valance. On the right side of the fabric, measure from the side of the valance a distance equal to this measurement; mark at the center of the rod pocket.

7 On the right side of the panel, stitch a buttonhole at the mark, from the top to the bottom of the rod pocket. Refold the upper edge of the panel along the pressed lines; pin.

8 Stitch close to the first fold; stitch again at the depth of the heading, using tape on the bed of the sewing machine as a stitching guide.

Installing a rod-pocket valance

Pole with wooden brackets and finials.
Remove the finials; insert the pole into the rod pocket with the ends of the pole extending through the buttonholes. Reattach the finials; mount the pole. Secure the return to the wooden bracket, using self-adhesive hook-and-loop tape.

Pole with keyhole bracket and finials.
Remove the finials; insert the pole into the rod pocket with the ends of the pole extending through the buttonholes. Reattach the finials. Insert the attachment screw through the fabric and into the back of the pole. Mount the pole by securing the screw in the keyhole. Attach a pin-on ring to the inner edge of the return, and secure it to a cup hook or tenter hook in the wall.

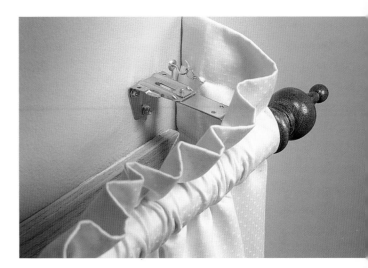

Pole with elbows.
Insert the pole through the rod pocket; pull the curtain back to expose the small attachment screws. Mount the pole on the brackets. Slide the curtain over the brackets.

Shaped Rod-Pocket Valances

A SOFT, CASUAL TREATMENT, the shaped rod-pocket valance forms a graceful arch. The curved hemline tapers into side tails. This version of a rod-pocket valance is lined-to-the-edge with a contrasting decorator fabric, which peeks out subtly along the lower edge. Shaped rod-pocket valances are often used over blinds or pleated shades to hide the top mechanism and soften the look. They are impressive when layered over floor-length draperies.

Lush and fringed (opposite)
Deep bullion fringe accents shaped hems in this formal sitting area. Without headings, the valances are more formal, yet their gathers soften the hardness of the louvered shutters.

Soft and feminine (left)
This shaped valance creates the perfect setting for a daybed. The modest heading adds frill without being excessive.

$\mathcal{W}$hat you need to know

The **design** most often seen is a single arch, with a center drop of one-third the window length and sides that extend down two-thirds the window length. For a narrower window, keep the arch relatively small to enhance and yet downplay the size. There can also be multiple small arches across a wider window. The tails can extend to the bottom of the window or even to the floor. The contemporary approach is a *fullness* of 1½ to 2 times the width of the window with short or no *headings*. The higher the heading, the more frilly and feminine the treatment will appear.

Lightweight and medium-weight decorator **fabrics** work best for both the face fabric and the *lining*.

Mount the valance on a 1" or 2½" (2.5 or 6.5 cm) utility curtain rod, as the fabric will completely cover the rod. You can also use a wooden pole.

Materials

- Decorator fabric for outer valance
- Chalk or removable marking pen
- Decorator fabric for lining
- Curtain rod or wooden pole
- Tools and hardware for installation

Cutting directions

- The *cut length* of each valance and lining piece is equal to the finished length at the longest point (from the underside of the rod to the hem) plus twice the rod-pocket depth plus twice the heading height plus 1" (2.5 cm).

- The *cut width* of the valance and lining is equal to the rod length plus twice the *projection* of the rod, multiplied by the amount of fullness desired, usually two to two-and-one-half times. After calculating the full cut width, divide this number by the fabric width and round to the nearest number of full and half widths to piece together.

- The cut length for the short center section of the valance is equal to the finished length at the shortest point plus twice the rod-pocket depth plus twice the heading height plus 1" (2.5 cm). This measurement is needed in step 1, opposite.

Making a shaped rod-pocket valance

1 Seam the fabric widths as necessary. Divide the valance panel into thirds and mark. Fold the valance in half lengthwise; mark the cut length for the center portion from the fold to the one-third marking. Measure and mark the depth of the *return* at the side. Draw a straight line from the return mark to the one-third marking at the center length.

2 Round the upper corner at the one-third marking and the lower corner at the return, using a dinner plate or saucer as a guide. Pin the fabric layers together. Cut along the marked lines. Cut the lining panel, using the valance panel as a pattern.

3 Place the valance and lining panels right sides together. Stitch around the sides and lower edge in a 1/2" (1.3 cm) seam, leaving the upper edge open.

4 Press the lining seam allowances toward the lining. Clip the seam allowances at the curves, and trim the corners at the returns diagonally.

5 Turn the valance right side out; press the seamed edges. Press the upper edge under 1/2" (1.3 cm), folding both layers as one. Then press under an amount equal to the rod-pocket depth plus the heading depth. Stitch close to the first fold. Stitch again at the depth of the heading, using tape on the bed of the machine as a stitching guide.

6 Insert the curtain rod through the rod pocket; install the rod on the brackets. Distribute the fullness evenly along the rod.

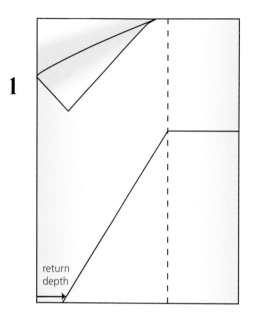

1

return depth

2

4

Gathered Pickup Valances

A GATHERED PICKUP valance looks quite complicated but is actually fairly easy to sew. It begins as a flat, lined rectangle with a rod pocket and heading. At evenly spaced intervals, vertical rows of tucks are sewn into the valance, drawing the lower section of the valance up into graceful bells. The fabric between the bells falls into gentle swags. Welting at the lower edge accents and supports the curves of the bells and swags. A contrasting fabric, used to line the valance, peeks from the inside of each bell.

Kingston (opposite)
A gathered pickup gives much the same look as this more complicated Kingston valance, which has graceful swags tucked up under box pleats. A Kingston valance requires a commercial pattern.

Rod-pocket pickup (top right)
A flat rectangle of fabric takes on a totally different look when gathered onto a rod and drawn up in bells. Fabric-covered welting emphasizes the undulating lower edge.

Board-mounted pickup (bottom right)
Matching valances above the sink and over the patio door tie the two areas of the room together.

What you need to know

When planning the **design** of the valance, work with enough full and half widths of fabric to equal about two-and-one-half times *fullness*. Bells are positioned at each seam and at each midpoint between seams. Though you usually shouldn't position prominent details of a window treatment at seams, this pattern of placement coincides with the placement of large motifs in most decorator fabrics, allowing the main motifs to fall in the center of each swag.

The valance hangs straight down at the *returns* to a length that is about 6" (15 cm) longer than the center of each swag. The shortest point at the back of each bell is about 2" (5 cm) shorter than the swags.

Medium-weight decorator **fabrics** work well for this valance. To add body and a slightly padded appearance, *interline* the valance with flannel. Select contrasting fabric for the *lining* and for the fabric-covered welting.

Mount the valance on a plain narrow pole with elbows or a utility rod just above and to the outside of the window frame.

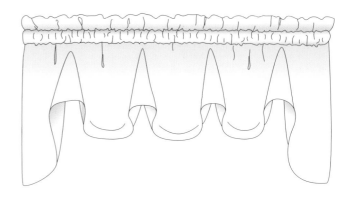

Materials

- Decorator fabric for valance
- Decorator fabric for contrasting lining
- Fabric-covered welting, twisted welting, or $1/2$" (1.3 cm) filler cord and fabric for making fabric-covered welting
- Flannel interlining, optional
- Curtain rod
- Tools and hardware for installation

Cutting directions

- The *cut length* of the valance fabric is equal to the finished length at the side (from the underside of the rod to the hem) plus twice the rod-pocket depth plus twice the *heading* height plus 1" (2.5 cm).

- The *cut width* of the valance is equal to the rod length plus twice the *projection* of the rod, multiplied by two-and-one-half times fullness. After calculating the full cut width, divide this number by the fabric width and round to the nearest number of full and half widths to piece together.

- Cut the fabric for the contrast lining to the same length and width as the valance fabric.

- If interlining is desired, the cut width of the interlining fabric is equal to the total width of the valance fabric after seaming. The cut length of the interlining fabric is equal to the finished length of the valance. If possible, *railroad* the interlining to avoid seams.

- Cut *bias* fabric strips if making fabric-covered welting, following step 1 on page 299.

- In fabrics with large motifs, one complete vertical repeat will have two rows of motifs with staggered placement. One row will have two full motifs, while the second row will have one full motif in the center and two halves of another motif matching at the selvages. Cut the valance pieces with the primary motifs in the lower 12" to 15" (30.5 to 38 cm), so they will be more visible in the finished valance.

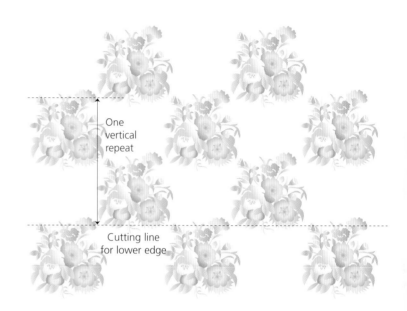

One vertical repeat

Cutting line for lower edge

Making a gathered pickup valance

1 Seam the valance fabric widths together. Repeat for the lining. Check to see that the valance and lining are exactly the same size.

2 Make fabric-covered welting (page 299), if desired, and stitch it to the lower edge of the valance; begin and end the welting ½" (1.3 cm) from the side edges. Alternatively, attach purchased welting. For a valance without interlining, omit step 3.

3 Seam the interlining, if necessary. Pin the interlining to the wrong side of the lining at the sides, with the lower edge of the interlining ½" (1.3 cm) above the lower edge of the lining. Baste within the ½" (1.3 cm) seam allowances on the sides.

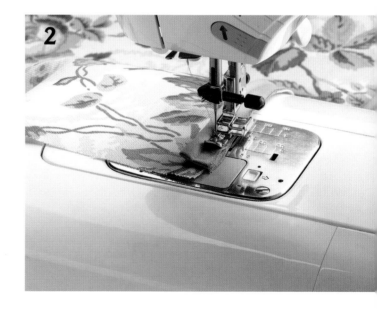

(continued)

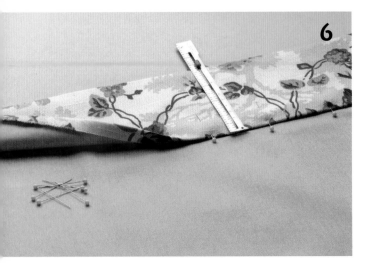

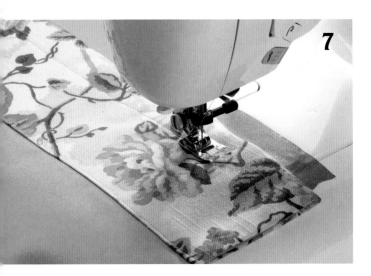

4 Place the valance and lining right sides together, matching the raw edges; pin along the sides and lower edge. Stitch ½" (1.3 cm) seams on the sides and lower edge, using a zipper foot and stitching with the valance fabric on top. Along the lower edge, stitch inside the previous stitching line, crowding the stitches against the welting.

5 Trim the lower corners diagonally. Turn the valance right side out. Press the sides and the lower edges. If the valance is interlined, smooth the interlining in place, checking to see that the upper edge of the interlining stops a distance from the upper edge of the valance equal to the heading depth plus the rod-pocket depth plus ½" (1.3 cm).

6 Press under ½" (1.3 cm) on the upper edge, turning under the valance and lining together. Then press under an amount equal to the heading depth plus the rod-pocket depth; pin.

7 Stitch close to the first fold; stitch again at the depth of the heading, using tape on the bed of the sewing machine as a stitching guide.

8 Lay the valance facedown on a flat surface. Mark for vertical rows of tucks at each seam and at each midpoint between the seams. The distance from the outer row of marks to the side edge equals the distance between rows. Measure up 10" (25.5 cm) from the lower edge for the placement of the first mark in each row. Place the remaining marks evenly spaced between the lower mark and the lower stitching line of the rod pocket, dividing the distance into three equal parts.

9 Thread a large-eyed needle with heavy thread. Insert the needle into the valance at the lowest mark in a row. Bring the needle back through to the lining side of the valance at the next mark and insert it back through 1/4" (6 mm) above it. Repeat, taking a small stitch at each mark and running the thread on the right side of the valance. Bring the needle through at the lower stitching line of the rod pocket. Insert the needle back through 1/4" (6 mm) to the side of the top stitch.

10 Make a second row of stitches alongside the first row back to the lowest mark. Cut the thread, leaving tails.

11 Repeat steps 9 and 10 for each marked row. Pull up the stitches to make three tucks in each row. Knot the thread securely.

12 Insert the rod into the rod pocket. Mount the rod; distribute the gathers evenly. Shape the bells and swags.

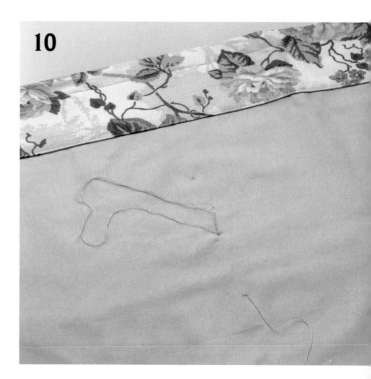

Pleated Valances

PLEATED VALANCES can be either crisply pressed and tailored or softly folded and elegant. Their symmetrical, geometrical look works well in many décors. These valances are easy to sew, too. They are just extra-wide self-lined rectangles with the excess width pleated out, stapled to mounting boards. Sketching the valance and making a pattern before sewing will ensure pleasing results.

Power of one (opposite)
A single inverted box pleat at the middle of a deep, banded valance makes a strong statement in this formal area. While centering the attention on the window, the valance also hides the hardware for the draperies and Roman shade.

Knife pleats (top)
Knife pleats play off of the plaid pattern.

Timeless toile (left)
Inverted box pleats in a lovely toile pattern grace not only the window, but also the canopy and dust ruffle. The crisp tailoring prevents so much fabric from overwhelming the small room.

What you need to know

Knife pleats and box pleats are the two basic **design** styles used for a pleated valance. Knife pleats are a series of sharp creases of equal size and spacing, usually 1" to 2" (2.5 to 5 cm), all turned in the same direction. For symmetry, knife-pleated valances are often divided in the center, with pleats turned toward the outer edges. Pleats can be arranged continuously from the center outward or in clusters of three or more pleats separated by spaces.

A box pleat looks like two knife pleats turned away from each other. Box pleats are generally deeper than knife pleats and are separated by wider spaces. This style is especially appealing when the folds are left unpressed for a softer look.

For inverted box pleats, the excess fabric of the pleat is folded to the inside. A valance can have continuous inverted box pleats of equal size and spacing, ending with one at each front corner. Fewer box pleats can be placed farther apart, perhaps accenting structural divisions of the window. For instance, you often see simple valances that have an inverted box pleat at each corner and one at the center.

It is necessary to make a paper pattern of the valance, following steps 1 to 3, opposite. The pattern will help determine pleat size, spacing, and placement of seams, allowing for adjustments before the panel width is cut. Any seams must be hidden in the folds of the pleats. If possible, *railroad* the fabric to eliminate seams.

To prevent the excess bulk of a hem, pleated valances are *self-lined*. They can be *interlined* with lightweight drapery *lining*, if necessary, to prevent the pattern on the back from showing through to the front.

Choose **fabric** for pleated valances according to the number and style of the pleats. Heavy pleating will obviously distort the pattern of the fabric, so plain colors or smaller,

all-over prints are more desirable than large prints. Larger prints are suitable for valances with fewer pleats. Striped and plaid fabrics can work very well for pleated valances as long as the pleats coincide with the fabric pattern.

Pleated valances are **mounted** on boards installed above and outside the window frame. If there is no *undertreatment*, a 1 × 4 board works well. If the valance goes over an existing treatment, it must have a deeper *projection*.

front view

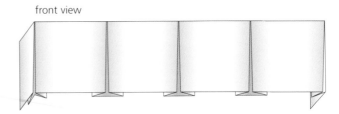

Materials

- Graph paper
- Roll of paper, such as adding machine paper
- Decorator fabric
- Drapery lining, for interlining valance, optional
- Decorative trim, for valance with unpressed pleats, optional
- Heavy paper, for pressing pleats
- Mounting board
- Heavy-duty stapler
- Tools and hardware for installation

Cutting directions

- The *cut length* of the valance fabric is twice the finished length plus 3" (7.5 cm).

- Cut full crosswise widths of fabric and piece them together so they are wider than the pattern. This will allow you to hide seams in pleats. Cut the fabric to the exact width in step 1, below.

- The cut length of the interlining is equal to the finished length plus 1½" (3.8 cm); the *cut width* is the same as the cut width of the valance fabric.

Making the pattern

1 Draw the valance to scale on graph paper, indicating the finished length, width, return depth, and placement of the pleats. *Returns* of 3½" (9 cm) or more can have two or more knife pleats or half of an inverted box pleat. Leave the valance flat on smaller returns. Plan the pleat depths, space sizes, and any seam placements; don't overlap pleats. For a striped or plaid valance, follow the fabric pattern to determine the pleat and space sizes. Check to see that the space measurements add up to the finished width.

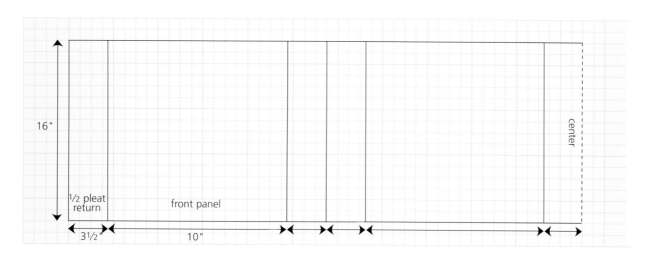

16"

½ pleat return   front panel   center

3½"   10"

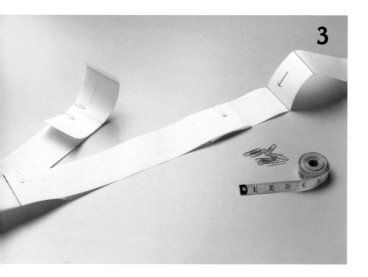

3

2 Unroll adding machine paper on a flat surface. Mark a ½" (1.3 cm) side seam allowance at the end. Measure and mark all spaces and pleats as determined in step 1. Mark the folds with solid lines; mark the placement lines with dotted lines. Indicate the direction of the folds with arrows. Mark the pattern for the entire width of the valance, ending with a ½" (1.3 cm) seam allowance at the opposite end; cut the paper.

3 Fold the pleats as marked. Measure the folded pattern to see that it equals the desired finished width, including the returns; adjust a few pleats, if necessary.

Making a pleated valance

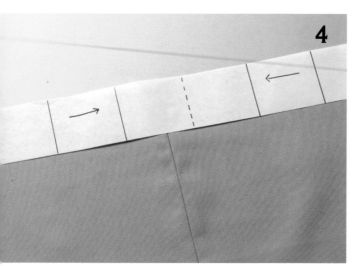

4

4 Seam the fabric widths as necessary. Trim the seam allowances to ¼" (6 mm); press them open. Lay the valance pattern over the seamed fabric, aligning the seams to points in the pattern where they will be hidden in pleats; cut the fabric to the width of the pattern.

5 Pin the interlining, if desired, to the wrong side of the valance, matching the upper edges and ends. Fold the end of the valance in half lengthwise, right sides together. Sew a ½" (1.3 cm) seam on the outer edge of the return. Repeat for the opposite end of the valance.

5

6 Turn the valance right side out; press. Match the upper raw edges. If your valance has interlining, it should extend to the lower fold of the valance. Machine-baste the layers together ½" (1.3 cm) from the upper raw edges. For a valance with unpressed pleats, apply trim to the lower edge, if desired.

7 Lay the valance faceup on a flat surface; lay the pattern over the upper edge of the valance, aligning the end seam lines to the seamed outer edges. Transfer the pattern markings to the valance. Repeat along the lower edge.

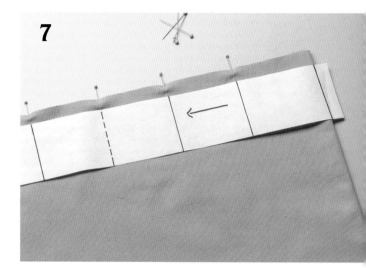

8 Pin the pleats in place along the upper and lower edges and center of the valance. Measure the valance width; adjust if necessary, distributing the adjusted amount among several pleats. If unpressed pleats are desired, omit step 9.

9 Press the pleats on the face of the valance, removing the pins from one pleat at a time; insert heavy paper under each pleat as it is pressed, to avoid imprinting. Replace the pins along the upper edge.

10 Stitch the pleats in place across the valance, 1½" (3.8 cm) from the upper edge; remove the pins. *Finish* the upper edge, by serging or zigzag stitching.

11 Cut the mounting board and cover it with fabric. Secure angle irons to the bottom of the mounting board, near the ends and at 45" (115 cm) intervals, using pan-head screws. Mount the board (page 296), centered above the window frame. Remove the screws that hold the mounting board to the angle irons, leaving the angle irons on the wall.

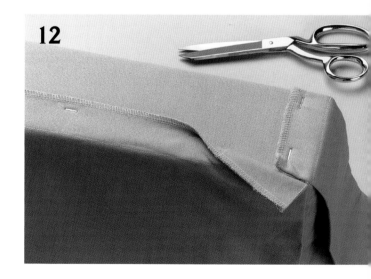

12 Position the valance on the mounting board, using the stitching line as a guide to extend the upper edge 1½" (3.8 cm) onto the top of the board; position the end pleats at the front corners of the board. Staple the valance in place at the returns. Clip the fabric at the corner pleats close to the stitching line to control the bulk. Staple the valance in place; ease or stretch the valance slightly to fit the board, if necessary. Mount the valance by re-attaching the board to the angle irons.

Pleated Valances with Shaped Hems

THESE VALANCES are often seen crowning a drapery, blinds, or shades. Less stiff than a cornice, the shaped hem valance frames the window with graceful curves and gentle lines.

For a stylish variation, the lower edge can be shaped into curves or angles.

Pleats and scallops (opposite)
Inverted-box-pleat valances with soothing scalloped hemlines top the sheer draperies in a girl's room. Pleats were planned to coincide with the horizontal pattern repeat of the blue floral fabric.

Sheffield valance (top right)
The hemline of the Sheffield valance swoops between kicky box pleats lined in a contrasting fabric. While often seen in formal settings, this Sheffield is very much at home in a country kitchen.

Softened squares (bottom right)
Dense brush fringe along the softly undulating hemlines softens the rigid square pattern of the fabric in these valances. Stacked box pleats near the sides add interesting dimension.

*W*hat you need to know

The **design** options for the lower edge are up to your imagination. Begin by sketching the valance to scale on graph paper. Determine the style and number of pleats. Shape the lower edge to complement the pleats and perhaps accent structural details of the window itself. For best results, avoid severe angles and sharp curves. Valance and *lining* pieces are cut using a full-size pattern.

Choose medium-weight decorator **fabric** in a plain color, small print, or a larger pattern that will work well with the design of your valance. Because the lining may be visible along the lower edge in some areas, line the valance with the same fabric or a coordinating fabric.

Pleated valances with shaped hems are **mounted** on boards installed above and outside the window frame. If there is no *undertreatment*, a 1 × 4 board works well. If the valance goes over an existing treatment, it must have a deeper *projection*.

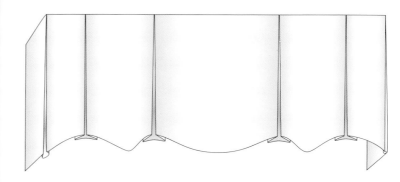

Materials

- Graph paper
- Roll of wide paper, such as inexpensive tablecloth paper or tracing paper
- Designing tool, such as flexible curve or curved ruler
- Decorator fabric
- Lightweight decorator fabric in accent color or coordinating print, for lining
- Heavy paper, for pressing pleats
- Mounting board
- Tools and hardware for installation
- Heavy-duty stapler

Making the pattern

1 Draw the valance to scale on graph paper, indicating the finished length, width, *return* depth, and placement of the pleats. Returns of 3½" (9 cm) or more can have two or more knife pleats or half of an inverted box pleat. Leave the valance flat on smaller returns. Plan the pleat depths, space sizes, and any seam placements; don't overlap pleats. For a striped or plaid valance, follow the fabric pattern to determine the pleat and space sizes. Check to

see that the space measurements add up to the
finished width. Draw the shape of the lower edge,
using one of these options or your own design.

(continued)

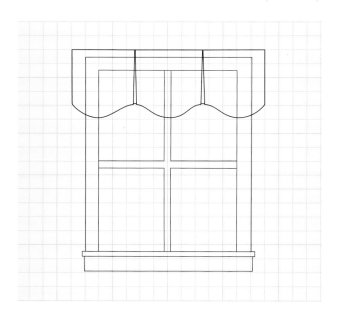

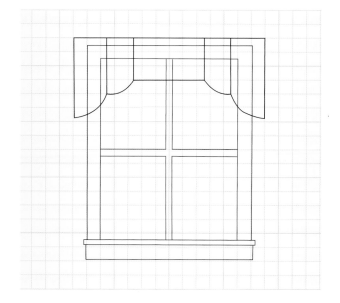

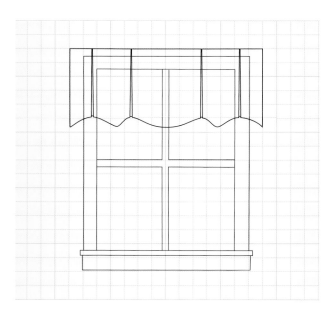

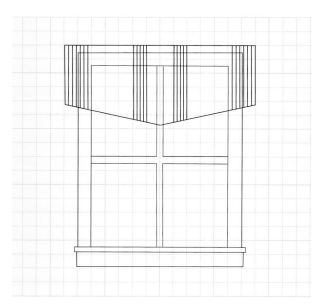

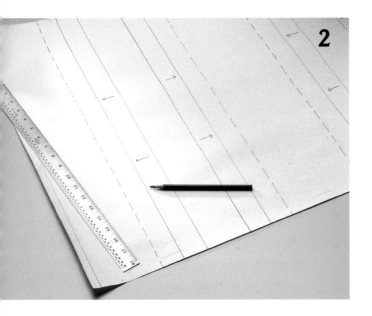

2 Unroll the wide paper; cut the paper with the length equal to the desired finished length of the valance at the long point plus 2" (5 cm). Mark a ½" (1.3 cm) side seam allowance at one end. Measure and mark all the spaces and pleats as determined in step 1. Mark the folds with solid lines; mark the placement lines with dotted lines. Indicate the direction of the folds with arrows. Mark the pattern for the entire width of the valance, ending with a ½" (1.3 cm) seam allowance at the opposite end; cut the paper.

3 Fold the pleats as marked. Measure the folded pattern to see that it equals the desired finished width, including the returns; adjust a few pleats, if necessary.

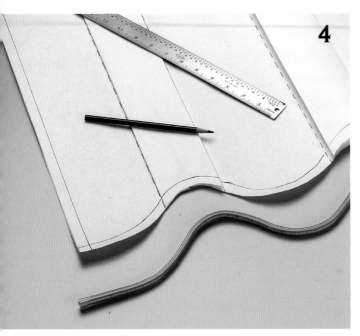

4 Draw the shaped seam line of the lower edge on the folded pattern, following your graphed sketch, with the longest point ½" (1.3 cm) above the cut edge of the paper. Draw curved lines, using a designing tool such as a flexible curve or curved ruler; draw angled lines, using a straightedge. Add a ½" (1.3 cm) seam allowance below the seam line. Cut out the pattern.

Cutting directions

- The *cut length* of the valance fabric is the finished length at the longest point plus 2" (5 cm).

- Cut full crosswise widths of fabric and piece them together so they are wider than the pattern. This will allow you to hide seams in pleats. Cut the fabric to the exact width in step 1, opposite.

- Cut the lining with the same length and width as the valance fabric.

Making a shaped pleated valance

1 Seam the fabric widths as necessary. Trim the seam allowances to ¼" (6 mm); press them open. Lay the valance pattern over the seamed fabric, aligning the seams to points in the pattern where they will be hidden in pleats; cut the fabric to the width of the pattern.

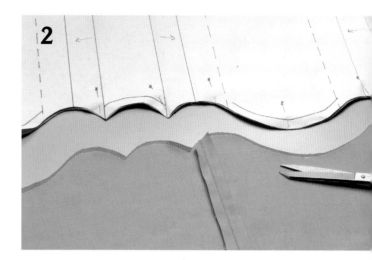

2 Place the valance fabric and lining right sides together; pin the pattern in place, aligning the upper edges and sides. Cut the valance fabric and lining along the lower edge of the pattern.

3 Remove the pattern. Pin the valance and lining together along the lower edge and sides; stitch a ½" (1.3 cm) seam.

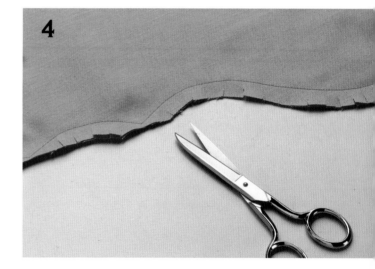

4 Trim the outer corners, clip into the inner corners, and clip the seam allowances on the curves. Complete the valance as on pages 84 and 85, steps 6 to 12.

Balloon Valances

WHEN A ROOM needs a focal point, the romantic balloon valance may be just right. The balloon valance is a series of inverted box pleats that are raised into soft billows along the lower edge. Graceful folds of fabric dip deeply into the top third of the window. The treatment can be sewn from one fabric, like the examples shown here, or with insets of contrasting fabric in the folds of each pleat to create more interest.

Focal point (opposite)
Multiple poufs conform to the contours of a bay window and show off the blue-on-yellow floral print, giving the room a definite focal point.

Padded effect (right)
Tassel fringe underlines the gentle curve of this generous balloon valance. The subtle gold check fabric has a soft, plump look because it has cushiony interlining.

*W*hat you need to know

To help you **design** your balloon valance, draw a diagram that shows the finished width, length, and *projection* of the valance. Your valance can have only two pleats (one at each corner) or several pleats spaced evenly at least 12" (30.5 cm) apart. After determining the number of pleats, to determine the exact space between pleats, divide this number into the valance width. Including the pleats at the outer front corners, there will be one more pleat in the valance than the number of spaces.

Balloon valances require at least two times *fullness*. They can be made from one **fabric** panel that is folded into inverted box pleats or the pleat inserts can be a contrasting fabric, as in the directions that follow. Choose lightweight to medium-weight fabrics that have enough body to hold the poufed shape without being too stiff.

Balloon valances are board **mounted,** which keeps light from shining up through the top of the treatment. The mounting board should extend 2" (5 cm) beyond the window frame or *undertreatment* on each side and have a *return* depth 2" (5 cm) deeper than the undertreatment or at least 4" (10 cm) if there is no undertreatment. A narrow utility curtain rod with returns equal to the depth of the mounting board stabilizes the lower edge and holds it away from the window or undertreatment.

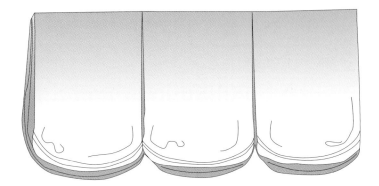

Materials

- Decorator fabric for main valance
- Contrasting decorator fabric for the pleat inserts
- Lining fabric
- Mounting board
- Plastic rings
- Shade cord
- Utility curtain rod with same projection as the mounting board
- Tools and hardware for installation
- Heavy-duty stapler

Cutting directions

- From the main valance fabric, cut a piece for each space section with the width equal to the finished width of the space plus 1" (2.5 cm). The *cut length* of each piece is equal to the finished length plus 14" (35.5 cm).

- Cut the fabric for each return section with the width equal to the projection of the mounting board plus 1" (2.5 cm). The cut length of each piece is equal to the finished length plus 14" (35.5 cm).

- Cut the contrasting fabric for the pleat inserts 21" (53.5 cm) wide with length equal to the finished length plus 14" (35.5 cm). If the projection of the mounting board is less than 5" (12.7 cm), trim the corner pleat inserts to equal twice the projection of the mounting board plus 11" (28 cm).

- Cut a piece of *lining* fabric to match each of the space sections, return sections, and pleat insert sections.

- Cut a facing strip 2½" (6.5 cm) wide and 1" (2.5 cm) longer than the finished width of the valance (including returns).

Making a balloon valance

1 Pin a decorator fabric piece and matching lining piece wrong sides together. *Finish* the sides together by serging or zigzag stitching. Repeat for each piece of the valance.

2 Pin the pleat insert for the left end of the valance over the left return section, right sides together. Stitch a ½" (1.3 cm) seam.

3 Pin a space section to the other side of the pleat insert, right sides together. Stitch a ½" (1.3 cm) seam. Continue to join sections, alternating pleat inserts and spaces. End with the right pleat insert and the right return section. Press the seam allowances open.

(continued)

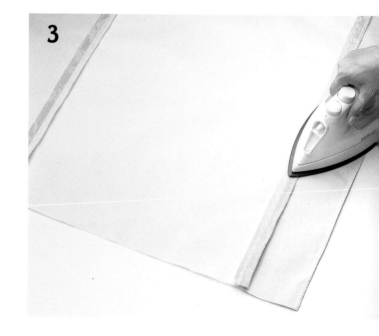

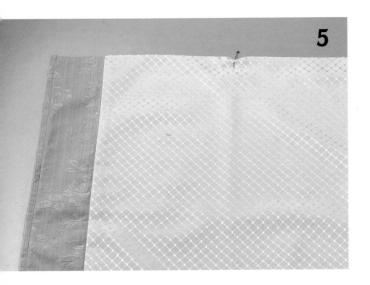

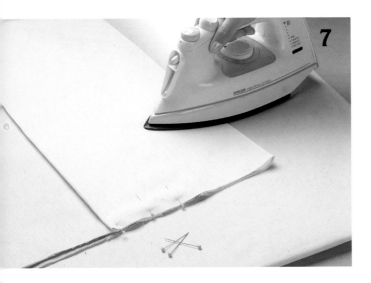

4 Turn under and press ½" (1.3 cm) side hems; stitch.

5 Mark the center of each pleat insert along the upper and lower edges. If the return is less than 5" (12.7 cm), measure from the inner seam of the return a distance equal to twice the return; mark.

6 Fold under the pleats at the seam lines; press. Bring the pressed seams together to the marks. Pin the pleats in place at the upper and lower edges. The side hems should be hidden under the end pleats.

7 Press the folded edges of all the pleat inserts, turning the valance back and pressing only on the pleat insert to avoid imprinting the edges to the right side of the valance.

8 Stitch the pleats in place across the valance, 1½" (3.8 cm) from the upper edge. Finish the upper edge by serging or zigzag stitching. Stitch ½" (1.3 cm) from the lower edge to secure the pleats.

9 Press under ½" (1.3 cm) on the short ends and one long side of the facing strip. Pin the other long side to the bottom of the valance, right sides together. Stitch a ½" (1.3 cm) seam. Turn the facing to the wrong side of the valance; press. Edgestitch along the inner fold, forming a casing for the lower rod.

10 Mark positions for four rings in columns at the center of each pleat insert, placing the bottom marks at the top of the casing and spacing the others 3" (7.5 cm) apart.

11 Stitch a ring at each mark, stitching only through the lining and insert fabric in the pleats.

12 Thread a length of shade cord through the rings of the first column and tie the rings together. Repeat for each column.

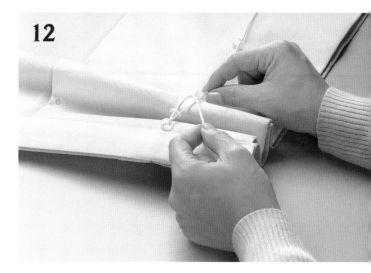

13 Cut the mounting board and cover it with fabric. Mount the board (page 296), centered above the window frame. Remove the board, leaving the angle irons on the wall.

14 Place the valance on the mounting board, using the stitching line as a guide to extend the upper edge 1½" (3.8 cm) onto the top of the board. Place the end pleats at the front corners of the board. Staple the valance in place.

15 Mount the valance on the angle irons, replacing the screws in their original holes. Insert the utility rod into the bottom casing. Adjust the billows at the lower edge of the valance.

Cloud Valances

THE CLOUD VALANCE is feminine, romantic, and eye-catching. It is gathered across the top, either by making a rod pocket and mounting the valance on a curtain rod (as in the directions that follow) or by gathering the top with shirring tape and securing it to a mounting board. The lower edge is raised into a series of soft billows by sewing in columns of rings and tying them together.

Different depths (opposite)
An extra-wide rod pocket creates a grand top for this sheer cloud valance. Three graceful swags of different depths are created by tying the two inner columns of rings tighter than the outer columns.

Ruffles (top)
Long cloud valances over sidelights draw the eye to the glass ceiling in this solarium. Ruffles emphasize the dramatic curves and folds at the lower edge.

Single pouf (left)
This single-pouf cloud valance is made by sewing a rod pocket at the top and bottom. In a deep window casing, tension rods hold the valance in place, the lower one tucked up and under the fabric to puff out the extra fullness and length.

𝒲hat you need to know

When you **design** a cloud valance, the pouf sizes can all be the same or they can vary in width and length. Columns of rings should be placed at seams between fabric widths and 18" to 24" (46 to 61 cm) apart, so, depending on the fabric width, there will either be two or three poufs per fabric width.

Lightweight **fabrics,** including sheers and semisheers, and soft medium-weight fabrics work best for cloud valances. The amount of *fullness* can vary. If using a medium-weight decorator fabric, two to two-and-one-half times fullness works well. For lighter fabric, three times fullness can be used. *Lining* gives the cloud valance extra body to hold the shape of the poufs and keeps light from shadowing through.

Mount the valance using a utility curtain rod. If the cloud valance will be installed over a shade or blind, the valance should be wide enough and project out far enough so it doesn't interfere with the operation of the *undertreatment*. A second curtain rod mounted under the lower edge of the cloud valance keeps the valance at the necessary *projection*.

Materials

- Decorator fabric for cloud valance
- Lining fabric, optional
- Plastic rings
- Shade cord
- Two utility curtain rods of equal projections
- Tools and hardware for installation

Cutting directions

- The *cut length* of each valance piece is equal to the finished length (from the underside of the rod to the hem) plus twice the rod-pocket depth plus twice the *heading* height plus 18" (46 cm).

- The *cut width* of the valance is equal to the rod length plus twice the projection of the rod, multiplied by the amount of fullness desired, usually two to two-and-one-half times. After calculating the full cut width, divide this number by the fabric width and round to the nearest number of full and half widths to piece together.

- Cut the lining the same width and length as the decorator fabric.

Making a cloud valance

1 Seam fabric widths together, using only full and half widths and adding the half widths at the sides. If an even number of full widths are needed, divide one in half and add a half width to each side of the center full width to avoid a seam in the center of the valance. Repeat for the lining, if desired.

2 Pin the valance and lining wrong sides together, aligning all edges. Trim any excess so the panels are the same size. Turn under and stitch 1" (2.5 cm) double-fold side hems, handling the decorator fabric and lining as one fabric.

3 Press under ½" (1.3 cm) on the upper edge. Then press under an amount equal to the rod-pocket depth plus the heading depth. Stitch close to the first fold; stitch again at the depth of the heading, using tape on the bed of the sewing machine as a stitching guide.

4 Turn under and stitch a 1" (2.5 cm) double-fold hem at the bottom.

5 Lay the valance facedown on the work surface. Mark positions for rings in columns at the side hems and at each seam, placing the bottom marks at the top of the bottom hem. Space one or two additional columns of marks between seams. Place four marks in each column, spaced 6" (15 cm) apart.

6 Stitch a ring at each mark, stitching through the lining and valance fabric.

7 Thread a length of shade cord through the rings of the first column and tie the rings together. Leave long tails of cord. Repeat for each column.

8 Insert the curtain rod in the upper rod pocket and mount the valance. Adjust the fullness evenly.

9 Mount the lower rod under the valance, even with the clusters of tied rings. Tie the cording tails to the rod to keep the poufs in position and away from the undertreatment. Adjust the poufs.

Upholstered Cornices

AN UPHOLSTERED CORNICE is a formal, tailored top treatment made by covering a wooden frame with fabric. The frame, like a box with an open back and bottom, is first padded with foam or batting to round the corners for a soft, upholstered look. Fabric-covered welting or twisted cord welting can be used to define the upper and lower edges of the cornice.

Building a cornice from plywood or pine boards takes only very basic carpentry skills. Any imperfections will be covered with padding and fabric. The front of your cornice can be cut straight across or can be shaped with curves and angles.

A cornice not only frames and finishes a window treatment by hiding the hardware, but also provides good insulation and light control because it encloses the top of the treatment.

Arched form (opposite)
These dramatic arched cornices are a grand focal point for a formal dining area. Ornate metal medallions accent the upper corners.

Nail head (top right)
A simple rectangular box cornice has been distinctively detailed with hammered brass nail heads.

Understated (bottom right)
Subtle shaping at the bottom of these cornices softens their appearance. Mounted at ceiling height, they hide the drapery hardware and create the illusion that the windows are higher than they are.

What you need to know

Design your cornice to clear the curtain or drapery hardware by 2" to 3" (5 to 7.5 cm) and extend at least 2" (5 cm) beyond the end of the drapery or window frame on each side. These measurements are the cornice *inside* measurements. Allow for the thickness of the wood when cutting.

In the directions that follow, the upper and lower edges of the cornice are defined with welting. Disregard the references to welting if you prefer your cornice without it.

Medium-weight, firmly woven decorator **fabrics** and upholstery fabrics are suitable for cornices. *Railroad* the fabric on a cornice to eliminate seams on plain fabrics and fabrics with nondirectional prints. If the fabric cannot be railroaded, place the seams inconspicuously, never in the center. Prints should be centered or balanced on the cornice front.

To **mount** your cornice, use enough angle irons to support and distribute the weight. It is difficult or impossible to insert screws into the wall working up inside a narrow box, so it is important to follow step 16 (page 107) when you install your cornice.

Materials

- Decorator fabric
- Lining fabric
- Contrasting fabric for welting
- Plywood or pine boards, 1/2" (1.3 cm) thick, for the front, top, and sides of the cornice box
- Carpenter's glue
- Sixpenny finishing nails
- Polyester upholstery batting or polyurethane foam, 1/2" (1.3 cm) thick
- Filler cord, 5/32" (3.8 mm) thick for making welting
- Heavy-duty stapler
- Cardboard upholstery stripping, enough to cover top and bottom edges
- Spray foam adhesive
- Tools and hardware for installation

Cutting directions

- For the face piece, cut decorator fabric 6" (15 cm) wider than the front and sides, and 3" (7.5 cm) longer than the height of the cornice.

- Cut a 4" (10 cm) inner *lining* strip from decorator fabric the same width as the face piece.

- Cut a strip of lining fabric the same width as the face piece and 2" (5 cm) shorter than the cornice height.

- Cut decorator fabric for the dustcover (fabric that covers the top of the cornice box) 1" (2.5 cm) larger than the cornice top.

- Cut a strip of batting or foam to cover the front and sides of the cornice.

- Cut 1½" (3.8 cm) bias strips of contrasting fabric to make fabric-covered welting. You will need a length slightly longer than the edges to be welted.

Making an upholstered cornice

1 For the cornice box, measure and cut the cornice top. Cut the front the same width as the top and the desired finished height. Shape the lower edge of the front, if desired. Cut the sides the same height as the cornice front and the depth of the top piece plus the thickness of the wood.

2 Glue the top to the front board first. Nail to secure. Then attach the sides, first gluing in place and then securing with nails. Allow the glue to set.

3 Prepare the welting as in steps 1 to 4 on page 299. Stitch the welting to the lower edge of the face piece in a ½" (1.3 cm) seam, raw edges even.

4 Sew the lower (welted) edge to the inner lining strip, right sides together. Sew the free edge of the inner strip to the lining strip. Press the seam allowances toward the lining.

5 Mark the center of the face piece at the top and bottom. Mark the center of the cornice at the top and bottom. Place the wrong side of the face fabric on the outside of the cornice, with the lower (welted) seam on the lower front edge of the cornice; match the center markings. Staple in place at the center.

(continued)

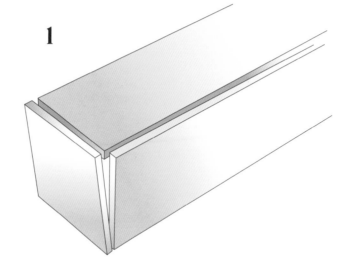

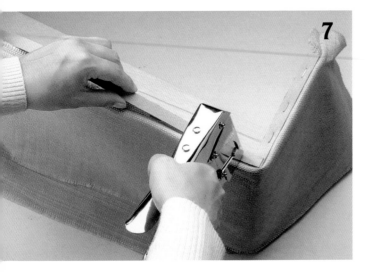

6 Pull the seam allowances taut to the corners of the cornice, and staple in place. Staple every 4" (10 cm) from the center to the ends, keeping the lower (welted) seam aligned to the front edge of the cornice.

7 Place cardboard stripping tight against the lower (welted) seam. Staple every 1" to 1½" (2.5 to 3.8 cm). Cut and overlap the stripping at the corners.

8 Fold the lining to the inside. Fold under the raw edge, and staple at the inside of the box where the top and face meet. At the lower corners, miter the fabric and staple close to the corner. Tuck excess fabric into the upper corners, and staple.

9 Open the welting seam back to the edge of the cornice. Trim the welting to 1" (2.5 cm). Trim out the cording even with cornice back edge to reduce bulk. Staple the lining to the back edge of the cornice; trim the excess lining. Staple the welting end to the back edge of the cornice.

10 Turn the cornice faceup. Apply spray adhesive to the front and sides. Place the padding over the glued surface, and smooth it taut over the front and sides. Allow the glue to set.

11 Fold the face fabric over the front of the cornice. Gently smooth the fabric toward the top of the cornice, keeping the padding tucked snug into the corners and along the lower edge.

12 Staple the face fabric to the cornice top at the center and ends, keeping the fabric taut but not stretched too tightly. Starting at the center, turn under the raw edge and staple it to the cornice top. Smoothing the fabric as you go, work first toward one end and then the other, placing staples 1½" (3.8 cm) apart.

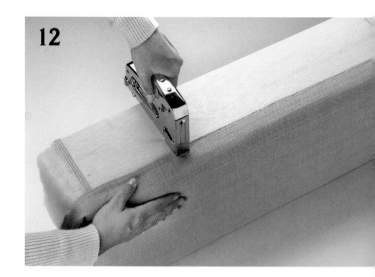

13 Pull the fabric around the cornice end to the top back corner, removing any slack; staple. Fold the side fabric to the back edge; staple. Trim the excess fabric at the back edge.

14 Fold the fabric diagonally at the corners to form miters. Staple at the corners and across the ends.

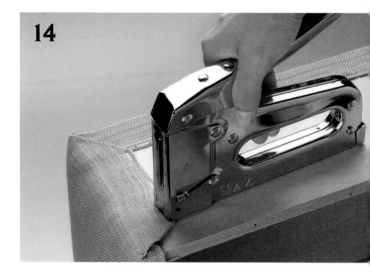

15 Staple welting to the sides and front of the cornice top, with the welting stitching line along the front and side edges. On the cornice front, place the dustcover over the welting, with right sides together and raw edges even. Staple cardboard stripping at the front. Fold under the sides of the dustcover even with the sides of the cornice. Insert cardboard stripping into the folds. Pull the fabric to the top of the cornice, and staple in place close to the folds. Fold under the back edge of the dustcover and staple it in place.

16 Screw angle irons to the underside of the cornice top near the ends and at 36" (91.5 cm) intervals, using pan-head screws. Hold the cornice in its proper position above the window, and mark the screw holes for the angle irons on the wall. Lower the cornice. Remove the angle irons, and attach them to the wall. Mount the cornice by reattaching it to the angle irons on the wall.

Rod-Pocket Mock Cornices

TOP TREATMENTS that resemble cornices can be made without carpentry or upholstery techniques. Mock cornices are mounted on flat curtain rods that are 4½" (11.5 cm) wide. Fusible fleece applied inside the rod pocket gives the treatment a padded look. The top and bottom of the rod pocket are accented with fabric-covered welting or twisted cord welting. For added flair and extra length, a pleated or gathered skirt is sewn below the rod pocket.

These versatile top treatments can be used to dress up windows that have existing treatments, such as vertical or horizontal blinds, pleated shades, or curtains. If you have sleeve valances on rods that are looking outdated, mock cornices will freshen the look without the expense of new rods.

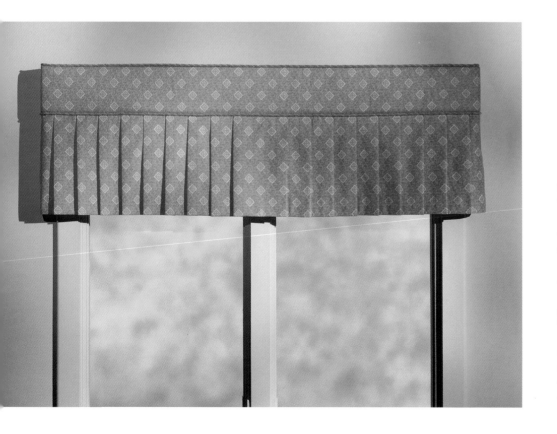

Gathered skirt (opposite)
The gathered skirt on this mock cornice has a soft, feminine appearance, providing a relaxed look while hiding the mechanisms of the shade.

Pleated skirt (left)
Knife pleating on the skirt of this mock cornice looks crisp and tailored. Narrow twisted cord welting accentuates the flat sleeve.

$\mathcal{W}$hat you need to know

Design your mock cornice with either a pleated or gathered skirt. Refer to the directions on page 83 for making a pattern for a pleated skirt.

For best results, select a lightweight to medium-weight **fabric** that can be *railroaded*. This will eliminate the need for seams in the rod pocket. The skirt can be seamed in the center if you hide the seam in a pleat or gathers. Two skirt lengths and both rod-pocket pieces can be cut from one width of railroaded 54" (137 cm) decorator fabric, if the skirt is not longer than 16" (40.5 cm).

Mount your mock cornice on a flat, 4½" (11.5 cm) utility rod. If the top treatment is going over an outside-mounted curtain or blind, adjust the mounting brackets to their deepest *projection*. Self-adhesive Velcro strips keep the ends of the sleeve secured to the brackets so the sleeve stays smooth and taut.

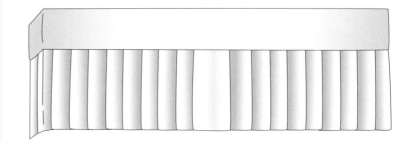

Materials

- Decorator fabric
- Lining fabric
- Fabric-covered welting, twisted welting, or 5/32" (3.8 mm) filler cord and fabric, for making fabric-covered welting
- Fusible fleece
- Flat curtain rod, 4½" (11.5 cm) wide, with adjustable mounting brackets to adjust the projection
- Tools and hardware for installation
- Self-adhesive hook-and-loop tape

Cutting directions

- Cut a strip of decorator fabric for the front of the rod pocket 6" (15 cm) wide, with the length equal to the *finished width* of the valance (including *returns*) plus 1½" (3.8 cm).

- Cut a strip of decorator fabric for the back of the rod pocket 6" (15 cm) wide, with the length equal to the *cut length* of the front rod-pocket strip plus 1" (2.5 cm).

- Cut a strip of *lining* fabric for the front rod-pocket facing, with the same length and width as the front rod-pocket strip.

- Cut decorator fabric for the skirt, with the length equal to the finished length plus 4½" (11.5 cm).

- For a pleated skirt, make a pattern to determine the cut width, as on page 83, steps 1 to 3. For a gathered skirt, the *cut width* of the skirt is equal to twice the finished width (including returns) plus 1" (2.5 cm).

- Cut lining for the skirt, with the length equal to the finished length of the skirt plus ½" (1.3 cm) and the cut width equal to the cut width of the decorator fabric.

- Cut *bias* fabric strips for fabric-covered welting, as on page 125, step 1.

- Cut a strip of fusible fleece, 5" (12.7 cm) wide, with the length equal to the finished width of the valance (including returns) plus ½" (1.3 cm).

Making a mock cornice– pleated skirt style

1 Center the fusible fleece strip on the wrong side of the front rod-pocket strip; fuse it in place, following the manufacturer's directions.

2 Make fabric-covered welting (page 299) and attach it to the upper and lower edges of the front rod-pocket strip; begin and end the welting ½" (1.3 cm) from the ends of the strip. Or attach purchased welting.

3 Place the front rod pocket over the front rod-pocket facing strip, right sides together, aligning the edges; pin along the lower edge and ends.

4 Stitch a ½" (1.3 cm) seam along the lower edge and ends, using a zipper foot and stitching with the facing side down. Crowd the cording by stitching just inside the previous stitches.

(continued)

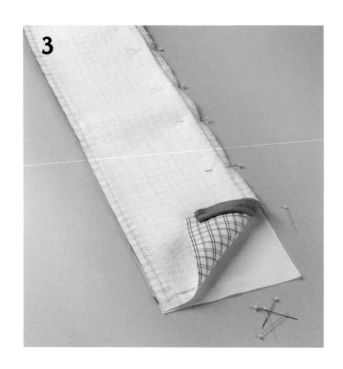

8

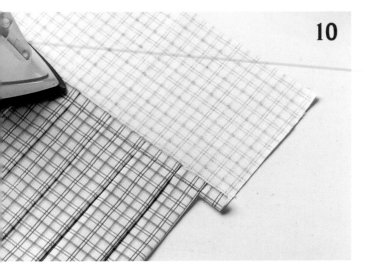

10

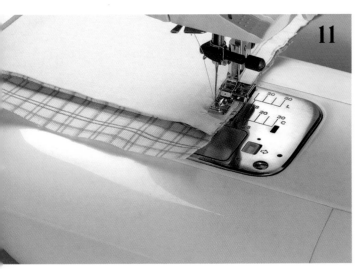

11

5 Trim the lower corners diagonally. Turn the front rod pocket right side out, and press. Baste the upper edges together within the 1/2" (1.3 cm) seam allowance.

6 Seam the fabric for the skirt, if necessary; repeat for the skirt lining. Pin the skirt and lining, right sides together, along the lower edge. Stitch 2" (5 cm) from the raw edges.

7 Press the 2" (5 cm) hem allowance away from the lining. Pin the skirt to the lining, right sides together, along the sides, aligning the upper edges; the skirt will form a fold even with the lower edge of the hem allowance. Stitch 1/2" (1.3 cm) side seams.

8 Trim the lower corners diagonally. Press the lining side seam allowances toward the lining. Turn the skirt right side out, realigning the upper edges; press. Baste the upper edges together.

9 Make a pattern for the pleated skirt, as on page 83, steps 1 to 3. Lay the skirt faceup on a flat surface; lay the pattern over the upper edge of the skirt, aligning the marked seam lines to the seamed outer edges. Transfer the pattern markings to the skirt. Repeat along the lower edge.

10 Pin the pleats in place along the upper and lower edges of the skirt; press. Baste along the upper edge. Pin the wrong side of the skirt to the right side of the back rod pocket along the lower edge, beginning and ending 1" (2.5 cm) from the end; stitch. Press the seam allowances toward the rod pocket.

11 Pin the back rod pocket to the front rod pocket along the upper edge, right sides together; the ends of the back rod pocket extend 1" (2.5 cm) beyond the ends of the front rod pocket. With the front rod pocket on top, stitch a 1/2" (1.3 cm) seam, using a zipper foot; crowd the welting.

12 Press the seam allowances toward the back rod pocket. Turn under the ends of the back rod-pocket strip ½" (1.3 cm) twice, encasing the ends of the seam allowances; stitch.

13 Turn the skirt and back rod pocket down behind the rod pocket. From the right side, pin the skirt in place along the seam line at the lower edge of the rod pocket, just above the welting.

14 Stitch in the ditch from the right side by stitching in the well of the seam above the welting, using a zipper foot.

15 Insert the curtain rod into the rod pocket. Mount the rod on the brackets. Pull taut toward the returns; secure the returns to the sides of the brackets, using self-adhesive hook-and-loop tape.

Making a mock cornice– gathered skirt style

1 Follow steps 1 to 8 on pages 111 and 112. Zigzag over a cord on the right side of the skirt within the ½" (1.3 cm) seam allowance of the upper edge.

2 Divide the skirt into eighths; pin-mark. Divide the lower edge of the back rod pocket into eighths, beginning and ending 1" (2.5 cm) from the ends. Pin the wrong side of the skirt to the right side of the back rod pocket along the lower edge, matching the pin marks and the raw edges.

3 Pull the gathering cord on the skirt to fit the lower edge of the back rod pocket; pin in place. Stitch ½" (1.3 cm) from the raw edges. Press the seam allowances toward the back rod pocket. Complete the mock cornice, following steps 11 to 15 above.

Soft Cornices

WHILE A PADDED CORNICE is mounted on a box frame, this variation is mounted on a board with side extensions. The look is lighter. A soft cornice can be made as either a single panel of fabric with a shaped lower edge or with over-lapping panels. Welting defines the lower edge of the soft cornice and can also trim the upper edge.

Easy angles (opposite)
This soft cornice conforms effortlessly to the angles of the bay window area. Tassel fringe with a decorative heading enhances the lower edge, drawing attention to the gentle curves.

Layers (top)
A tasseled triangle-point hangs freely over a straight plaid panel in this layered soft cor-nice. Though subtle, the color scheme draws the room together.

Multipurpose (left)
A single-layer soft cornice placed at ceiling level elongates the window area and hides both drapery and shade mechanisms. Pretty tassel fringe defines the edge.

What you need to know

To **design** a soft cornice, first draw it to scale. Tape a full-size paper pattern over the window before beginning the actual project, to check the measurements and proportion.

Use firmly woven decorator **fabric** and back it with fleece for a padded effect. To prevent the shadowing of any seams or overlapped panels, the panels are lined with blackout drapery *lining*.

The **mounting** board for the soft cornice is constructed with legs at the *return* ends to give the treatment added support. The finished width of the soft cornice must be at least 3" (7.5 cm) wider than the outside measurement of the window frame or *undertreatment*; this allows the necessary space for the legs and angle irons.

Materials

- Graph paper
- Wide kraft paper or newsprint for making pattern
- Flexible curve or curved ruler
- Decorator fabric for the soft cornice, hem facing, covered mounting board and legs, and dustcover
- Contrasting decorator fabric for the welting
- Filler cord, 1/2" (1.3 cm) thick
- Fusible fleece
- Blackout lining
- Paper-backed fusible adhesive strip, optional
- Glue stick
- Heavy-duty stapler
- Mounting board and side legs
- Four 2¹/2" (6.5 cm) flathead screws for connecting legs to mounting board
- Cardboard stripping
- Self-adhesive hook-and-loop tape
- Tools and hardware for installation

Making the pattern

1 Draw the soft cornice to scale on graph paper. Indicate the finished length at the longest and shortest points, the *projection* of the mounting board, and the finished width of the cornice including returns. Indicate the placement of welting with heavy lines; include 1/2" (1.3 cm) welting at the lower edge and returns in the finished length and width measurements. For a cor-

nice with overlapping panels, draw the shape of the overlapped panels with dotted lines, and indicate the measurements of each panel.

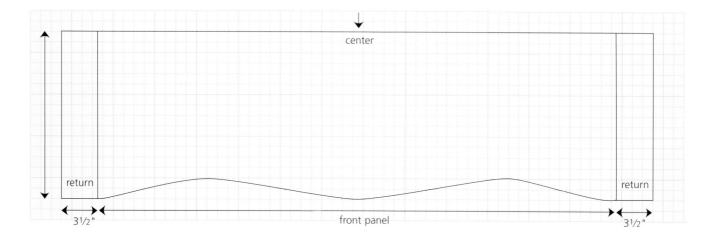

2 Draw a full-size pattern of the soft cornice, including returns, following your scale drawing. Use a designing tool, such as a flexible curve or curved ruler, to draw curved lines along the lower edge of the pattern. Round the corners. For a cornice with overlapping panels, draw a pattern for each piece.

3 Cut out the pattern. Do not add seam allowances because the ½" (1.3 cm) allowance for the welting compensates for the seam allowances. Hang the pattern in the desired location at the top of the window. Check for accurate measurements and proportion.

(continued)

Cutting directions

Single panel

- Cut the fabric with the length equal to the finished length at the longest point plus 4" (10 cm).

- The *cut width* of the fabric is equal to the finished width plus twice the projection of the mounting board, plus 4" (10 cm). If the cut width exceeds the fabric width, *railroad* the fabric whenever possible, to avoid any seams. For fabric that cannot be railroaded, cut one fabric width for the center of the panel and seam equal partial widths to each side, matching the pattern in the fabric.

- Cut the fusible fleece to the same size as the decorator fabric.

- Cut the blackout lining to the same size as the decorator fabric.

- Cut one facing strip from the decorator fabric the same width as the lining. To find the cut length of the strip, subtract the shortest point of the cornice from the longest point; then add 3½" (9 cm).

Overlapping panels

- Make a separate pattern for each piece. Cut the fabric, adding a 2" (5 cm) margin around each pattern piece.

- Cut the fusible fleece to the same size as the decorator fabric.

- Cut the blackout lining to the same size as the decorator fabric.

- Cut facing strips for the panels on the return ends only.

Both styles

- From the contrasting fabric, cut *bias* strips, 2½" (6.5 cm) wide to cover the cording for the welting.

- Cut the mounting board. Cut two side legs with the same projection as the mounting board, each 3" (7.5 cm) shorter than the finished length of the soft cornice at the return.

- Cut the fabric for the dustcover 1" (2.5 cm) wider and longer than the width and length of the mounting board.

Making a soft cornice

1 Place the fabric facedown on a pressing surface. Apply fusible fleece to the wrong side of the fabric, following the manufacturer's directions.

2 Place the pattern on the right side of the padded fabric; pin in place within the seam allowances. Cut out the soft cornice along the sides and lower edge; do not trim off the excess fabric at the top.

3 For a one-piece soft cornice or for the return pieces of a multi-piece soft cornice, press under a ½" (1.3 cm) seam allowance along the upper edge of the facing strip. Lay the facing strip over the lining, right side up, matching the lower edge and sides. Stitch close to the fold or secure with paper-backed fusible adhesive strip.

4 Place the pattern facedown over the right side of the lining piece, aligning the lower edges; pin within the seam allowances. Cut out the lining along the sides and lower edge; do not trim off excess fabric at the top. Glue-baste the lower edge of the facing strip to the lining.

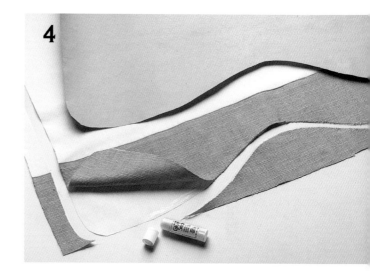

5 Prepare welting as on page 299, steps 1 to 4. Machine-baste the welting to the right side of the padded fabric along the sides and lower edge, matching raw edges and stitching a scant ½" (1.3 cm) from the edges. Clip and ease the welting at the corners and curves.

6 Pin the welted fabric to the lining within the seam allowances, right sides together. Stitch a ½" (1.3 cm) seam along the sides and lower edge, crowding the welting. Clip the seam allowances on the curves; trim the corners. Turn the soft cornice right side out, and press.

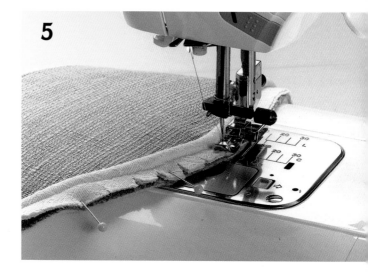

7 Measure the desired finished length from the lower edge of the cornice; mark a line on the lining side. Mark a second line 1½" (3.8 cm) above the first line. Cut along the second line through all layers.

(continued)

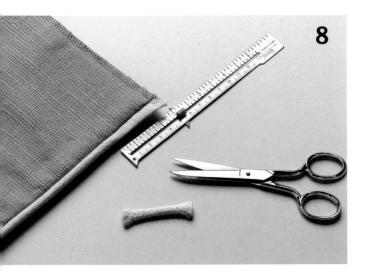

8 Pull out the cord at the ends of the welting; cut off 2" (5 cm) of cording. Pull the seam to draw the cut ends of the cord back into the welting. *Finish* the upper edge by serging or zigzagging through all layers.

9 Cover the mounting board with lining. Cover the legs with decorator fabric. The smooth sides of the legs will face inward. On the outward surface of each leg, staple the hook side of hook-and-loop tape ½" (1.3 cm) from the back edge. Stand the mounting board and legs on edge. Butt the tops of the legs to the underside of the mounting board, outer edges even. Predrill holes for two screws through the mounting board into the end of one leg. Insert the screws. Repeat for the other leg.

10 Cut two strips of loop tape to the same length as the hook tape applied to the legs. Affix the tape to the lining at the return edges of the soft cornice, just inside the welting, with the top of the tape at the marked line.

11 Place the mounting board on the lining side of the soft cornice, with the front edge of the board facedown and the upper edge of the top board even with the marked line. Secure the returns to the legs with the hook-and-loop tape.

12 Support the mounting board on the edge of the work surface. Staple the upper edge of the soft cornice to the top of the mounting board, clipping and overlapping fabric at the corners.

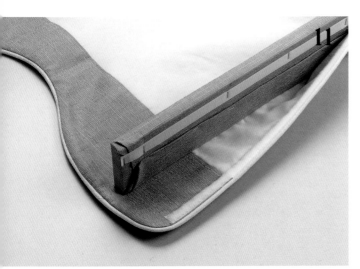

13 Trim ½" (1.3 cm) of cording out of the end of the welting; tuck the fabric into the end, encasing the cord. Staple the welting to the top of the mounting board, along the outer edge, beginning at the back of the board. Allow the welting to overhang the board slightly. Staple to within 3" (7.5 cm) of the opposite end.

14 Cut the welting ½" (1.3 cm) beyond the back edge of the board. Trim ½" (1.3 cm) of cording out of the end. Tuck the fabric into the end, encasing the cord. Finish stapling the welting to the board.

15 On the cornice front, place the dustcover over the welting, with right sides together and raw edges even. Staple cardboard stripping at the front. Fold under the sides of the dustcover even with the sides of the cornice. Insert cardboard stripping into the folds. Pull the fabric to the top of the cornice, and staple in place close to the folds. Fold under the back edge of the dustcover and staple it in place.

16 Secure angle irons to the underside of the mounting board just inside the legs and at 36" (91.5 cm) intervals, using pan-head screws. Hold the soft cornice in its proper position above the window, and mark the screw holes for the angle irons on the wall. Lower the cornice. Remove the angle irons, and attach them to the wall. Mount the cornice by reattaching it to the angle irons on the wall.

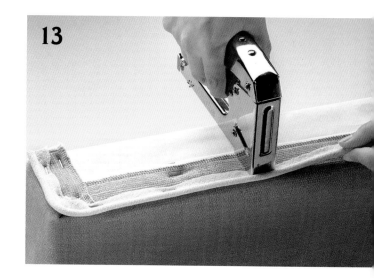

13

Curtains
and
Draperies

Flat Panel Curtains

ONE OF THE EASIEST curtains to make is also one of the most versatile. Flat panel curtains are just pieces of fabric that are hemmed on all four edges and hung from decorative rods with clip-on or sew-on rings. That's as basic as you can get, yet this style of curtain can easily be adapted to create a variety of looks: unlined sheers or semisheers that cover the window, lined or unlined side panels that reveal most or all of the glass, panels formally styled into uniform folds, or panels allowed to casually drape and slouch.

Side framing (opposite)
Slouchy, casual curtain panels that puddle onto the floor are attached to wall hooks that echo the arch of the window frame. These curtains, drawn to the side with simple tiebacks, are stationary—the pleated shades provide the privacy and sun control.

Slim and trim (top)
Single widths of fabric, hemmed on all sides and hanging from crane rods, break up a window-wall covered with pleated shades. Such a simple treatment makes a big difference in the overall appearance of the room.

Simplicity (left)
Some windows need just a touch of fabric. These casual side panels, with their clean lines and neutral tone, conceal the window frame and enhance the padded cornice and pleated shade. So simple but so effective.

*W*hat you need to know

Flat panel curtains can be **designed** as simple, casual, sill-length panels; semi-formal floor-length styles, perfect for a contemporary interior; or spilling-onto-the-floor luxurious draperies. The look is strongly influenced by the *fullness* of the curtains, which can be sleek and spartan at one-and-one-half times fullness, full and opulent at three times fullness, or anywhere in between. See the examples for fullness and ring spacing on page 127.

Select firmly woven medium-weight **fabric** to create a simple tailored look, with an upper edge that can be styled into gentle rolling folds. Lightweight, slinky fabric will result in a relaxed, soft look, with an upper edge that dips gracefully between attachment points. Depending on the desired fullness, one full width of decorator fabric will cover an area 18" to 32" (46 to 81.5 cm) wide. If more width is desired, seam together full or half widths of fabric for each panel. You may prefer to line the curtain panels to add body and prevent the decorator fabric from fading.

The panels can be hung from a decorative rod with clip-on or sew-on curtain rings, which are available in many styles. Choose the hardware and **mount** the rod before you begin so you can accurately measure for the finished length. The rod is usually mounted above the window frame far enough that the top of the curtain covers the wood. Before you drill any holes, it is a good idea to *mock up* a small sample to determine the exact location of the curtain top in relation to the rod; the type of ring used also affects the measurement.

Materials

- Decorative curtain rod
- Tools and hardware for installation
- Decorator fabric
- Drapery lining for lined curtains
- Drapery weights for floor-length curtains
- Clip-on or sew-on rings

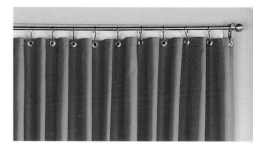

Different fabric fullnesses and same spacing between hooks. For a flatter panel, one-and-one-half times fullness is used (left); this means the width of the curtain measures one-and-one-half times the length of the rod. For a fuller panel, use two times fullness (center) or two-and-one-half times fullness (right). In these photos, all rings are spaced 15½" (39.3 cm) apart.

Cutting directions

- The *cut length* of the fabric is equal to the finished length of the curtain plus the lower hem allowance (see chart below) plus 3" (7.5 cm) for the upper hem.

- The *cut width* of the fabric is equal to the amount of space you want to cover multiplied by the desired fullness (see examples above). Divide this amount by the width of the fabric and round up or down to the nearest whole or half width to find the number of fabric widths you need. Use full or half widths of fabric for each curtain panel.

- Multiply the cut length by the total number of widths needed to determine the amount of fabric to buy. Buy an extra *pattern repeat* per fabric width for matching patterns (page 298).

- For lined curtains, cut the lining fabric 5" (12.7 cm) shorter than the decorator fabric for floor-length curtains; 3" (7.5 cm) shorter than the decorator fabric for sill- or apron-length curtains; or the same length as the decorator fabric for curtains that puddle on the floor. The cut width of the lining is the same as the decorator fabric.

HEM ALLOWANCES

Curtain length	Bottom hem allowance
to sill or apron	6" (15 cm)
½" (1.3 cm) above floor	8" (20.5 cm)
brushing floor	8" (20.5 cm)
puddling on floor	1" (2.5 cm)

Different spacing between rings and same fabric fullness. For a controlled look along the top of the curtain, use more rings and space them close together (left). For a softer look, use fewer rings with more space between them (center). For dramatic swoops in the fabric, use a minimum of rings, spaced even farther apart (right). All of these curtain panels have two times fullness.

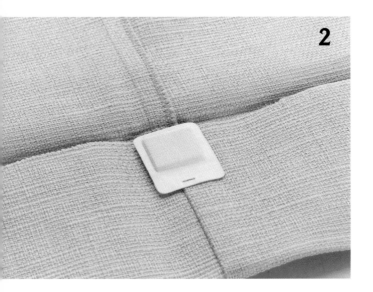

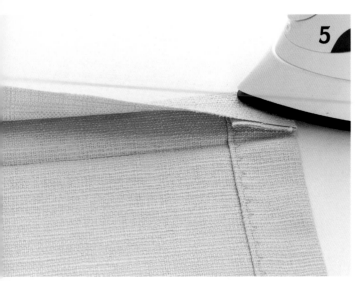

Making unlined flat panel curtains

1 Seam the fabric widths together, if necessary, for each curtain panel. If half widths are needed, add them at the sides of the panels. Finish the seams together, and press them toward the side of the panel.

2 Press under the lower edge the full amount of the hem allowance. Then unfold the pressed edge and turn the cut edge back, aligning it to the pressed fold line. Press the outer fold. If you are making floor-length curtains with more than one fabric width, tack a drapery weight to the upper layer of fabric at the base of each seam, with the bottom of the weight near the inner fold.

3 Refold the lower edge, forming a double-fold hem. Pin. Stitch, using a blindstitch for an invisible hem or a straight stitch for a visible hem.

4 Press under 3" (7.5 cm) on one side. Then unfold the pressed edge and turn the cut edge back, aligning it to the pressed fold line. Press the outer fold. If you are making floor-length curtains, insert a drapery weight between the layers of the lower hem and tack it in place. Refold the edge, forming a 1½" (3.8 cm) double-fold side hem. Stitch, using a blindstitch. Repeat for each side of each curtain panel.

5 Press under a 1½" (3.8 cm) double-fold hem in the upper edge. Stitch the upper hem.

6 Mark the placement for sew-on or clip-on rings along the top hem, placing the end marks ¾" (2 cm) from the sides. Space the remaining marks evenly 6" to 10" (15 to 25.5 cm) apart. Try different spacing patterns, using safety pins, to help you decide. See the examples on page 127. Attach a ring at each mark.

7 Slide the rings onto the drapery rod, and mount the rod on the brackets.

Making lined flat panel curtains

1 Follow steps 1 to 3 for unlined flat panel curtains on page 128. Repeat for the lining, but make a 2" (5 cm) double-fold hem in the lining.

2 Place the curtain panel and lining panel wrong sides together, matching the raw edges at the sides and upper edge; pin. The lining panel will be 1" (2.5 cm) shorter than the curtain panel. Complete the curtain as on page 128, steps 4 to 7, handling the decorator fabric and lining as one fabric.

Making puddled curtains

1 Follow step 1 on page 128 for both decorator fabric and lining. Place the lining and decorator fabric wrong sides together, matching the raw edges. Complete steps 2 to 7, treating both fabrics as one.

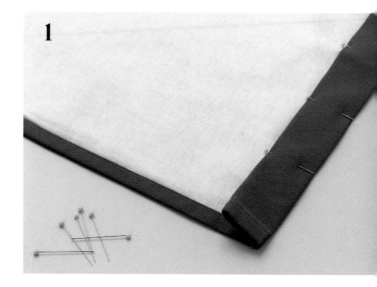

Grommet Curtains

F LAT CURTAIN PANELS with grommets in the top hem can be hung from a decorative rod with cording laced through the grommets or with fancy S-hooks. A popular look is curtains with very large grommets that are speared by the rod. A convenient grommet heading tape product, available in fabric stores, makes this project easy.

Muted geometrics (opposite)
Retro geometric patterns are back. The tones here are muted, so the pattern is not overwhelming. The grommet heading is threaded onto steel cables—totally chic.

Double up (top)
Sheers to filter sunlight and calm the breeze, sun-blocking panels for sleeping in late—these grommet curtains have it all. The casual puddling on the floor adds to the carefree attitude.

Accent on hardware (right)
Grommet tape, which comes with a choice of ring colors, assures uniform folds in these understated curtains. A boldly striped fabric is paired with a metal rod and sculpted finials; this treatment is as much about the hardware as it is the fabric.

What you need to know

Grommet curtains can be made in two styles: those with small grommets that are attached to the rod with hooks or cording, and those with large grommets that are speared by the rod. For either **design**, it is important to have an even number of grommets so both sides of the curtain can turn toward the wall. The space between grommets can be varied for small-grommet curtains. Closer spacing will hold the upper edge in a straighter line; wider spacing will allow the curtain to slouch between grommets. For large-grommet curtains, the space is determined by the grommet tape and cannot be altered. The tape has plastic spacer tabs that make the curtain top fold back and forth in gentle rolls and keep the upper edge straight.

Small-grommet curtains can be made from lightweight to medium-weight **fabric**. Lightweight slinky fabrics will slouch gracefully between grommets. Firmer fabric will hold a straighter line at the upper edge. To be sure the fabric is not too heavy, buy a small amount of fabric to test first; fold it into three layers, and attach a grommet. Use medium-weight fabric for grommet-tape curtains.

Before you cut into the fabric, **mount** the rod so you can take accurate measurements. To determine the proper height for the rod, *mock up* a sample the way you intend to hang the curtain, so you'll know the distance between the curtain top and the bottom of the rod for small-grommet curtains. For large-grommet curtains, the top of the rod will be even with the top of the grommet hole; the top of the curtain will be 1" (2.5 cm) above the rod.

Materials

- Decorative rod
- Tools and hardware for installation
- S-hooks for hanging curtain with small grommets
- Decorator fabric
- Drapery weights for floor-length curtains
- Drapery lining for lined curtains
- Safety pins
- Grommets, size 0 or $^1/_4$" (6 mm) and attaching tool for curtains with small grommets
- Grommet heading tape for curtains with large grommets

Cutting directions

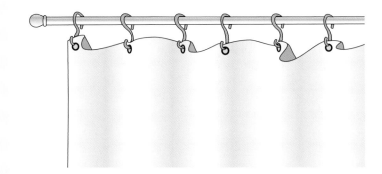

Small-grommet curtains

- The *cut length* of the fabric is equal to the finished length of the curtain plus the lower hem allowance (see chart on page 127) plus an upper hem allowance of two times the diameter of the grommet plus 2" (5 cm).

- The *cut width* of the fabric is equal to the amount of space you want to cover multiplied by the desired *fullness* (see examples on page 127). Divide this amount by the width of the fabric and round up or down to the nearest whole or half width, to determine the number of fabric widths you need. Use full or half widths of fabric for each curtain panel.

- Multiply the cut length by the total number of widths needed to determine the amount of fabric to buy. Buy an extra *pattern repeat* per fabric width for matching patterns.

Large-grommet curtains

- The *cut length* of the fabric is equal to the *finished length* of the curtain plus the lower hem allowance (see chart on page 127) plus 2" (5 cm) for the upper hem.

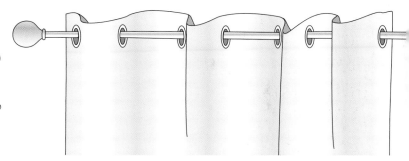

- The *finished width* of the curtain panel is equal to the amount of space you want to cover multiplied by two times fullness (required by the grommet tape). Measure this length of grommet tape. You must have an even number of grommets, and you must begin and end 2" (5 cm) beyond a space tab on each outer edge. Cut the grommet tape to this length.

- The *cut width* of the curtain panel is equal to the length of the grommet tape plus 6" (15 cm) for side hems. Divide this amount by the width of the fabric to determine the number of fabric widths you need. Don't cut the panel to the exact width until step 1 on page 134.

- Multiply the cut length by the total number of widths needed to determine the amount of fabric to buy. Buy an extra pattern repeat per fabric width for matching patterns.

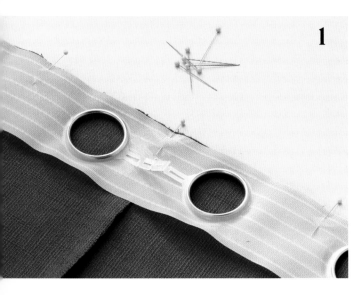

Making curtains with small grommets

1 Follow steps 1 to 4 on page 128 for flat panel curtains. Press the double-fold hem into the upper edge. Unfold the fabric at the upper corners. Trim out the excess fabric of the side hem to within ⅜" (1 cm) of the first fold. Refold and stitch the upper hem.

2 Mark the placement for an even number of grommets along the top hem, placing the end marks ¾" (2 cm) from the sides. Space the remaining marks evenly 6" to 10" (15 to 25.5 cm) apart. Try different spacing patterns, using safety pins to help you decide.

3 Insert the grommets, following the manufacturer's directions.

Making curtains with large grommets

1 Seam the fabric widths together, if necessary, for each curtain panel. Finish the seams together, and press them toward the side of the panel. Lay out the grommet tape along the upper edge of the panel, and adjust the placement so seams in the panel only fall between pairs of grommets that are spaced closer together. Mark the curtain panel 3" (7.5 cm) beyond the ends of the tape, and trim off excess fabric evenly down the sides.

2 Press under the lower edge the full amount of the hem allowance. Then unfold the pressed edge and turn the cut edge back, aligning it to the pressed fold line. Press the outer fold. If you are making floor-length curtains with more than one fabric width, tack a drapery weight to the upper layer of fabric at the base of each seam, with the bottom of the weight near the inner fold.

3 Refold the lower edge, forming a double-fold hem. Pin. Stitch, using a blindstitch for an invisible hem or a straight stitch for a visible hem.

4 Press under 3" (7.5 cm) on one side. Then unfold the pressed edge and turn the cut edge back, aligning it to the pressed fold line. Press the outer fold of the double-fold hem. Repeat on the other side. Unfold the side hems.

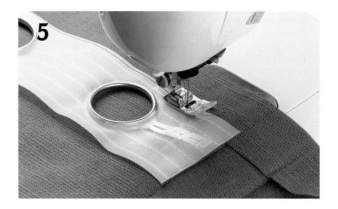

5 Turn under the upper edge 2" (5 cm) and press. Pin the grommet tape, tabs up, on the wrong side of the panel, aligning the cut ends to the inner folds of the side hems, with the upper edge of the tape 1½" (3.8 cm) from the upper pressed fold. Stitch close to the top and bottom edges of the tape.

6 Refold the side hems. Insert a drapery weight between the layers of the lower hem, and tack it in place. Stitch, using a blindstitch or straight stitch. Straight stitch the hems in place over the grommet tape, keeping the spacer tabs free.

7 Trim away the fabric from inside the grommet openings.

8 Working on a flat surface, clip the decorative rings over the grommet openings, encasing the raw edges of the fabric.

9 Hook the plastic spacers together to ripple-fold the curtain. Insert the rod through the grommets and hang the rod.

Curtains with Cuffs

AN ATTACHED CUFF of matching or contrasting fabric drapes gracefully along the top of a relaxed curtain. By varying the fullness or the way the curtains are hung, you can adapt this basic style to create different looks. Simply attach sew-on or clip-on rings to the upper edge and hang the curtain from a decorative rod or a series of interesting knobs or wall hooks. For a techno look, install grommets along the upper edge (page 134) and hang the curtain using cording or decorative hooks.

Dramatic draping (opposite)
The vibrant color and over-the-top styling of these curtains is in the same spirit as the art and furniture. Lavish draping makes the curtains sensuous and playful all at once. Hung from decorative wall hooks, the cuffs droop to reveal their contrast lining.

Feminine and pretty (top)
The tiny floral pattern of these semi-sheer curtains works so well with the wide stripes of the wallcovering and the floral-motif finials of the narrow rod. The curtains swish into shallow puddles on the floor. Their ruffly cuffed tops are edged with ribbon for a delicate finish.

Fringe benefits (left)
Bullion fringe caught in the seam traces the undulating curves of the burgundy silk cuffs that top off these citrine silk curtains. This lush treatment has a gilded ornate rod mounted close to the ceiling.

What you need to know

Cuffed curtains are a very casual and dramatic **design**. Because the upper edge slouches between hooks, the lower edge will also be uneven and should be allowed to break at or puddle on the floor. Use two or two-and-one-half times *fullness* and space the rings 12" to 16" (30.5 to 40.5 cm) apart for a gentle draping effect along the upper edge of the cuff. If you prefer a more controlled upper edge, use less fullness or space the grommets or rings closer together. The cuff length can range from 6" to 15" (15 to 38 cm) to suit the curtain length and the tone you want to create—short, casual, and perky to long, formal, and sophisticated.

Lightweight, drapable **fabrics** are most effective for this treatment, for both the curtain and cuff. If you want the curtain to hold a more rigid pattern of swoops and rolls, choose a firmer fabric so you will be able to arrange the cuffs a certain way. Lining the curtain and *interlining* the cuff with a lightweight drapery lining will also create more body.

Before you cut into the fabric, **mount** the rod or wall hooks so you can take accurate measurements. To determine the proper height for the hardware, *mock up* a sample the way you intend to hang the curtain, so you'll know the distance between the curtain top and the bottom of the rod or the hooks. For curtains that puddle on the floor, the exact length measurement is not as crucial.

Materials

- Decorative curtain rod
- Tools and hardware for installation
- Lightweight fabric that drapes softly for the curtain
- Matching or contrasting lightweight fabric for the cuff
- Drapery lining for lined curtains
- Drapery weights for floor-length curtains
- Clip-on or sew-on rings or grommets and attaching tool

Cutting directions

- The *cut length* of the fabric is equal to the finished length of the curtain plus the lower hem allowance (see chart on page 127) minus 2½" (6.5 cm). Include 2" (5 cm) for curtains that break at the floor or 12" to 20" (30.5 to 51 cm) for curtains that puddle on the floor.

- The *cut width* of the fabric is equal to the amount of space you want to cover multiplied by the desired fullness (see examples on page 127). Divide this amount by the width of the fabric and round up or down to the nearest whole or half width, to determine the number of fabric widths you need. Use full or half widths of fabric for each curtain panel.

- Multiply the cut length by the total number of widths needed to determine the amount of fabric to buy. Buy an extra *pattern repeat* per fabric width for matching patterns.

- The cut length of the cuff is equal to the finished length from the top of the curtain plus 3½" (9 cm) multiplied by 2. Use the same number of fabric widths as for the curtain, and seam them together so the cut width of the cuff is equal to the hemmed width of the curtain plus 1" (2.5 cm) for seam allowances on the sides.

- For lined curtains, cut the lining fabric 5" (12.7 cm) shorter than the decorator fabric for floor-length curtains; 3" (7.5 cm) shorter than the decorator fabric for sill- or apron-length curtains; or the same length as the decorator fabric for curtains that puddle on the floor. The cut width of the lining is the same as the decorator fabric.

Making curtains with cuffs

1 Seam the fabric widths together, if necessary, for each curtain panel. If half widths are needed, add them at the sides of the panels. Finish the seam allowances together, and press them toward the side of the panel.

2 Press under the lower edge the full amount of the hem allowance. Then unfold the pressed edge and turn the cut edge back, aligning it to the pressed fold line. Press the outer fold. If you are making floor-length curtains with more than one fabric width, tack a drapery weight to the upper layer of fabric at the base of each seam, with the bottom of the weight near the inner fold.

3 Refold the lower edge, forming a double-fold hem. Pin. Stitch, using a blindstitch for an invisible hem or a straight stitch for a visible hem. Omit steps 4 and 5 if the curtains are unlined.

4 For lined curtains, repeat steps 1 to 3 for the lining, making a 2" (5 cm) double-fold hem. For puddle curtains, layer the fabric and lining and treat them as one for hemming.

5 Place the curtain panel and lining panel wrong sides together, matching the raw edges at the sides and upper edge; pin. At the bottom, the lining panel will be 1" (2.5 cm) shorter than the curtain panel.

6 Press under 3" (7.5 cm) on one side. Then unfold the pressed edge and turn the cut edge back, aligning it to the pressed fold line. Press the outer fold. Insert a drapery weight between the layers of the lower hem, and tack it in place. Refold the edge, forming a 1½" (3.8 cm) double-fold side hem. Stitch, using a blindstitch. Repeat for each side of each curtain panel. If making lined curtains, treat the lining and face fabric as one.

7 Seam the fabric widths together for the cuff, using ½" (1.3 cm) seam allowances. Press the seams open. Fold the cuff in half crosswise, right sides together. Stitch ½" (1.3 cm) seams at the ends.

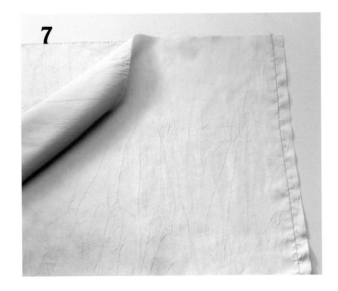

7

8 Turn the cuff right side out and press the seams at the ends. Baste the raw edges together and press along the fold.

9 Pin the cuff to the top of the curtain panel, matching raw edges, with the right side of the cuff facing down on the wrong side of the curtain panel. Stitch ½" (1.3 cm) seam; finish the seam, using zigzag or overlock stitch.

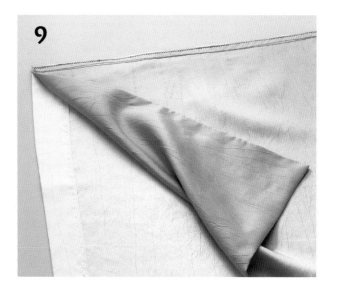

10 Fold the cuff 3" (7.5 cm) above the seam line as shown. Pin in place; do not press the fold.

11 Mark the upper fold ½" (1.3 cm) from each side of the curtain panel for the placement of the end grommets or rings.

12 Mark the placement for the remaining grommets or rings 12" to 16" (30.5 to 40.5 cm) apart, spacing the marks evenly.

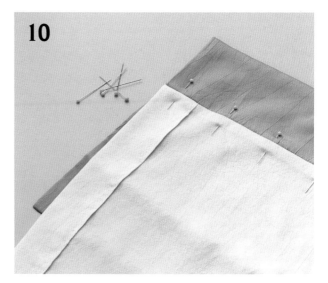

13 Install the grommets through all layers, with the top of each grommet ½" (1.3 cm) below the upper folded edge. Or secure clip-on rings or sew-on rings at markings. Remove the pins.

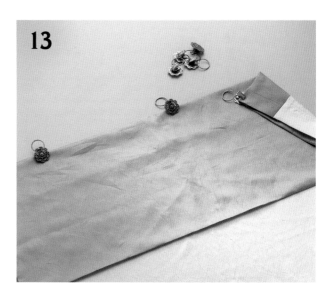

Tab Curtains

THE EYE is drawn upward when a window is dressed with tab curtains. Narrow straps that loop or tie over a decorative rod give this treatment the no-frill appeal of blending form with function. The tabs can loop, tie, or be buttoned.

Classic country (opposite)
These sunny curtains for a country kitchen are floor-to-ceiling. Tied up simply with scarves that match the shade, these tab curtains are classic, uncluttered, and cheerful.

Retro with a twist (top)
The paisley panels of the seventies never looked this sophisticated. In updated styling, this decorator print is edged with a subtle geometric that is repeated in the slender tie tabs.

Tailored serenity (left)
Earth tones of cream, brown, and yellow create a calm and inviting space. Button accents on the tabs add just the right amount of detail to these understated curtains.

$\mathcal{W}$hat you need to know

Tab curtains are not intended to be opened and closed repeatedly, because the friction would put too much strain on the tabs. Therefore, this curtain style is often **designed** as two stationary panels at the sides of a window. For a narrow window, one panel can cover the entire width at the top and be drawn to one side to let light in. The tabs can be a continuous loop, two straps that are tied over the rod, or a single strap attached at one end and seemingly buttoned to the curtain at the front. (To avoid strain on the buttons, the tabs are sewn in place and the buttons are just decorative.) Each fabric width has five or six evenly spaced tabs.

Tab curtains can be lined or unlined, depending on the **fabric** selection and the degree of light control and privacy required. Medium-weight decorator fabrics offer the needed strength for the tabs and will keep the upper edge of the curtain in a controlled line. If a soft drape between tabs is desired, choose a lighter weight, drapable fabric for the curtain.

It is wise to *mock up* the treatment and hang the rod before cutting for accurate length measurements (see the steps below). **Mount** the rod high enough so the top of the window frame will not be visible above the curtain.

Materials

- Decorative curtain rod
- Tools and hardware for installation
- Decorator fabric
- Drapery lining for lined curtains
- Drapery weights for floor-length curtains
- Buttons or covered button kits for button tab curtains

Measuring

1 Determine the tab length by wrapping a cloth tape measure over the rod the desired distance to the top of the curtain. Add 1" (2.5 cm) for seam allowances and 2¾" (7 cm) more for button tabs. For tie tabs, mock up a tab with wide ribbon or strips of fabric in the style of knot you want to use. Then measure the length of each piece and add 1" (2.5 cm) for end seams.

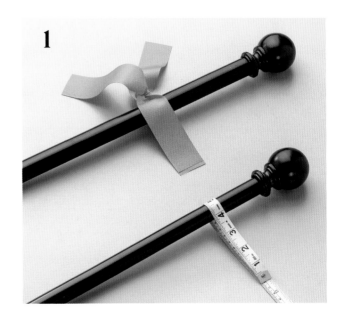

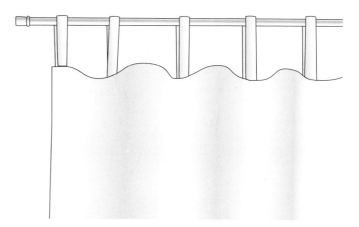

2 Measure the distance from the underside of the rod to the top of the curtain. Mount the rod a distance above the window equal to this distance plus 1" (2.5 cm). This ensures that the window frame will not show above the curtain.

Cutting directions

- The *cut length* of each curtain panel is equal to the finished length plus the bottom hem allowance (see chart on page 127) plus 3" (7.5 cm).

- The *cut width* of the fabric is equal to the amount of space you want to cover multiplied by 2. Divide this amount by the width of the fabric and round up or down to the nearest whole or half width, to determine the number of fabric widths you need. Use full or half widths of fabric for each curtain panel.

- For lined tab curtains, the cut length of the lining is equal to the finished length of the curtain plus 3½" (9 cm). The cut width is the same as for the decorator fabric.

- You will need five tabs for the first full width plus four tabs for each additional full width and two tabs for each additional half width in each curtain panel. For loop or button tabs 1½" (3.8 cm) wide, cut a 4" (10 cm) strip of fabric for each tab, using the length measurement from step 1, opposite. For tie tabs 1" (2.5 cm) wide, cut two 2½" (6.5 cm) strips for each tab, using the length measurement found in step 1, opposite.

- Multiply the cut length by the number of fabric widths needed to determine the total amount required for the curtains. For the tabs, add 12" (30.5 cm) for every two fabric widths needed to determine the total length to buy.

Making unlined loop tab curtains

1 Seam the fabric widths together as necessary for each curtain panel, adding any half widths at the *return* ends of the panels. Finish the seam allowances together, and press them toward the side of the panel.

2 Press under the lower edge 8" (20.5 cm) for the hem. Then unfold the pressed edge and turn the cut edge back, aligning it to the pressed fold line. Press the outer fold. If the panel has more than one fabric width, tack a drapery weight to the upper layer of fabric at the base of each seam, with the bottom of the weight near the inner fold.

3 Refold the lower edge, forming a 4" (10 cm) double-fold hem, encasing the weights at the seams. Pin. Stitch, using a blindstitch for an invisible hem or a straight stitch for a visible hem.

4 Press under ½" (1.3 cm) on the upper edge. Then fold 2" (5 cm) to the right side, forming a facing. At the outer corners, stitch the facing to the curtain 3" (7.5 cm) from the edges (arrow). Trim the facing to within ¼" (6 mm) of the stitching; trim off the top 1" (2.5 cm) of the side hem allowance (see photo on next page).

5 Fold each tab in half lengthwise, right sides together. Stitch a ½" (1.3 cm) seam along the cut edge.

(continued)

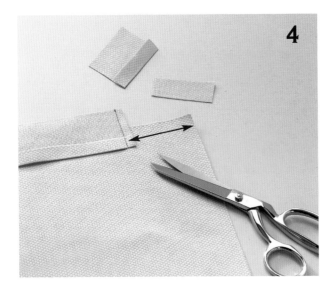

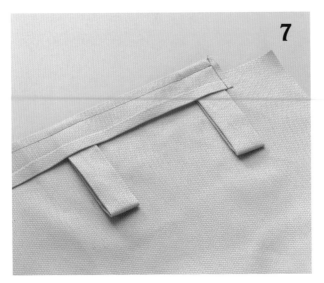

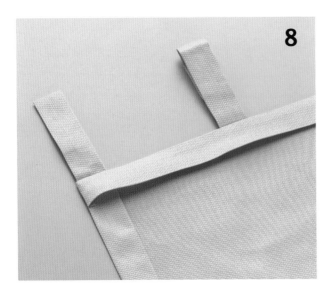

6 Turn the tabs right side out. Center the seam in the back of each tab; press.

7 Mark the placement for the tabs evenly spaced along the upper hem of the curtain, with the first and last tabs flush with the outer edges. Fold the tabs in half and slide them under the facing with the raw edges in the fold; pin. Stitch across the curtain top, ½" (1.3 cm) from the fold.

8 Press under 1½" (3.8 cm) double-fold side hems. Turn the facing to the curtain back; press. Stitch the side hems, encasing a drapery weight in the hem layers at the lower corners of floor-length curtains. At the upper corners, the hem will disappear under the facing. Stitch along the lower fold of the facing.

9 Hang the curtain from the rod. Space the tabs evenly on the rod. Train the curtain to fall in soft folds, with the fabric at the tabs rolling forward and the fabric between the tabs rolling toward the window.

Making lined tab curtains

1 Follow steps 1 to 3 for unlined tab curtains on page 145. Repeat for the lining, but make a 2" (5 cm) double-fold hem in the lining and omit drapery weights in the lining.

2 Place the curtain panel and lining panel wrong sides together, matching the raw edges at the sides. The upper edge of the lining will be 2½" (6.5 cm) below the upper edge of the curtain panel. At the bottom, the lining panel will be 1" (2.5 cm) shorter than the curtain panel. Pin.

3 Complete the curtain as on pages 145 and above, steps 4 to 9, handling the decorator fabric and lining as one fabric.

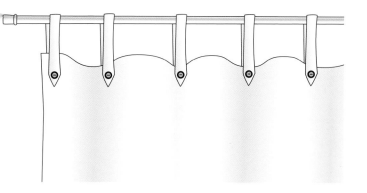

Making button tab curtains

1 Follow steps 1 to 5 on page 145. Center the seam in the back of the tab; press, avoiding sharp creases on the outer edges. Mark a point $\frac{1}{4}$" (6 mm) from the lower edge on the seam; mark points $1\frac{1}{4}$" (3.2 cm) from the lower edge on the outer folds.

2 Sew from the mark on the outer fold to the mark on the seam; pivot, and stitch to the mark on the opposite fold, forming the point of the tab. Trim the seam to $\frac{1}{4}$" (6 mm). Turn the tab right side out; press.

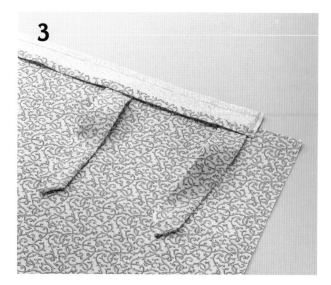

3 Follow step 7, but secure only the open end of the tabs under the facing, with the seam against the right side of the curtain.

4 Finish the curtains as in step 8. Turn the tabs down over the top of the curtain. Tack the tabs securely with the sewing machine. Sew buttons over the stitches. Hang the curtains as in step 9.

Making tie tab curtains

1 Follow steps 1 to 4 for loop tab curtains. Fold each tab in half lengthwise, right sides together. Stitch a $\frac{1}{4}$" (6 mm) seam along the cut edge and one end. Turn the tabs right side out and press.

2 Follow step 7, but stack two tabs, securing only the open ends under the facing.

3 Finish the curtains as in step 8. Hang the curtains as in step 9, tying the tabs over the rod.

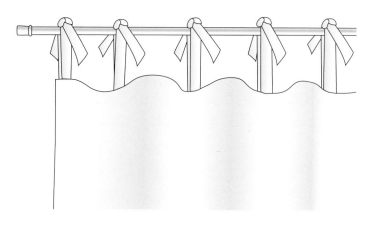

Scalloped Curtains

*S*CALLOPS EXAGGERATE the droops between tabs or rings along the upper edge of a curtain. The dips can be deep and dramatic on formal curtains that brush the floor or shallow and sweet on a set of café curtains. This style works for stationary curtains that are attached to a rod by tabs or by clip-on or sew-on rings. Curtains attached by rings can also traverse the rod to cover the window when necessary.

Black pinstripes (opposite)
Tall and tailored, scalloped curtains dress up and frame in the formal seating area of this greatroom. Pinstripes draw your eye upward to the scalloped, tabbed tops while seemingly raising the ceiling.

Café style (top)
Café curtains with scallop shaping and ribbon tie tabs are perfect in a room where light is necessary but privacy is, too. The blue and white print fabric is lined for added privacy, yet light can flood the room through the top window panes.

Filtered light (left)
Semisheer plaid curtains filter the morning sun streaming through bedroom windows. The curtains' scalloped upper edges droop softly between tie tabs, adding to the relaxed, laid-back atmosphere of the room.

*W*hat you need to know

For this **design**, you will need to make a paper pattern to shape the top of the curtain. For curtains with two panels that meet in the center, both panels should end with a tab or ring at the center edge. Seams are least visible if they are 3" (7.5 cm) from the nearest tab or ring. This will cause the scallop widths in the center of a multi-width panel to be slightly narrower than the other scallops. Scallop depths are all equal, however, and tabs or rings are spaced evenly along the rod, so the difference in scallop widths is not noticeable. Scalloped curtains can be lined or unlined, in a casual length just below the window frame, to a more formal length just above the floor, or breaking at the floor with 2" (5 cm) of extra length.

Select medium-weight **fabric** with enough body to hold the shape of the scallop. The scalloped edge is finished with a facing, using the same fabric as the curtain or a coordinating fabric.

Before **mounting** the rod above the window, consider the distance any rings or clips hang below the rod, as this will determine the highest point of the curtain's upper edge. If making tab curtains, wrap a cloth tape measure over the rod to determine the desired length of the tab. Also determine the depth of the scallops. Shallow scallops of 2½" to 3" (6.5 to 7.5 cm) work well for café curtains on a small window. Deep 8" (20.5 cm) scallops create a dramatic effect for floor-length curtains. Depending on how high the rod is mounted and the depth of the scallops, part of the upper window frame and even the glass may be exposed by the scallops.

Materials

- Decorative curtain rod
- Tools and hardware for installation
- Decorator fabric
- Matching or contrasting fabric for facing
- Matching or contrasting fabric for tabs, optional
- Paper, pencil, and string for making scallop pattern
- Drapery weights for floor-length curtains
- Drapery lining for lined curtains
- Clip-on or sew-on rings, optional
- Pin-on rings and cup hooks or tenter hooks for securing returns to wall

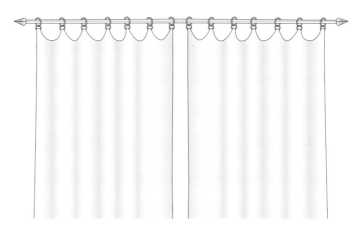

Cutting directions

- The *cut length* of the fabric is equal to the finished length of the curtain plus the bottom hem allowance (see chart on page 127) plus ½" (1.3 cm) for the seam allowance at the upper edge.

- The *cut width* of the fabric is equal to the amount of space you want to cover multiplied by two times *fullness*. Divide this amount by the width of

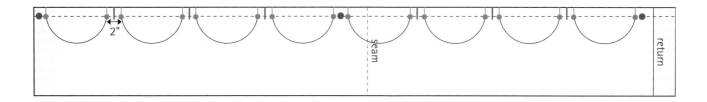

the fabric and round up or down to the nearest whole or half width, to find the number of fabric widths you need. Use full or half widths of fabric for each curtain panel.

- Cut fabric for the facing, with the length equal to the scallop depth plus 4" (10 cm) and the width equal to the cut width of the curtain fabric.

- The cut length of the lining is equal to the cut length of the decorator fabric minus the scallop depth minus 8" (20.5 cm).

- If making tab curtains, cut a 3" (7.5 cm) strip of fabric for each tab, 1" (2.5 cm) longer than the desired finished length. You will need five tabs for the first full width plus four tabs for each additional full width and two tabs for each additional half width in each curtain panel.

- Cut paper for the pattern, 2" (5 cm) longer than the desired scallop depth and 6" (15 cm) narrower than the seamed width of the curtain panel. This equals the finished width of the curtain after hemming.

Making unlined scalloped curtains

1 Seam the fabric widths together as necessary for each curtain panel, adding any half widths at the *return* ends of the panels. Repeat for the facings. Finish the seam allowances together, and press them toward the side of the panel.

2 Press under the lower edge 8" (20.5 cm) for the hem. Then unfold the pressed edge and turn the cut edge back, aligning it to the pressed fold line. Press the outer fold. For floor-length curtains, if the panel has more than one fabric width,

tack a drapery weight to the upper layer of fabric at the base of each seam, with the bottom of the weight near the inner fold.

3 Refold the lower edge, forming a 4" (10 cm) double-fold hem, encasing the weights at the seams. Pin. Stitch, using a blindstitch for an invisible hem or a straight stitch for a visible hem.

4 Finish the lower edge of the facing by serging, or turn the edge under ¼" (6 mm) twice and stitch.

5 Mark a ½" (1.3 cm) seam allowance across the upper edge of the pattern. Mark the depth of the return on one end of the pattern; mark the seam positions.

6 Mark a point on the upper seam line ½" (1.3 cm) away from the return. Mark a point 3" (7.5 cm) beyond the first seam from the return.

7 Fold the paper to divide the space between marks into four equal parts if the space represents a whole width, or into two equal parts if the space represents a half width; crease to mark. Unfold.

8 Divide any additional whole widths, falling between the return end and the opposite end of the panel, into four equal parts, placing the marks for the tabs or rings nearest the seams 3" (7.5 cm) beyond the seams.

9 Mark a point ½" (1.3 cm) from the end; divide the end width into four equal parts.

10 Mark the scallop end points on the upper seam line, 1" (2.5 cm) on each side of the marks. This allows for ½" (1.3 cm) seam allowances in the scalloped edge and 1" (2.5 cm) space for the tabs or rings.

(continued)

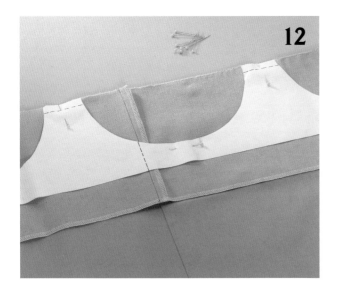

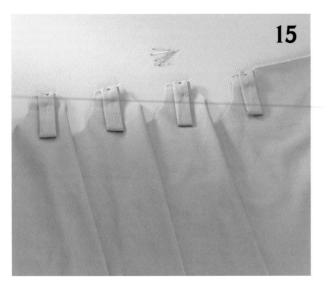

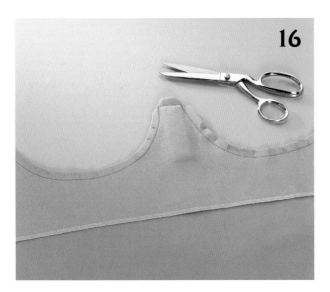

11 Mark the depth of the scallop in the first space from the return, measuring from the upper edge of the pattern; draw the scallop from the end points through the depth mark. Refold, and cut the first set of scallops. Repeat for each set of scallops.

12 Place the facing over the curtain panel, right sides together, matching the upper and side edges. Pin the pattern over the facing, aligning the upper edges and seam marks; cut the scallops through both layers. Transfer the mark for the return. Remove the facing. For curtains without tabs, omit steps 13 to 15.

13 Fold each tab in half lengthwise, right sides together. Stitch a ½" (1.3 cm) seam along the cut edge.

14 Turn the tabs right side out. Center the seam in the back of each tab; press.

15 Fold each tab in half, aligning the raw edges. Pin or baste the tabs in place on the right side of the curtain, aligning the raw edges of the tabs to the upper edge of the curtain and centering the tabs between the scallops. Pin the tab at the return end with the outer edges on the return mark. Pin the tab at the opposite end 3" (7.5 cm) from the side of the panel.

16 Pin the facing to the upper edge of the curtain, right sides together, aligning the raw edges. Stitch a ½" (1.3 cm) seam. A zipper foot may be used to stitch close to the tab. Trim the seam; clip the curves. Turn the curtain right side out, aligning the outer raw edges; press.

17 Press under 3" (7.5 cm) on one side. Then unfold the pressed edge and turn the cut edge back, aligning it to the pressed fold line. Press the outer fold. Insert a drapery weight between the layers of the lower hem, and tack it in place. Refold the edge, forming a 1½" (3.8 cm) double-fold side hem. Stitch, using a blindstitch. Repeat for each side of each curtain panel. Fold the hem under diagonally at the upper corners, if necessary; hand-stitch.

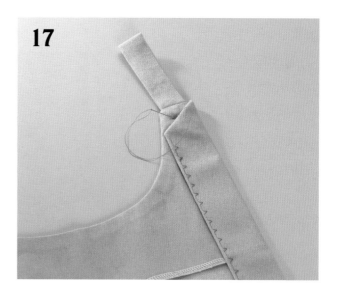

18 Hang the curtain from the rod, using tabs or clip-on or sew-on rings. Attach a pin-on ring to the inner edge of the return, and secure it to a tenter hook or cup hook in the wall.

19 Space the tabs or rings evenly on the rod. Train the curtain so the fabric in the scallops rolls toward the window; fabric at the tabs or rings rolls outward, forming soft folds.

Making lined scalloped curtains

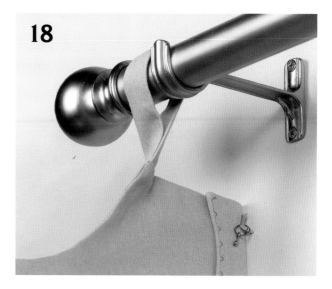

1 Follow steps 1 to 3 for unlined scalloped curtains on page 151. Repeat for the lining, but make a 2" (5 cm) double-fold hem in the lining and omit drapery weights in the lining.

2 Pin the facing to the upper edge of the lining, right sides together. Stitch a ½" (1.3 cm) seam. Press the seam allowances toward the facing.

3 Follow steps 5 to 16 on pages 151 and 152. Align the outer edges of the facing and lining to the outer edges of the curtain. The lining will be 1" (2.5 cm) shorter than the curtain panel. Complete the curtain, following steps 17 to 19, folding the lining and decorator fabric as one.

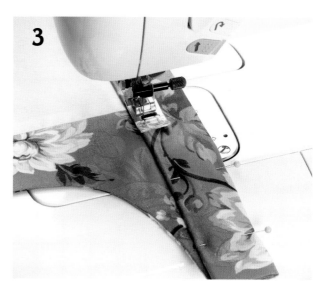

Styling Tape Curtains

CLEVER AND PRACTICAL, styling tapes help even rookie sewers create curtains with gorgeous, intricate headings. The tapes have woven-in cords that are pulled to draw the fabric fullness into pleats, gathers, or distinctive folds. Some tape styles imitate European hand-smocking; some create tiny, continuous pencil pleats; others fold the fabric into three-finger pinch pleats—all at a tug of the cords!

Well-dressed bay (opposite)
Window walls, like this expansive bay, can be a design challenge. Multiple layers at the window make the room cozy. Only the underlayer needs to open and close. The sumptuous curtains have a styling tape heading accented with a contrasting fabric band.

Delightful dining room (top)
The cheerful cabbage rose pattern of these tied-back curtains creates an inviting atmosphere for dining. The smocked curtain heading, mounted just under the crown molding, was created effortlessly with styling tape.

Exotic silk (left)
Semisheer silk curtains with a wide shirred heading are global-chic. Styling tape made the sewing quick and easy.

What you need to know

Styling tapes in various pleating and gathering styles are available in the decorating areas of fabric stores as precut packaged lengths or to be bought by the yard. Instructions for using the tape are included to help you **design** your curtains. The amount of *fullness* needed in the curtain depends on the style of tape you select—most require two to three times fullness.

For best results, use medium-weight to lightweight **fabric**.

Mount the hardware before you cut to ensure accurate measurements. The curtains can be installed on standard or decorative curtain rods or on pole sets with rings. Some tapes have loops woven into them for securing drapery pins, and some manufacturers provide special pins for installation.

Styling tapes

Materials

- Standard curtain rod, decorative rod, or pole set with rings
- Tools and hardware for installation
- Decorator fabric
- Drapery weights
- Styling tape
- Thin cardboard
- 2 small plastic bags
- Drapery hooks

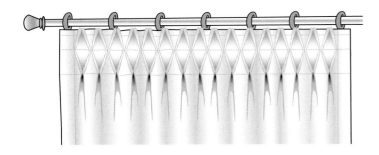

Cutting directions

- The *cut length* of the decorator fabric is equal to the desired *finished length* of the curtain plus the bottom hem allowance (see chart on page 127) plus ¾" (2 cm) for turn-under at the upper edge. If using a standard curtain rod, measure the finished length of the curtain from the top of the rod; then add ½" (1.3 cm) so the curtain will extend above the rod. If using a decorative curtain rod or a pole set with rings, measure the length from the pin holes in the slides or rings.

- The *cut width* of the fabric is equal to the width to be covered multiplied by the recommended fullness of the styling tape plus 6" (15 cm) for side hems. If it is necessary to seam the fabric widths together to make each panel, allow 1" (2.5 cm) for each seam. If a standard or decorative curtain rod is used, also add twice the *projection* of the rod for *returns*.

- The cut length of the lining is 5¾" (14.5 cm) shorter than the cut length of the decorator fabric. The cut width of the lining is the same as the decorator fabric.

Making styling tape curtains

1 Seam fabric widths together, if necessary, for each panel. Finish the seam allowances together, and press them toward the side of the panel.

2 Press under the lower edge the full amount of the hem allowance. Then unfold the pressed edge and turn the cut edge back, aligning it to the pressed fold line. Press the outer fold. If you are making floor-length curtains with more than one fabric width, tack a drapery weight to the upper layer of fabric at the base of each seam, with the bottom of the weight near the inner fold.

3 Refold the lower edge, forming a double-fold hem, encasing the weights at the seams. Pin. Stitch, using a blindstitch for an invisible hem or a straight stitch for a visible hem.

4 Press under 3" (7.5 cm) on one side. Then unfold the pressed edge and turn the cut edge back, aligning it to the pressed fold line. Press the outer fold. Insert a drapery weight between the layers of the lower hem, and tack it in place. Refold the edge, forming a $1\frac{1}{2}$" (3.8 cm) double-fold side hem. Repeat for each side of each curtain panel.

5 Press under $\frac{3}{4}$" (2 cm) on the upper edge of the curtain panel. Cut the styling tape to the width of the hemmed panel plus 2" (5 cm). Turn under 1" (2.5 cm) on each end of the tape, and use a pin to pick out the cords. Position the tape right side up on the wrong side of the panel, with the upper edge of the tape $\frac{1}{4}$" (6 mm) from the top.

6 Stitch the tape to the curtain, stitching just inside the top and bottom edges and next to any additional cords.

7 Knot all cords together, or knot them in pairs, at each end of the styling tape. At one end, pull evenly on the cords to pleat or gather the curtain panel to its determined finished width.

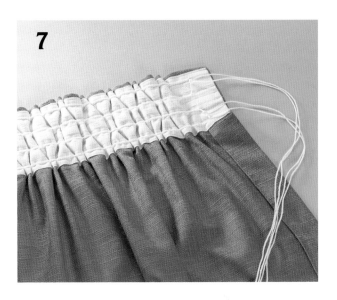

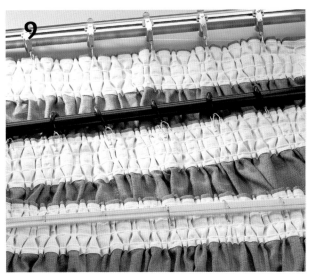

8 Knot the cords securely at the side. Wind the excess cord around a square of thin cardboard, and tuck it into a small plastic bag pinned to the side hem out of sight.

9 Insert drapery pins at the ends of the panels and at 3" (7.5 cm) intervals. If the styling tape has loops, insert drapery pins into them. Insert the drapery pins into the eyes of the slides on a decorative curtain rod (top) or the eyes of the rings for a pole set (middle). Or use drapery pins with round tops and hook them over a standard curtain rod.

Classic Rod-Pocket Curtains

R OD-POCKET curtains are often chosen for a stationary window treatment that is stylish and easy to sew. With ample fullness and a deep, ruffly heading, classic rod-pocket curtains take on a feminine, romantic appearance. With less fullness and a shorter heading, the look becomes more tailored and modern. Either way, the fluid lines and gathered fabric soften the hard surfaces and edges of the window.

Sunny sheers (opposite)
These sheer rod-pocket curtains bring sunshine into this quaint bedroom. The vibrant yellow is tempered by the blue (the complementary color) of the walls, Roman shade, and bedding. With their short heading and spilling-onto-the-floor length, this treatment is definitely a departure from the rod-pocket curtains of the past.

Classic florals (top)
Rod-pocket side panels mounted over traversing draperies create a soft focal point for this bedroom. Sewn from pretty floral fabric, they have a modest heading, and the inner edges are accented with decorator ball fringe.

Retro linens (right)
These curtains were made from colorful tablecloths in patterns from the forties. Cinched with fruit ties that conjure up Carmen Miranda, they make a bold statement in this charming kitchen.

What you need to know

Rod-pocket curtains have a *heading* and *rod pocket*. The heading is the portion at the top of a rod-pocket curtain that forms a ruffle when the curtain is on the rod. The depth of the heading is the distance from the top of the curtain to the top stitching line of the rod pocket. The rod pocket is the "tunnel" where the rod or pole is inserted; stitching lines at the top and bottom of the rod pocket keep the rod in place. To determine the depth of the rod pocket, measure around the widest part of the rod or pole; add ½" (1.3 cm) ease to this measurement, and divide by two.

To **design** your rod-pocket curtains, first decide how you will hang them. Several types of rods can be used, including flat rods in widths of 1", 2½", and 4½" (2.5, 6.5, and 11.5 cm). Wood and metal pole sets with elbows or finials can also be used and are available in several diameters. When a curtain rod or pole set with elbows is used, sides of the curtain panels wrap to the wall. This portion is called the *return*. For curtains mounted on poles with finials, returns can be created by making an opening in the front of the rod pocket for inserting the pole.

Rod-pocket curtains work well with a variety of **fabrics**. Unlined rod-pocket curtains can be made from sheers or laces, creating a lightweight treatment that allows filtered light to enter the room. For curtains made from medium-weight decorator fabrics, lining can be used to make the curtains more durable and opaque, add extra body, and support the side hems and heading. For sheer fabrics, allow two-and-one-half to three times the length of the rod for *fullness*; for heavier fabrics, allow two to two-and-one-half times.

Before cutting the fabric, decide where the window treatment should be positioned and **mount** the curtain rod or pole. Brackets are usually mounted on the wall just outside the window frame so the bottom of the rod is even with the top of the frame. Measure from the lower edge of the rod to where you want the lower edge of the curtain. To determine the *finished length* of the curtain, add the desired depth of the heading and rod pocket to this measurement.

Materials

- Standard curtain rod or pole set with finials or elbows
- Tools and hardware for installation
- Decorator fabric
- Drapery lining for lined curtains
- Drapery weights for floor-length curtains
- Fusible interfacing

Cutting directions

- The *cut length* of the fabric is equal to the finished length of the curtain plus the lower hem allowance (see chart on page 13) plus the depth of the heading and the rod pocket plus ½" (1.3 cm) for turn-under at the upper edge.

- The *cut width* of the fabric is equal to the amount of space you want to cover (including returns) multiplied by the desired fullness. Divide this amount by the width of the fabric and round up or down to the nearest whole or half width to find the number of fabric widths you need. Use full or half widths of fabric for each curtain panel.

- Multiply the cut length by the total number of widths needed to determine the amount of fabric to buy. Buy an extra *pattern repeat* per fabric width for matching patterns (page 298).

- For lined curtains, cut the lining fabric 5" (12.7 cm) shorter than the decorator fabric. The cut width of the lining is the same as the decorator fabric.

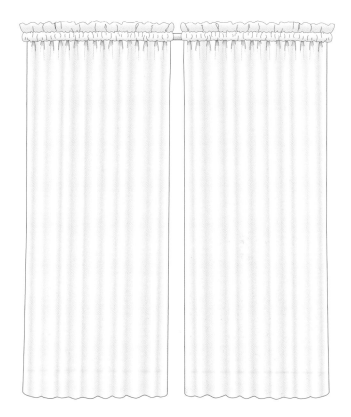

Making unlined rod-pocket curtains

1 Seam the fabric widths together, if necessary, for each curtain panel. If half widths are needed, add them at the sides of the panels. Finish the seam allowances together, and press them toward the side of the panel.

2 Press under the lower edge the full amount of the hem allowance. Then unfold the pressed edge and turn the cut edge back, aligning it to the pressed fold line. Press the outer fold. If you are making floor-length curtains with more than one fabric width, tack a drapery weight to the upper layer of fabric at the base of each seam, with the bottom of the weight near the inner fold.

3 Refold the lower edge, forming a double-fold hem, encasing the weights at the seams. Pin. Stitch, using a blindstitch for an invisible hem or a straight stitch for a visible hem.

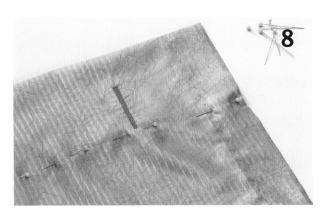

4 Press under 3" (7.5 cm) on one side. Then unfold the pressed edge and turn the cut edge back, aligning it to the pressed fold line. Press the outer fold. Insert a drapery weight between the layers of the lower hem, and tack it in place. Refold the edge, forming a 1½" (3.8 cm) double-fold side hem. Stitch, using a blindstitch. Repeat for each side of each curtain panel.

5 Press under ½" (1.3 cm) on the upper edge. Then press under an amount equal to the rod-pocket depth plus the heading depth. If the curtain will be mounted on a pole with elbow returns, omit steps 6 to 8.

6 Mount the rod on a wooden, keyhole, or elbow bracket. Measure the distance from the wall to the center of the pole.

7 Unfold the upper edge of the curtain on the return side of the panel. On the right side of the fabric, measure from the side of the curtain a distance equal to the measurement in step 6; mark at the center of the rod pocket. If the curtain will be mounted on a rod with keyhole brackets, omit step 8.

8 Cut a 1" (2.5 cm) strip of fusible interfacing, 1" (2.5 cm) longer than the depth of the rod pocket. Fuse the strip to the wrong side of the curtain panel, centering it directly under the mark made in step 7. On the right side of the panel, stitch a buttonhole at the mark, from the top to the bottom of the rod pocket. Refold the upper edge of the panel along the pressed lines; pin.

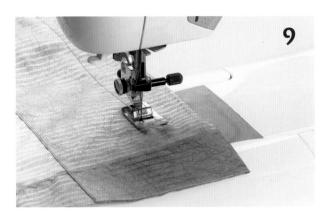

9 Stitch close to the first fold; stitch again at the depth of the heading, using tape on the bed of the sewing machine as a stitching guide.

Making lined rod-pocket curtains

1 Follow steps 1 to 3 for unlined rod-pocket curtains on page 161. Repeat for the lining, but make a 2" (5 cm) double-fold hem in the lining and omit drapery weights in the lining.

2 Place the curtain panel and lining panel wrong sides together, matching the raw edges at the sides and upper edge; pin. At the bottom, the lining panel will be 1" (2.5 cm) shorter than the curtain panel. Complete the curtain as on page 162, steps 4 to 9, handling the decorator fabric and lining as one fabric.

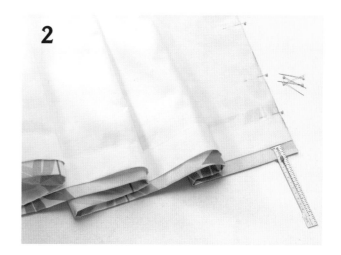

Installing rod-pocket curtains

Pole with wooden brackets and finials (left)
Remove the finials; insert the pole into the rod pocket with ends of the pole extending through the buttonholes. Reattach the finials; mount the pole. Secure the return to the wooden bracket, using self-adhesive hook and loop tape.

Pole with keyhole bracket and finials (center)
Slit the center of the rod pocket at the point marked in step 7, opposite. Insert the pole into the pocket.

Pull the return over the end of pole, aligning slit to the finial screw hole; attach the finials through the slits, and mount the pole. Attach a pin-on ring to the inner edge of the return and secure to a cup hook or tenter hook in wall.

Pole with elbows (right)
Insert the pole through the rod pocket; pull the curtain back to expose the small screws. Mount the pole on brackets. Slide the curtain over brackets.

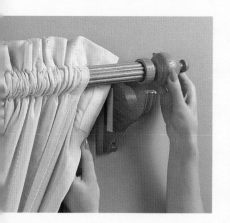

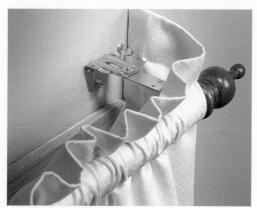

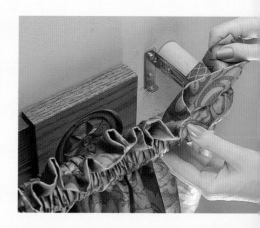

Rod-Pocket Curtains with Fancy Headings

ASY CHANGES in the headings of rod-pocket curtains can change their look. For some styles, such as a flounce heading or a popped heading, a softer, more feminine look is created by simply increasing the depth of the heading and shaping it on the rod. With a few extra steps, you can make a contrasting flounce or a welted heading, changing an ordinary rod-pocket curtain into an impressive room accent. Make the heading extra long and shape it to a point in the center, and you have a waterfall.

Intimate setting (opposite)
Lush rod-pocket curtains in a gold-tone fabric—always a popular color—make this small dining area feel intimate. The extending heading falls gently forward, topping off the low-slung side panels with casual grace. The effect is not overpowering—just a nice focal point.

Popped heading (top)
Decorators are incorporating fashion details into window treatments—like these popped headings that could be on an evening gown at the Oscars! The elegantly feminine treatment is perfect for this boudoir.

Waterfall headings (left)
The contrasting, extended headings on these rod-pocket curtains, often called waterfalls, are the crowning glory of this otherwise plain window treatment. As a strong design element, they tie together the two stories of windows, making the large space cozier.

$\mathcal{W}$hat you need to know

Here are some guidelines to help you **design** this treatment:

• A popped *heading* is created by pulling the layers of the heading apart after inserting the rod into the pocket. Allow a heading depth of 6" to 8" (15 to 20.5 cm). Do not press the upper edge of the curtain when turning under the heading and rod-pocket depth.

• An extended heading drapes down over the front of the rod pocket, creating a short flounce, a mock valance, or a much longer waterfall. Allow a heading depth of 12" to 16" (30.5 to 40.5 cm) for a flounce or mock valance; up to 36" (91.5 cm) for a waterfall.

• A contrasting flounce, mock valance, or waterfall can repeat a fabric that is used in the tieback for a coordinated look. A separate facing of contrasting fabric is sewn to the curtain at the top of the heading.

• A welted heading, measuring 4" to 6" (10 to 15 cm) deep, droops into dramatic curves above the rod pocket. Contrasting welting is sewn into the seam at the top of the heading between the curtain and the facing.

Use medium-weight **fabrics** that have enough body to hold the shape of extended or popped headings. Lining adds body to flounce and welted headings and prevents show-through when a light-colored fabric is used. Sheer or semisheer fabric with body can be used for a curtain with a popped heading.

Refer to rod-pocket curtains (page 160) for how to measure the depth of the rod pocket and heading, where to **mount** the rod, and how to measure for finished length.

Materials

- Standard curtain rod or pole set
- Tools and hardware for installation
- Decorator fabric
- Drapery lining for lined curtains
- Contrasting decorator fabric for facing of contrast flounce and welted styles
- Contrasting fabric and ¼" (6 mm) cording for welted style
- Drapery weights for floor-length curtains

Cutting directions

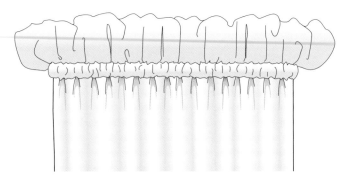

Popped heading

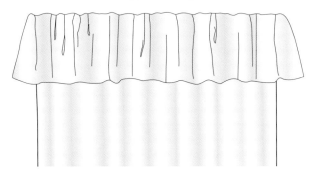

Flounce heading

Popped, flounce, mock valance, or waterfall heading

• Cut the decorator fabric and lining as for rod pocket curtains on page 161; allow for heading depths as given at left.

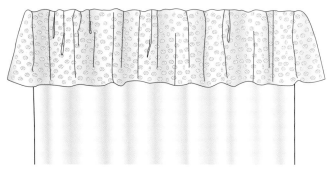

Contrasting flounce heading

Contrasting flounce, mock valance, or waterfall heading

- The *cut length* is equal to the desired finished length of the curtain plus the hem allowance plus the rod-pocket depth plus the extended heading allowance plus ½" (1.3 cm) for the seam allowance at the top.

- The *cut width* is the same as for other rod-pocket curtains (page 161).

- Cut the fabric for the heading facing with the length equal to the depth of the heading plus the depth of the rod pocket plus 1" (2.5 cm) for turn-under and seam allowance. The cut width of the facing is the same as the cut width of the decorator fabric.

- Cut the lining fabric 5" (12.7 cm) shorter than the decorator fabric. The cut width of the lining is the same as the decorator fabric.

Welted heading

- Cut the decorator fabric, facing, and lining as for rod-pocket curtains with a contrasting flounce, mock valance, or waterfall heading.

- From contrasting fabric, cut bias fabric strips, 1⅝" (4 cm) wide, to cover the cording for the welting.

- For lined curtains, cut the lining fabric 5" (12.7 cm) shorter than the decorator fabric for floor-length curtains; 3" (7.5 cm) shorter than the decorator fabric for sill- or apron-length curtains; the same length as the decorator fabric for curtains that puddle on the floor. The cut width of the lining is the same as the decorator fabric.

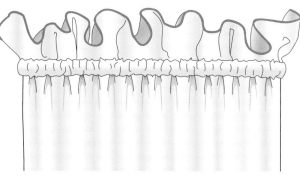

Welted heading

Making a contrasting extended heading

1 Follow steps 1 to 3 for unlined rod-pocket curtains on page 161. Repeat for the lining, but make a 2" (5 cm) double-fold hem in the lining and omit drapery weights in the lining.

2 Place the curtain panel and lining panel wrong sides together, matching the raw edges at the sides and upper edge; pin. At the bottom, the lining panel will be 1" (2.5 cm) shorter than the curtain panel.

3 Pin the facing to the top of the curtain panel, right sides together; if the facing fabric has a one-way design, make sure it will run in the right direction when the flounce falls forward. Stitch a ½" (1.3 cm) seam; press the seam open.

4 Press under 1½" (3.8 cm) twice on the sides, folding the lining and curtain fabric as one. Open out the hem, and trim the facing seam allowance in the hem area. Tack drapery weights inside the side hems, about 3" (7.5 cm) from the lower edge. Stitch to make double-fold side hems.

5 Press under ½" (1.3 cm) on the lower edge of the facing. Turn under the facing along the seam line; press. Pin the facing to the curtain panel along the pressed edge. Mark the upper stitching line for the rod pocket on the facing. Pin along the line to keep all the layers together.

6 Stitch close to the lower pressed edge. Stitch again along the marked line, creating the rod pocket.

7 Insert the rod or pole through the rod pocket. Mount the rod or pole on the brackets, draping the flounce toward the front, and arrange the gathers.

Making a welted heading

1 Seam the bias fabric strips together. Center the cording on the wrong side of the fabric strip, with the end of the cording 1" (2.5 cm) from the end of the strip; fold the end of the strip back over the cording.

2 Fold the fabric strip around the cording, wrong sides together, matching the raw edges and encasing the end of the cording.

3 Machine-baste close to the cording, using a zipper foot or welting foot, to create welting.

4 Follow steps 1 and 2 opposite. Stitch the welting to the right side of the curtain at the upper edge, matching raw edges; place the encased end of the welting 3" (7.5 cm) from the side of the panel. Stop stitching 5" (12.7 cm) from the opposite side of the panel.

5 Mark the upper edge of the curtain 3" (7.5 cm) from the side; cut the welting 1" (2.5 cm) beyond the mark.

6 Remove the stitching from the end of the welting, and cut the cording even with the mark on the curtain panel.

7 Fold the end of the fabric strip over the cording, encasing the end of the cording. Finish stitching the welting to the curtain panel, stopping 3" (7.5 cm) from the side.

8 Follow steps 3 and 4 on page 168 for the contrasting flounce. When stitching side hems, stitch up to the welting and secure the threads; start stitching again on the other side of the welting.

9 Complete the curtains as in steps 5 and 6, opposite. Insert the rod through the pocket, gathering the fabric evenly. Mount the rod.

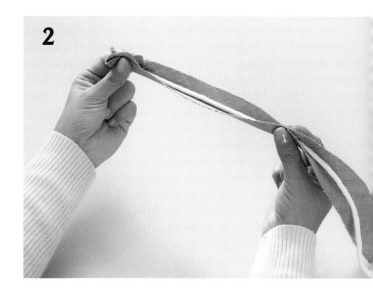

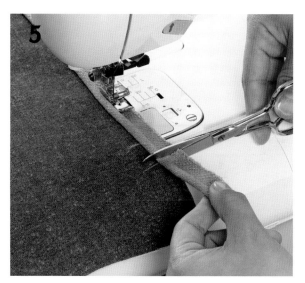

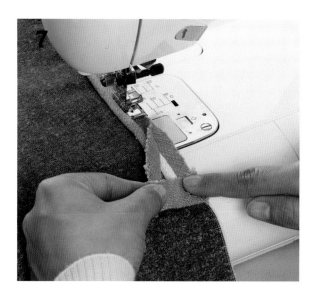

Ruffled Rod-Pocket Curtains

R UFFLES ARE FRILLY, feminine, and charming. The look can be relaxed and luxurious in floor-length silk curtains for a master suite or fresh and cute for a nursery or little girl's room.

Feminine floral (opposite)
Lined rod-pocket curtains with ruffles along the inner edges and bottom dress a simple casement window in a guest bedroom. A layer of eyelet trim added to the ruffle is a sweet touch. Tiebacks in the same plaid as the ruffle are a contrasting companion to the floral print.

Pristine white (top)
Floor-length, semisheer, ruffled curtains enhance the inviting outdoor view from this cozy cottage bedroom. Shades behind the curtains provide the light control and privacy when needed.

Country clever (right)
Simple ruffled curtains work well in a country-style kitchen. Small windows like these can't handle anything heavier or more imposing than this wispy, sheer treatment. So the windows can open in, the curtains are mounted directly onto the window frames.

What you need to know

The instructions that follow are for lined rod-pocket curtains with a self-faced ruffle along one edge and the bottom of each panel. You can **design** your curtains as one panel pulled back to the side with a tieback or holdback or as two panels that meet in the middle and are pulled back to the sides. The *return* sides are not ruffled. When two panels meet in the middle, the heights of the ruffles are staggered so one laps over the other from the *rod pocket* to the top of the *heading*. The width of the ruffle is a matter of personal taste and the look you want to achieve. Narrow ruffles simply accent the curtain edges, much like fringe. Longer ruffles make a more romantic statement.

Use lightweight to medium-weight **fabrics** for both the curtain and ruffle, using less *fullness* for heavier fabric to accommodate the bulk of the ruffle seam. Soft, drapable fabric will give the ruffles a luxurious droop. Crisp fabrics make perkier ruffles.

Follow the guidelines for classic rod-pocket curtains (page 160) for **mounting** the hardware and measuring the treatment.

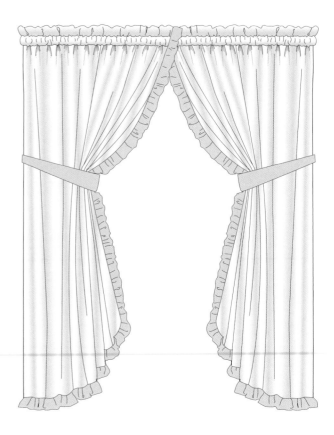

Materials

- Standard curtain rod or pole set with finials or elbows
- Tools and hardware for installation
- Decorator fabric for curtain
- Matching or contrasting fabric for ruffle
- Drapery lining
- Heavy thread or cord, such as crochet cord
- Pencil and string
- Drapery weights for floor-length curtains

Cutting directions

- The *cut length* of the curtain is equal to the *finished length* minus the finished width of the ruffle plus the depth of the rod pocket and heading plus 1" (2.5 cm) for seam allowance and turn-under.

- The *cut width* of the fabric is equal to the amount of space you want to cover multiplied by the desired fullness. Divide this amount by the width of the fabric and round up or down to the nearest whole or half width to determine the number of fabric widths you need. Use full or half widths of fabric for each curtain panel.

- Cut the lining for each panel to the same length and width as the decorator fabric.

- Cut fabric strips for the ruffles on the *lengthwise* or *crosswise grain* of the fabric with the width equal to twice the desired finished width plus 1" (2.5 cm). Cut as many strips as necessary for a continuous length of two to two-and-one-half times the length to be ruffled.

Making ruffled lined rod-pocket curtains

1 Pin two ruffle strips right sides together at right angles to each other, with the short ends extending ¼" (6 mm). Mark a diagonal line connecting the inner intersecting corners. Stitch. Trim the excess fabric to within ¼" (6 mm) of the stitching line. Press the seam allowances open. The diagonal seam minimizes the bulk.

2 Repeat step 1 to join all the ruffle strips. Fold the ends of the strip in half lengthwise, right sides together, and stitch across the ends in ¼" (6 mm) seams. Turn the ruffle strip right side out, aligning the raw edges, and press.

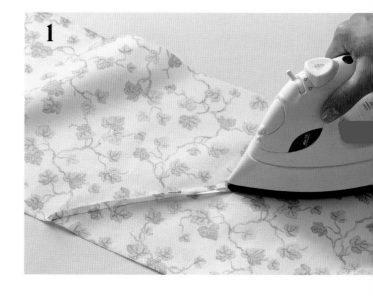

(continued)

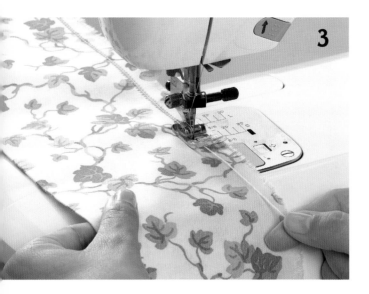

3 Zigzag over a cord within the ½" (1.3 cm) seam allowance, stitching through both layers of the ruffle strip.

4 Seam the fabric widths together, if necessary, for each curtain panel. If half widths are needed, add them at the sides of the panels. Finish the seam allowances together, and press them toward the side of the panel.

5 Repeat step 4 for the lining panels.

6 Mark a curve on the inside lower edge of one curtain panel with a pencil and string from a pivot point 12" (30.5 cm) up from the bottom and 12" (30.5 cm) in from the side.

7 Place the curtain panel over the lining, wrong sides together, matching the edges. Cut along the marked line through both layers. If your curtain has two panels, curve the opposite corner of the other panel in the same way. Separate the layers.

8 Press under ½" (1.3 cm) on the upper edge of the curtain. Then press under an amount equal to the rod-pocket depth plus the heading depth. If you are making a curtain panel with the ruffle beginning below the rod pocket, pin-mark the location of the lower stitching line for the rod pocket. Unfold the pressed edge.

9 Divide the ruffle strip into eighths, and pin-mark. Divide the curtain edge to be ruffled into eighths, beginning at the top of the heading or at the lower stitching line of the rod pocket and ending on the lower edge 3" (7.5 cm) from the raw edge on the return side of the panel. Pin the ruffle strip to the right side of the curtain, matching pin marks and raw edges.

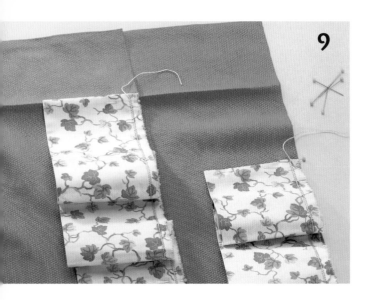

10 Pull the gathering cord on the ruffle to fit the edge of the curtain. Ease in the fullness and pin the rest of the ruffle in place. Stitch the ruffle to the curtain a scant 1/2" (1.3 cm) from the raw edges.

11 Pin the lining to the curtain panel, right sides together, matching the raw edges on the ruffled side of the panel. Stitch a 1/2" (1.3 cm) seam on the ruffled edges.

12 Turn the curtain right side out, matching the remaining raw edges of the curtain and lining. Press the seam.

13 Press under 3" (7.5 cm) on the other side, folding the curtain and lining as one. Then unfold the pressed edge and turn the cut edge back, aligning it to the pressed fold line. Press the outer fold. Tack a drapery weight to the hem allowance, just above the lower edge. Refold the edge, forming a 1 1/2" (3.8 cm) double-fold side hem. Stitch, using a blindstitch.

14 Finish the curtains as in steps 5 to 9 on page 162 for rod pocket curtains, treating the curtain and lining as one. Hang the curtains as on page 163. For curtains with two panels that meet in the middle, lap the ruffle that starts at the top of the heading over the shorter ruffle of the other panel.

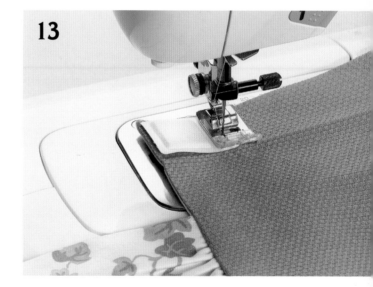

Relaxed Rod-Pocket Curtains

*U*PDATED rod-pocket curtains have no heading ruffling above the rod. Relaxed rod-pocket curtains are also made with less fullness—sometimes no fullness—and the pockets are deep and loose instead of snug fitting. These contemporary curtains are often paired with sleek, narrow decorator rods for a casual look. Dress them up or down through your choice of fabric.

Soft touch (opposite)
Imagine this room without the curtains—much less soft and comfortable! Also, mounting the curtains high and puddling them on the floor visually raises the height of the ceiling and makes the room feel more spacious.

Casual elegance (top)
These silk curtains are interlined for plumpness and puddled onto the floor. Drawn back with rope-style tasseled tiebacks to reveal the contrasting lining, they enhance this gorgeous room.

Ultra-modern (left)
With clean, simple lines and up-to-the-minute color, this room exudes confidence and class. The relaxed rod-pocket side panels on thin metal rods are so contemporary.

*W*hat you need to know

This curtain has no *heading*, only a *rod pocket*. The pocket should be very roomy, so the stitching line hangs 1" (2.5 cm) or more below the rod. Because rod-pocket styles are stationary by nature, they can be **designed** as separate panels hung at the sides of a window or as abutting panels that are parted and pulled back to the sides. One continuous panel can cover the window or be drawn to one side or to the center. For a casual or luxurious look, the curtains can be cut with 2" (5 cm) of extra length so the hem brushes the floor or with 12" to 15" (30.5 to 38 cm) of extra length for puddles. Another modern application is to hang flat rod-pocket panels on stationary rods or on rods that swing open or slide sideways on a track.

A single width of decorator fabric, gathered onto a rod at one-and-one-half to two times *fullness* will cover 32" to 24" (81.5 to 61 cm).

Choose **fabrics** that are very fluid and drapable, including sheer or semi-sheer fabrics. This style is often unlined, but you can line them and even inter-line (page 218) them for more body.

Choose a decorative rod and **mount** it before you cut the fabric, to be sure of accurate measurements. If the rod has finials and you don't want side *returns* on the curtains, extend the rod farther outside the window frame to minimize side light. Consider crane rods (page 294) for side treatments on curtains over doors or in-swinging windows.

Materials

- Decorative curtain rod
- Tools and hardware for installation
- Decorator fabric
- Drapery weights for floor-length curtains

Cutting directions

- The *cut length* of the fabric is equal to the finished length of the curtain plus the lower hem allowance (see chart on page 127) plus the depth of the rod pocket plus $\frac{1}{2}$" (1.3 cm) for turn-under at the upper edge.

- The *cut width* of the fabric is equal to the amount of space you want to cover (including returns) multiplied by the desired fullness. Divide this amount by the width of the fabric and round up or down to the nearest whole or half width, to find the number of fabric widths you need. Use full or half widths of fabric for each curtain panel.

- Multiply the cut length by the total number of widths needed to determine the amount of fabric to buy. Buy an extra *pattern repeat* per fabric width for matching patterns (page 298).

Making relaxed rod-pocket curtains

1 Seam the fabric widths together, if necessary, for each curtain panel. If half widths are needed, add them at the sides of the panels. Finish the seam allowances together, and press them toward the side of the panel.

2 Press under the lower edge the full amount of the hem allowance. Then unfold the pressed edge and turn the cut edge back, aligning it to the pressed fold line. Press the outer fold. If you are making floor-length curtains with more than one fabric width, tack a drapery weight to the upper layer of fabric at the base of each seam, with the bottom of the weight near the inner fold.

3 Refold the lower edge, forming a double-fold hem, encasing the weights at the seams. Pin. Stitch, using a blindstitch for an invisible hem or a straight stitch for a visible hem.

4 Press under 3" (7.5 cm) on one side. Then unfold the pressed edge and turn the cut edge back, aligning it to the pressed fold line. Press the outer fold. Insert a drapery weight between the layers of the lower hem, and tack it in place. Refold the edge, forming a 1½" (3.8 cm) double-fold side hem. Stitch, using a blindstitch. Repeat for each side of each curtain panel.

5 Press under ½" (1.3 cm) at the upper edge. Then fold under the remaining rod-pocket allowance and pin; do not press a crease into the upper fold. Stitch close to the lower fold, forming the rod pocket.

6 Insert the rod through the pocket and mount the curtain. Distribute fullness evenly along the rod. Style the curtains as desired.

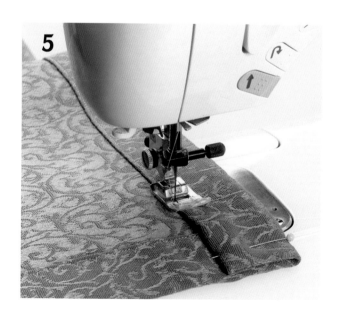

Stretched Curtains

CURTAINS STRETCHED taut from top to bottom over the window filter sunlight and provide privacy and softness. Often made of sheer or semisheer fabric, stretched curtains are a wonderful solution for French doors, door sidelights, and slim windows that do not open.

Filtered light (opposite)
Stretched rod-pocket curtains of pinstriped sheer fabric softly filter the light coming through French doors. Textured sheers dress up a window and look attractive from both sides.

Masking the view (top)
Lightweight stretched curtains on the lower halves of the windows let in light and provide privacy without blocking the view entirely. Double-hung windows like these can be opened from the top for air flow.

$\mathcal{W}$hat you need to know

This **design** is a *rod-pocket* curtain with a pocket and *heading* on the bottom as well as the top. The headings should be only ½" to 1" (1.3 to 2.5 cm) deep, or they can be eliminated if you prefer. Stretched curtains are not suitable for casement or double-hung windows because the curtain fits tightly over the window from top to bottom. Stretched curtains can be used on door windows, sidelights, or in-swinging windows if the rods are attached directly to the window molding instead of the frame.

Use lightweight sheer or semisheer **fabrics**, including novelty sheers, casements, and laces. The curtains can be completely flat if you want a very sleek, contemporary look or if you want to show off a beautiful lace fabric. Otherwise use one-and-one-half to two times *fullness*.

Stretched curtains are **mounted** on narrow rods, called sash rods, at the top and bottom. These come with brackets that will hold the curtain the right distance from the glass. There are also spring-tension rods that can be used if the window frame is deep enough to accommodate them, thus eliminating the need to drill holes. When you install the rods, leave room at the top and bottom for a narrow heading, if you wish, or leave just enough room for the fabric gathered on the rod. Install the rods first so you can measure accurately for the curtains.

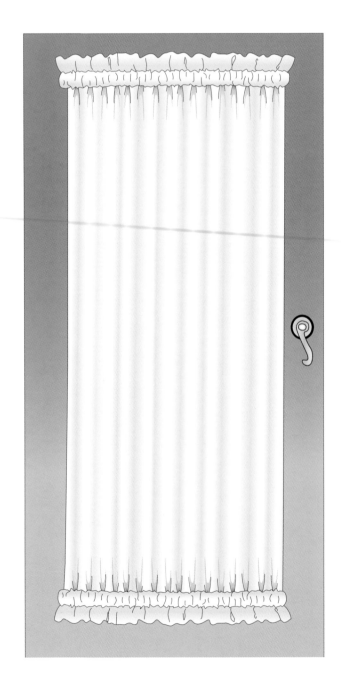

Materials

- Two sash rods or spring-tension rods
- Sheer or semisheer decorator fabric

Cutting directions

- The *cut length* is equal to the distance between rods, measured from the bottom of the top rod to the top of the bottom rod, plus four times the allowance for rod pocket and heading plus 1" (2.5 cm).

- The *cut width* is equal to the *finished width* multiplied by the desired fullness plus 4" (10 cm) for 1" (1.3 cm) double-fold side hems.

Making stretched curtains

1 Seam the fabric widths together, if necessary, using French seams in this manner: Place the panels wrong sides together. Stitch a scant ¼" (6 mm) seam. Press the seam allowances open. Turn the panels right sides together along the seam line, and stitch again ¼" (6 mm) from the edge, encasing the raw edges.

2 Press under 1" (2.5 cm) twice on the sides of the curtain panel; stitch to make double-fold hems, using a straight stitch or blindstitch.

3 Press under ½" (1.3 cm) on the upper edge. Then press under an amount equal to the rod-pocket depth plus the heading depth; pin.

4 Stitch close to the first fold. Stitch again at the depth of the heading.

5 Repeat step 3 for the lower edge of the curtain panel.

6 Insert the rods through the rod pockets. Install the upper rod, then the lower rod. Adjust the fullness evenly.

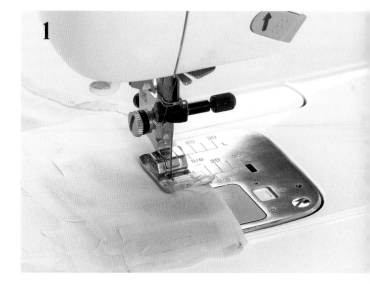

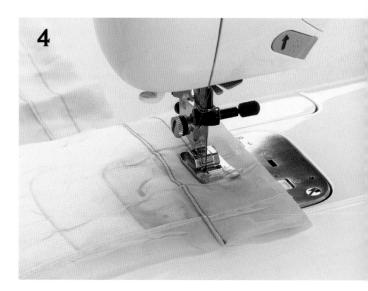

Hourglass Curtains

THESE GRACEFUL stretched curtains are cinched in at the "waistline." Often seen on French doors, they are also great for atrium doors and in-swinging windows or for sidelights and other narrow windows that do not open and close.

Dressing the view (opposite)
When privacy and light control aren't the issues, beautiful hourglass curtains like these entice you to take a closer, longer look at the doors and what lies beyond them. The sheer fabric filters light without hiding the door details.

Dressing the room (bottom)
The plaid hourglass curtains on these windows keep all the interest inside the room while letting in light at their sides. Jumbo cording covered with fabric is knotted attractively around each curtain. Though the matching door treatment is made to move with the door, the furniture arrangement suggests the homeowner rarely uses the door or opens the windows.

What you need to know

This is not just a stretched curtain (page 182) that is tied at the middle. The sides are made longer than the center so the curtain is equally taut in all areas. For this **design**, you need to take two length measurements, as shown on page 187.

Hourglass curtains are especially attractive in lace and sheer **fabrics**. They are often visible from both sides, so take that into consideration when selecting the fabric.

Mount the curtain with sash rods or other curtain rods with very shallow *projections* if the treatment is for a door. Use spring-tension rods for mounting the curtain inside a window frame. Install the rods and measure the window (opposite) before cutting the fabric.

Materials

- Two sash rods, curtain rods with up to 1¹/4" (3.2 cm) projection, or spring-tension rods
- Tools and hardware for installation
- Ribbon or twill tape for *mocking up* the shape
- Straightedge
- Sheer to lightweight decorator fabric
- White heavyweight sew-in interfacing

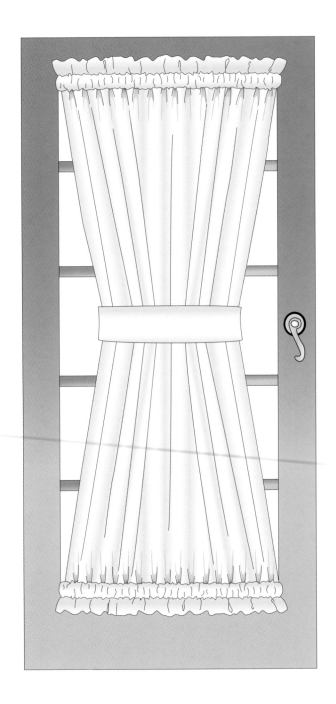

Measuring the window

1 Install the rods. Tape a strip of ribbon or twill tape to the door or window, outlining the desired shape of the curtain. Begin at the lower outside corner of the top rod, angling in the desired

distance to the center, and then out to the upper outside corner of the bottom rod. Repeat for the opposite side.

2 Measure the width of the curtain across the top or bottom; this is referred to as measurement 1. Measure the width of the curtain across the center; this is referred to as measurement 2. Subtract measurement 2 from measurement 1; record the difference.

3 Measure the length of the ribbon down one angled side; this is referred to as measurement 3. Measure the length of the curtain down the center, measuring from the lower edge of the top rod to the upper edge of the bottom rod; this is referred to as measurement 4. Subtract measurement 4 from measurement 3; record the difference.

Cutting directions

- The *cut length* of the fabric is equal to measurement 3 plus four times the rod-pocket depth and four times the desired heading depth plus 1" (2.5 cm) for turn-under.

- The *cut width* of the fabric is equal to measurement 1 multiplied by two to two-and-one-half times fullness plus 4" (10 cm) for 1" (2.5 cm) double-fold side hems.

- Cut a strip of fabric for the tieback, with the length equal to two times measurement 2 plus 1½" (3.8 cm) and the width equal to the desired finished width plus 1" (2.5 cm).

- Cut a strip of heavyweight sew-in interfacing 1" (2.5 cm) shorter than the cut length of the tieback strip and ⅛" (3 mm) narrower than the finished width of the tieback.

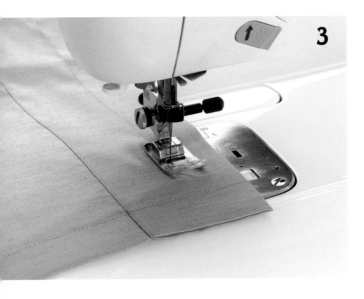

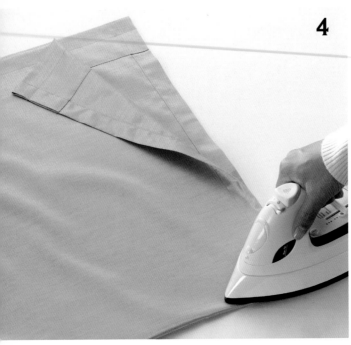

Making hourglass curtains

1 Seam the fabric widths together, if necessary, using French seams (page 183). Press under 1" (2.5 cm) twice on the sides of the curtain panel; stitch to make double-fold hems, using a straight stitch or blindstitch.

2 Press under ½" (1.3 cm) on the upper edge. Then press under an amount equal to the rod-pocket depth plus the heading depth; pin.

3 Stitch close to the first fold. Stitch again at the depth of the heading.

4 Repeat steps 2 and 3 for the lower edge of the curtain panel. Fold the curtain in half crosswise, right sides together, matching the top and the bottom rod pockets and headings. Press the fold line across the center of the curtain.

5 Divide the difference between measurement 1 and measurement 2 in half. Then multiply this number by the amount of fullness allowed for the curtain. Measure this distance along the pressed fold from one side toward the center; pin-mark. Repeat for the opposite side.

6 Divide the difference between measurement 3 and measurement 4 in half. Measure up from the fold at the pin marks a distance equal to this measurement; mark. Draw a line between the upper marks, parallel to the fold line.

7 Using a straightedge, extend the line to the pressed fold at the inner edges of the side hems, if sash rods or spring-tension rods are used. If the rods have up to a 1¼" (3.2 cm) projection, taper the line to 4" (10 cm) from the side hems. Stitch on the marked line, making a long dart.

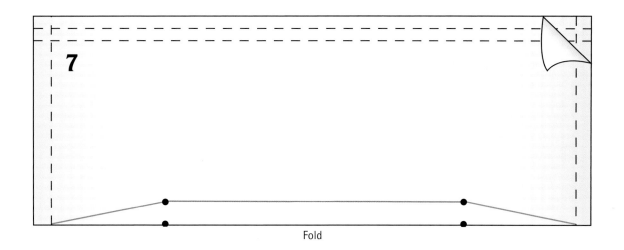

7

Fold

8 Press under ½" (1.3 cm) on one short end of the tieback. Fold the tieback in half lengthwise, right sides together; pin. Sew a ½" (1.3 cm) seam on the long edge; press the seam open.

9 Turn the tieback right side out, using a safety pin or bodkin. Center the seam on the back of the tieback; press. Insert the interfacing strip into the tieback.

10 Insert the unfinished end of the tieback into the pressed end, overlapping ½" (1.3 cm). Slipstitch the ends together, making a circular tieback.

11 Place the curtain through the tieback. Insert the spring-tension rods or sash rods in the top and bottom rod pockets. Mount the curtain, and check the fit.

12 Adjust the stitching of the dart, if necessary. Trim the fabric ½" (1.3 cm) from the stitched dart; finish the raw edges together, and press.

13 Reinstall the curtain. Secure the tieback to the center of the curtain, using a concealed safety pin.

9
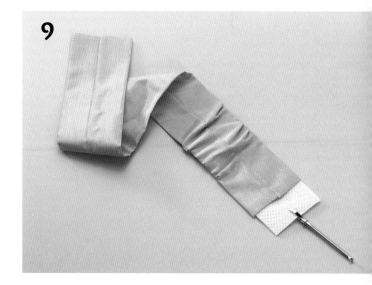

10
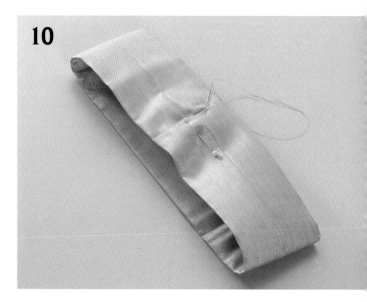

Tent-Flap Curtains

TRIM AND TAILORED tent-flap curtains are great for bedrooms, bathrooms, or home theaters where you want optimum light control and privacy. These flat panels attached to a mounting board are lined with decorative fabric because both sides show when the flaps are open. A great way to use two coordinating prints!

Partial view (opposite)
The curtain is drawn back for you—take a peek! This tent-flap curtain dresses a window with a deep ledge. A drapery holdback works as an attachment point for the curtain as well as a focal point. The simple styling is serene.

Tassel tabs (top)
Here's an innovative way to hang a simple lined rectangle of fabric. Tassel and medallion accents at the top also tie the tent flap to the pole. A matching cord medallion and tassel at the side anchor the flap.

Pretty frame (left)
What a pretty way to frame a window—and so simple, too. This tent-flap curtain is tailored and feminine all at once. The narrow ties at the sides can be purely decorative if you never intend to close the curtain, or make them workable if the room requires privacy and light control.

$\mathcal{W}$hat you need to know

Tent-flap curtains work especially well for windows that are taller than they are wide. They can be **designed** in many ways. One panel can be drawn back from a corner or from partway up one side. Two slightly overlapping panels can be mounted side by side and drawn apart. Separate panels made to fit individual frames in a bank of windows can be drawn open in symmetrical or asymmetrical patterns. The flaps can be held open by slipping a buttonhole, grommet, or metal ring over a button or small wall hook.

Choose medium-weight, firmly woven decorator **fabrics** for both the front and lining. If the window receives strong light, avoid dark or bright colors for the lining because the curtain may fade noticeably. If you choose two print fabrics, layer them and hold them up to the light to see if the pattern from the back fabric shadows through to the front. You may need to *interline* them with plain drapery lining or blackout lining for maximum light control.

The curtains are attached to a 1 × 2 board for **mounting** and installed with angle irons. Cut the mounting board 2" (5 cm) wider than the window to allow room for the angle irons at the ends to fit just outside the window frame.

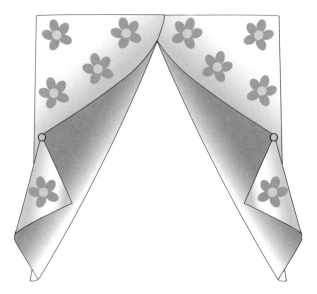

Cutting directions

• Cut one piece each of the two decorator fabrics for each curtain panel. The *cut length* of each panel is equal to the desired *finished length* plus the depth of the mounting board plus 1" (2.5 cm).

• For a curtain with two panels, the *cut width* of each panel is equal to one-half the width of the mounting board plus the depth of the mounting board plus 2" (5 cm). For a curtain with one panel, the cut width is equal to the width of the mounting board plus twice the depth of the board plus 1" (2.5 cm) for seam allowances.

• Cut a piece of drapery lining to the same size for each panel if interlining is necessary.

Making tent-flap curtains

1 Cover the mounting board with fabric. Attach angle irons at the ends, and mount the board above the window. Remove the board, leaving the angle irons on the wall.

Materials

• Mounting board
• Tools and hardware for installation
• Two different decorator fabrics
• Drapery lining, optional
• Staple gun and staples
• Findings for securing the curtain open, such as grommets, metal rings, buttons, wall hooks, cup hooks, or Velcro
• Self-adhesive Velcro

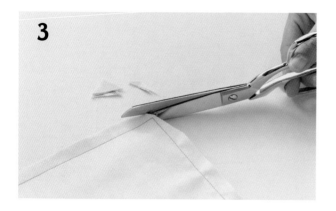

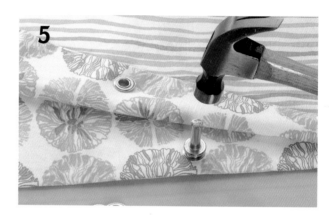

2 If interlining is needed, pin the interlining to the wrong side of the curtain front piece. Stitch them together, ⅜" (1 cm) from the edges.

3 Pin the front to the back, wrong sides together, matching raw edges. Stitch ½" (1.3 cm) seams on all sides, leaving an opening at the top for turning. Trim seam allowances diagonally at the corners.

4 Press the seam allowances open. Turn the panel right side out. Press the edges, pressing in the seam allowances at the opening.

5 Repeat steps 2 to 4 for any additional panels. Hold the panels up to the window to decide on the best position for holding the curtains open. Mark the locations for buttons, grommets, or rings. Stitch buttonholes, insert a grommets, or hand-stitch metal rings at the marks.

6 Center the panels on the mounting board, aligning the upper edges to the board back and wrapping the sides around the board ends. The panels will overlap 1" (2.5 cm) at the center. Staple the panels to the board, mitering the corners.

7 Install the curtain above the window, re-attaching the board to the angle irons. Attach the desired findings to the curtain and wall for holding the curtain open.

8 Cut two blocks of 1 × 2 board. Secure an angle iron to the narrow edge of each block, and attach one block on each side of the window frame at the height of the button. Secure the panel to the wood with self-adhesive Velcro.

Pinch-Pleated Draperies

CLASSIC PLEATED DRAPERIES are the ultimate window treatment for versatility and style. Installed on traverse rods, they easily open to reveal the full window view. When closed, they offer privacy, light control, and even insulation. They can also be made as stationary draperies. Traditional threefold pinch pleats will create uniform, graceful folds.

Tall and tasteful (opposite)
Perfectly styled pinch pleats, mounted at ceiling level for extra height and drama, afford full access to the doors, yet can be closed completely when needed. With their small-scale geometric pattern and rich, buttery color, these draperies provide a tasteful background for the room's furnishings.

Stately elegance (top)
Floor-to-ceiling draperies work well in this sunny atrium. They draw attention to the impressive ceiling and offer a break from the expanse of white woodwork and glass. Tied low with hefty cord and tassel tiebacks and spilling onto the marble floor, these stationary treatments add to the stately elegance of the room.

Unifying solution (bottom)
The different size doors and windows in this bedroom posed a decorating problem solved by the pinch-pleated, traversing draperies. Though there are shades over the glass to filter light and give privacy, closing the draperies also darkens and warms the room. The light fabric color that contrasts with the walls moves the eye around the room.

*W*hat you need to know

The instructions that follow are for a pair of drapery panels mounted on a two-way-draw traverse rod. When **designing** the treatment, allow for the *stacking space* at the sides of the window so the draperies will clear the window when they are open. The actual stacking space varies, depending on the weight of the fabric, the *fullness* of the draperies, and whether or not they are *lined* but is estimated at one-third the width of the windows; allow for one-half of the stacking space on each side of the window.

A wide range of decorator **fabrics** can be used, including sheers, casements, semisheers, and medium-weight fabrics in both prints and solids. Two-and-one-half times fullness is used for most draperies, but for sheers, three times fullness can be used. For lace draperies, use two-and-one-half times fullness so the pattern of the lace is noticeable in the finished draperies.

After you measure the window and determine the stacking space, purchase the rod and **mount** it on the wall above and to the outside of the window frame. If the draperies will hang from a conventional traverse rod, measure for the finished length from the top of the rod to where you want the lower edge of the draperies; then add ½" (1.3 cm) so the draperies will extend above the rod. If the draperies will hang from a decorative rod, measure from the bottom of the rod to the desired finished length. If the draperies will hang from a pole set with rings, measure from the pin holes in the rings to the desired finished length.

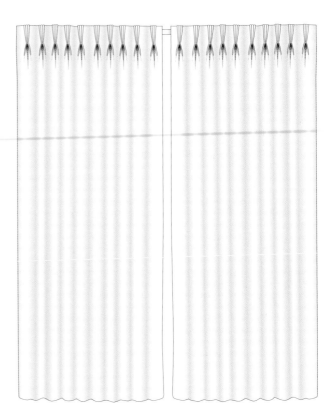

Materials

- Conventional or decorative traverse rod
- Tools and hardware for installation
- Decorator fabric
- Drapery weights
- Drapery lining for lined curtains
- *Buckram*, 4" (10 cm) wide
- Drapery hooks

Cutting directions

- Use the Fabric Worksheet (page 197) to find the necessary measurements. Several widths of fabric are often required. Cut the number of fabric widths you need to the calculated *cut length* of the draperies.

Making unlined pinch-pleated draperies

1 Seam the fabric widths together as necessary. If half widths are needed, add them at the sides of the panels. Finish the seams together, and press them toward the side of the panel.

2 Press under the lower edge 8" (20.5 cm) for the hem. Then unfold the pressed edge and turn the cut edge back, aligning it to the pressed fold line. Press the outer fold. If the panel has more than one fabric width, tack a drapery weight to the upper layer of fabric at the base of each seam, with the bottom of the weight near the inner fold.

3 Refold the lower edge, forming a 4" (10 cm) double-fold hem, encasing the weights at the seams. Pin. Stitch, using a blindstitch for an invisible hem or a straight stitch for a visible hem.

4 Press under the upper edge 8" (20.5 cm). Then unfold the pressed edge and turn the cut edge back, aligning it to the pressed fold line. Press the outer fold. Cut *buckram* the width of each drapery panel. Slip the buckram under the first fold, and then refold the top, encasing the buckram. Pin in place.

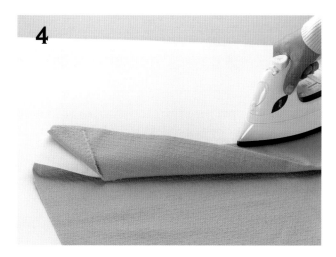

4

Drapery length

Desired *finished length*

+ 8" (20.5 cm) for heading

+ 8" (20.5 cm) for 4" (10 cm) double-fold lower hem

= *cut length* of drapery *

*If you buy fabric with a *pattern repeat*, your cut length must be rounded up to the next number evenly divisible by the pattern repeat.

Drapery width

Rod width (from end bracket to end bracket on conventional rods; from end ring to end ring on decorative rods)

+ allowance for two *returns* [*projection* of rod plus $1/2$" (1.3 cm) for each return]

+ $3^1/2$" (9 cm) for overlap

= *finished width* of drapery

Total number of drapery fabric widths

Finished drapery width

× multiplied by $2^1/2$ to 3 times *fullness*

÷ divided by width of fabric

= total number of fabric widths needed, rounded up or down to nearest full width

Number of fabric widths per panel

Total number of fabric widths

÷ divided by 2

= number of fabric widths per panel

Amount to purchase

Total number of fabric widths

× multiplied by cut length

= amount to purchase

Lining length

Cut length of drapery

- 5" (12.7 cm)

= cut length of lining

Number of lining widths

Same as for total number of drapery fabric widths (above).

Lining fabric width must be the same as the decorator fabric width.

PLEATS WORKSHEET

Finished panel width

Finished drapery width (see chart on page 197)

÷ divided by 2

= finished panel width

Number of pleats per panel

Number of drapery fabric widths per panel (see chart on page 197)

× multiplied by number of pleats per width*

= number of pleats per panel

Space between pleats

Finished panel width (see chart on page 197)

- overlap and return

= width to be pleated

÷ divided by number of spaces per panel (one less than number of pleats per panel)

= space between pleats

Pleat size

Flat width of hemmed panel

- finished panel width (figured above)

= total amount allowed for pleats

÷ divided by number of pleats per panel (figured above)

= pleat size

* Plan 5 pleats per width of 48" (122 cm) fabric, 6 pleats per width of 54" (137 cm) fabric. For example, for 54" (137 cm) fabric, 3 widths per panel = 18 pleats. If you have a half width of fabric, plan 2 or 3 pleats in that half width.

5 Press under 3" (7.5 cm) on one side. Then unfold the pressed edge and turn the cut edge back, aligning it to the pressed fold line. Press the outer fold. Insert a drapery weight between the layers of the lower hem, and tack it in place. Refold the edge, forming a 1½" (3.8 cm) double-fold side hem. Stitch. Repeat for each side of each curtain panel.

6 Determine the number and size of pleats and spaces between them by working through the chart below. The recommended amount of fabric for each pleat is 4" to 6" (10 to 15 cm). The recommended space between pleats is 3½" to 4" (9 to 10 cm). If the calculation from the worksheets results in pleats or spaces that are greater than the amount recommended, add one more pleat and space. If the calculation results in pleats or spaces smaller than the amount recommended, subtract one pleat and space.

7 Cut buckram templates in sizes to match the determined pleats and spaces; cut five of each for 48" (122 cm) fabric or six of each for 54" (137 cm) fabric. Mark the overlap and return on the right side of one panel, using chalk. Arrange the templates on the first fabric width, with the first pleat starting at the overlap line and the last pleat ending at the seam line. There will be one less space. Adjust the pleat sizes to arrange the spaces evenly; spaces must remain uniform. Mark the heading even with the outer edges of the space templates.

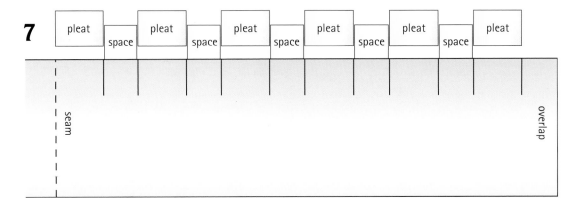

8

pleat		pleat		pleat		pleat		pleat		pleat	
	space		space		space		space		space		space

return

seam

8   Arrange the templates on the second fabric
     width from the overlap, with the first space
starting at the first seam line from the overlap and
the last pleat ending at the next seam line; use the
same number of pleats as spaces. Repeat for each
panel. (The last pleat ends at the return mark in the
last fabric width.) Adjust the pleats as necessary;
mark the spaces. If the return end of the panel has
a half width of fabric, plan for two pleats if the fabric is 48" (122 cm) wide or for three pleats if the
fabric is 54" (137 cm) wide. Transfer the markings
to the opposite panel in mirror-image placement.

9   Fold each pleat by bringing the pleat lines
     together; pin. Crease the buckram on the fold.

10   Stitch on the pleat line from the top of the
     heading to the lower edge of the buckram;
backstitch to secure. Repeat for each pleat in each
panel.

11   Check the finished width of the panel along
     the heading. Adjust the size of a few pleats
if necessary to adjust the width of the panel.

12   To divide each stitched pleat into three
     even pleats, grasp the center crease and
push it down toward the stitching line, forcing
the sides to spread out. Form the fabric into three
even pleats and press creases in the buckram with
your fingers.

(continued)

10
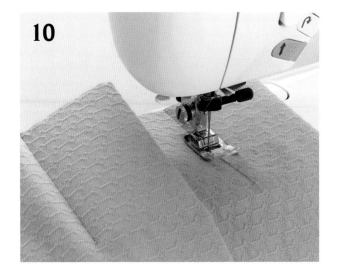

12
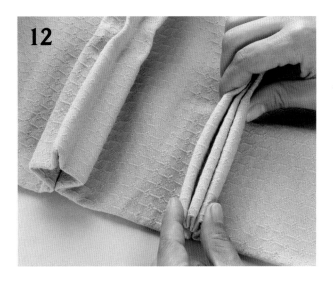

13 Bar-tack pleats by machine just above the lower edge of the buckram; or tack pleats by hand, using a stabstitch and heavy-duty thimble.

Hanging and dressing the draperies

1 Insert drapery hooks, with one hook at each pleat and one hook near each end of the panel. On a conventional traverse rod, the top of the hook is 1¾" (4.5 cm) from the upper edge of the overdrapery or 1¼" (3.2 cm) from the upper edge of the underdrapery. On a pole set with rings, the top of the hook is ¼" (6 mm) from the upper edge. On a decorator traverse rod, the top of the hook is ¾" to 1" (2 to 2.5 cm) from the upper edge.

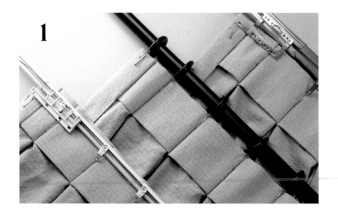

2 Crease the buckram midway between each pleat; fold it forward if a conventional traverse rod is being used, or fold it to the back if a decorative traverse rod is being used. This is often referred to as "cracking" the buckram. After cracking the buckram, press the draperies, using a warm, dry iron.

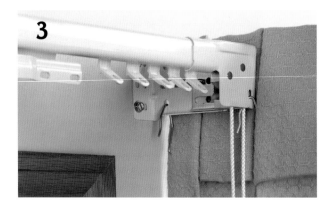

3 Hang the end hook at the return in the hole on the side of the bracket. Hang the hook of the first pleat in the hole at the front corner of the bracket.

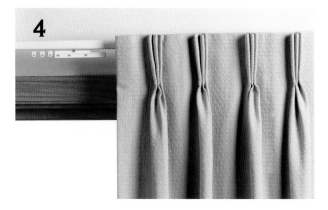

4 Hang the hooks for middle pleats on the slides; remove any slides that are not used. Hang the hook for the last pleat in the first hole of the master slide. Hang the end hook on the overlap of the drapery in the end hole of the master slide. Pinch the hooks on the master slides closed to keep them from catching when the draperies are drawn; also, pull the front master slide slightly forward, if necessary.

5 Open the draperies completely into the stacked position. Check the heading to be sure the buckram is folded as it was cracked in step 2. Starting at the heading, guide the pleats into evenly spaced soft folds of equal depth; follow the grain line of the fabric to keep the pleats perpendicular to the floor.

6 Staple a narrow strip of matching fabric or muslin around the drapery panel, midway between the heading and hem, to hold the pleats in place. Avoid pulling the fabric too tightly or you will create unwanted wrinkles.

7 Staple a second strip of fabric at the hemline. Check to see that the draperies hang straight down from the rod. Leave the draperies in this position for two weeks to set the pleats. In humid conditions, one week may be sufficient.

Making lined pleated draperies

1 Prepare the drapery panels as in steps 1 to 3 on page 197. Repeat for the lining panels, making 2" (5 cm) double-fold lower hems and omitting weights.

2 Place the drapery panel on a large flat surface. Lay the lining panel on top of the drapery panel, wrong sides together, with the lower edge of the lining 1" (2.5 cm) above the lower edge of the drapery panel; raw edges should be even at the sides.

3 Mark the lining panel 8" (20.5 cm) from the upper edge of the drapery panel. Trim on the marked line. This will be even with the top fold of the heading.

4 Finish the draperies as in steps 4 to 13 on pages 197 to 200, treating the decorator fabric and lining as one. The lining will be caught in the stitches of the pleats and in the side hems.

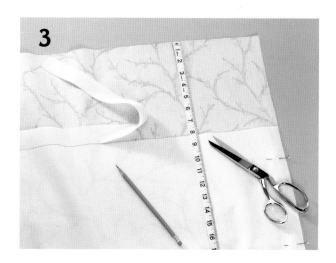

3

Pleat Alternatives

GO BEYOND the classic pinch pleat with these variations that really add a designer touch. Options for creative drapery headings include goblet pleats, fan pleats, butterfly pleats, inverted pinch pleats, and cartridge pleats.

Fringed cartridge pleats (opposite)
The heading of this cartridge-pleat drapery is stitched into cylinders that extend into the body of the drapery as soft, rounded folds. Cleverly placed wide fringe trim calls attention to the heading and changes the drapery from a quiet backdrop to an energizing room accent.

Fan pleats (top)
Also called Euro pleats or Parisian pleats, fan pleats are pinch pleats that are tacked at the top. They fan downward into soft, rolling folds that have a more contemporary look. This is a very popular style.

Silk goblets (left)
Open tubes that are pinched into pleats at the bottom resemble wine glasses—thus the name "goblet pleats." Shown here in a silky, yellow, giant plaid fabric, goblet pleats give the draperies a dressed-up look. For added detailing, the base of each goblet is often embellished with a covered button.

$\mathcal{W}$hat you need to know

Design the draperies following the guidelines and worksheets for pinch-pleated draperies (page 197). The only difference here is the method and style of pleating, which is the last phase of the construction.

• Goblet pleats are similar to three-fold pinch pleats at the base, but the tops are belled out to resemble wine glasses.

• Fan pleats (also called Euro pleats) are pinch pleated with the tacking done at the top instead of the base.

• Butterfly pleats can have two or three folds with tacking done about 1" (2.5 cm) above the base. The folds are drawn to the sides and tacked at the top of the heading to resemble wings.

• Inverted pinch pleats are just like standard pinch pleats, only the pleat is formed on the back of the heading.

• Cartridge pleats are tubular; they are not divided into folds.

To draw attention to the pleats, you can add dressmaker detailing, such as covered buttons at the base of goblet pleats or a decorative trim along the base of cartridge pleats.

Choose lightweight or medium-weight decorator **fabrics** for any of these styles. The draperies can be lined and interlined, depending on the look you want.

Mount the drapery hardware, following the same guidelines for pinch-pleated draperies. With the exception of inverted pinch pleats, any of the pleat styles can be hung from conventional traverse rods or decorative rods. Because of the bulk on the back of the heading, avoid conventional traverse rods for inverted pinch pleats.

Materials

- Conventional traverse rod or decorative rod
- Tools and hardware for installation
- Decorator fabric
- Drapery weights
- Drapery lining for lined curtains
- *Buckram*, 4" (10 cm) wide
- Tissue paper or sections of foam pipe insulation
- Drapery hooks

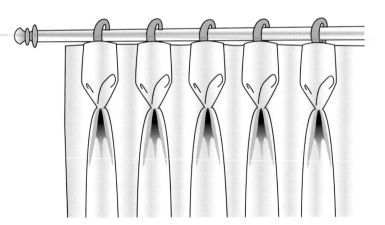

Making goblet pleats

1 Follow the charts and directions for making pinch-pleated draperies on pages 197 to 200, up through step 11, but do not crease the buckram in step 9.

2 Pinch the fabric at the bottom of the buckram into three or four small pleats. Tack the pleats by hand, using a stabstitch and heavy-duty thimble; or bar-tack the pleats by machine just above the lower edge of the buckram.

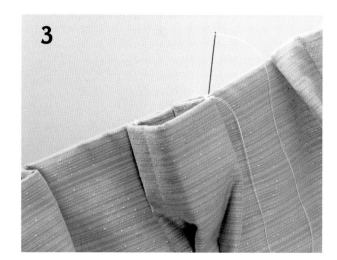

3 Form each pleat into a rounded, goblet shape. Hand-stitch the pleat along the upper edge of the drapery, up to ½" (1.3 cm) on each side of the stitching line.

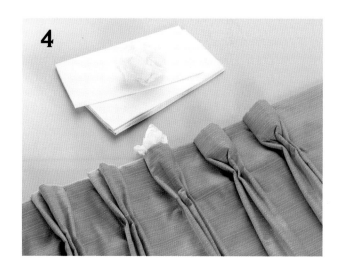

4 Insert wadded tissue paper or sections of foam pipe insulation into the pleats to help them retain the shape.

5 Hang and dress the draperies as on pages 200 and 201.

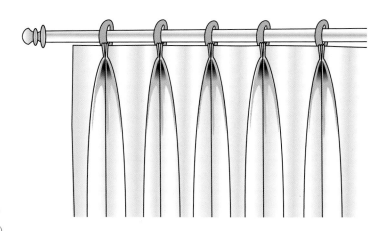

Making fan pleats

1 Follow the charts and directions for making pinch-pleated draperies on pages 197 to 199, through step 11.

2 At the top of each pleat, form the fabric into three even pleats and press creases in the buckram with your fingers.

3 Bar-tack the pleats by machine near the top of the curtain; or tack pleats by hand, using a

(continued)

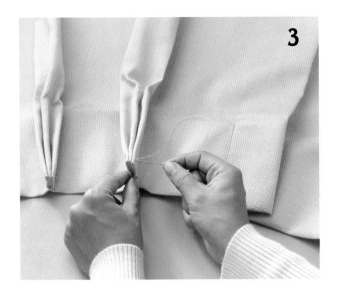

3

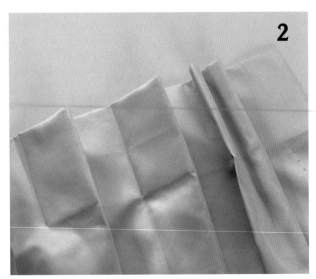

2

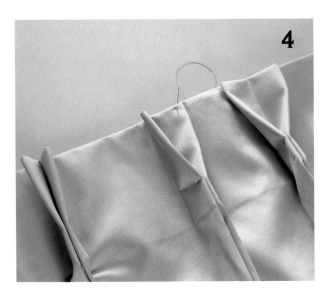

4

stabstitch and heavy-duty thimble. The pleats will fan outward from the top.

4 Hang and dress the draperies as on pages 200 and 201.

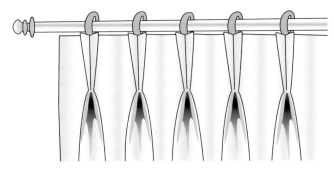

Making butterfly pleats

1 Follow the charts and directions for making pinch-pleated draperies on pages 197 to 200, through step 11.

2 Push the center of each pleat down over the pleat stitching line, forcing the sides outward. Then form the sides into two even pleats.

3 Bar-tack the pleats by machine 1" (2.5 cm) above the lower edge of the buckram; or tack pleats by hand, using a stabstitch and heavy-duty thimble.

4 Turn the pleats to the sides at the top and hand-stitch them to the heading. The pleats will fan out above and below the tack, like the wings of a butterfly.

5 Hang and dress the draperies as on pages 200 and 201.

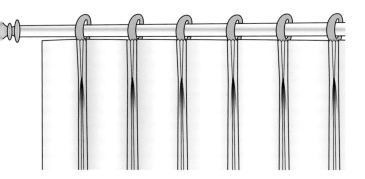

Making inverted pinch pleats

2

1 Follow the charts and directions for making pinch-pleated draperies on pages 197 to 199, through step 8. In steps 7 and 8, make the marks on the wrong side of the heading.

2 Follow steps 9 to 13, pages 199 and 200, but fold the pleats to the back side of the heading.

3 Hang and dress the draperies as on pages 200 and 201.

Making cartridge pleats

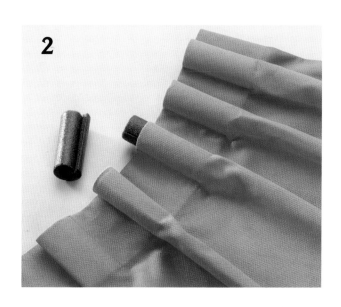

2

1 Follow the charts and directions for making pinch-pleated draperies on pages 197 to 200, through step 11. You'll probably want the pleats closer, so plan on one more pleat per fabric width and half width. In step 9, don't crease the buckram.

2 To hold the shape of the cartridge pleats, insert a section of foam pipe insulation into each pleat.

3 Hang and dress the draperies as on pages 200 and 201.

Inverted Box-Pleat Draperies

BOX PLEATS have long been used for valances, dust ruffles, or skirts on upholstered furniture; now they're popular for full-length draperies as well. In an inverted pleat, the fullness is folded out to the back of the heading, creating a smooth line on the front, perfect for a tailored, modern look.

Modern tailoring (opposite)
Color-blocked panels in red and taupe provide a colorful solution for this family room patio door. The inverted box pleats at the drapery heading reflect the modern tone of the room.

Quietly tasteful (top)
A classy treatment for a bank of windows, these inverted box-pleat drapery panels are stationary layers over traversing sheer pinch-pleat draperies. In an ivory color that melds with the wallcovering, they are understated and lovely.

Beaded accent (right)
A closer look reveals the beaded trim that accents the box-pleat heading and dresses up the drapery panels like a string of pearls at a neckline.

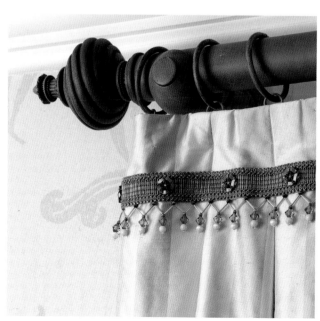

What you need to know

Follow the guidelines and worksheets for pinch-pleated draperies (pages 197 to 200). **Design** these draperies with two-and-one-half to three times *fullness*. The more fullness in the pleats, the more cumbersome the draperies will be to stack back, so if they are meant to traverse, use less fullness. This style is often used as elegant side panels or as single panels on a narrow window, drawn to one side with a tieback or holdback.

Medium-weight decorator **fabrics** work best, though you can beef up an elegant lightweight silk fabric with flannel interlining for a truly posh look. Because of its sleek lines, this drapery style is a good candidate for banding along the sides and bottom or for added details, such as buttons or decorator trims at the heading.

Follow the same guidelines for **mounting** the rod as for other draperies (page 293). Avoid conventional traverse rods, as the added bulk on the back of the heading will make it difficult to draw the draperies.

Materials

- Decorative rod or conventional rod
- Tools and hardware for installation
- Decorator fabric
- Lining
- Interlining, optional
- *Buckram*
- Drapery weights
- Drapery hooks or sew-on or clip-on rings

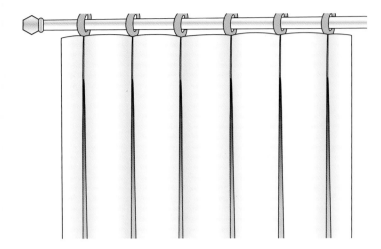

Making inverted box-pleat draperies

1   If interlined, follow cutting directions and steps for interlined draperies, page 216, to prepare the panels. If not interlined, follow the cutting directions and steps for lined draperies on page 201.

2   Calculate the pleat and space sizes, using the chart on page 197. Plan four pleats per width of 48" (122 cm) fabric, five pleats per width of 54" (137 cm) fabric, two pleats in any half widths.

3   Cut templates in sizes to match the pleats and spaces. Mark the overlap and return on the wrong side of one panel, using chalk. Arrange the templates on the first fabric width, with the first pleat starting at the overlap line and the last pleat spanning the seam. There will be one less space. Adjust the pleat sizes to arrange the spaces evenly; spaces must remain uniform. Mark the heading even with the outer edges of the space templates.

4   Arrange the templates on the second fabric width from the overlap, with the first space abutting the last pleat of the first panel and the last pleat incorporating the next seam line; use the same number of pleats as spaces. Repeat for each panel. (The last pleat ends at the return mark in the last fabric width.) Adjust the pleats as necessary; mark the spaces. Transfer the markings to the opposite panel in mirror-image placement.

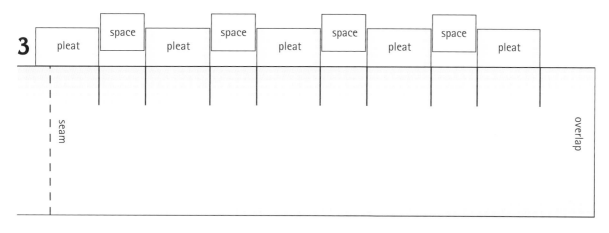

3

pleat   space   pleat   space   pleat   space   pleat   space   pleat

seam

overlap

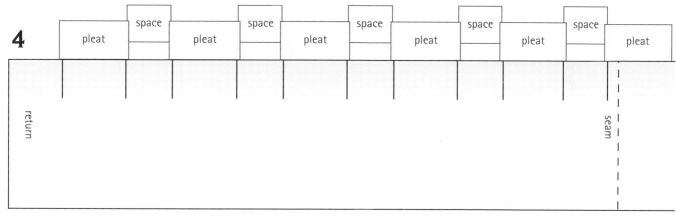

4

pleat   space   pleat   space   pleat   space   pleat   space   pleat   space   pleat

return

seam

5   Fold each pleat to the back of the heading by bringing the pleat lines together; pin. Stitch on the pleat line from the top of the heading to the lower edge of the buckram; backstitch to secure.

6   Check the finished width of the panel along the heading. Adjust the size of a few pleats, if necessary, to adjust the width of the panel.

7   Flatten each pleat, distributing the fullness evenly to the sides. Stitch in the ditch of the pleat seam from the right side to keep the pleat flat against the back of the heading.

8   Insert a drapery hook into the back of the heading next to the center stitching line of each pleat. Or attach sew-on or clip-on rings at the center of each pleat. Hang the drapery.

5

8

Banded Treatments

BANDING DEFINES the edges of a curtain or drapery. A solid-color band can accent a patterned panel, giving visual weight to the sides and anchoring the lower edge. A patterned band can add excitement to otherwise plain draperies while connecting them to the room's decor. A versatile design addition, banding is suitable for many styles of window treatments.

Formal in brocade (opposite)
Brocade curtains, detailed with banding and tassel trim, provide an elegant backdrop for this formal sitting room. Extra fullness is shaped into deep, even folds. Hidden wands make it easy to close the curtains for privacy.

Bias banding (top)
What a clever way to turn a hole-in-the wall window into an attractive room feature. This sweet, simple treatment—a combination tab (page 142) and tent-flap (page 190 subtly edged with reversible banding cut on the *bias*.

Well defined (left)
Inverted box-pleat draperies (page 208) with contrast banding dress the corner windows in this graceful, tailored living room. Just as the dark wood of the chairs defines the upholstered seats and backs, the drapery banding defines its borders.

*W*hat you need to know

In this **design**, faced banding is applied to the sides and lower edge of the window treatment, eliminating the need for side and bottom hems. For a professional finish, the corners are mitered. The width of the banding is a matter of personal taste. To help you decide, *mock up* some samples at the window and stand back to choose which one you like best. Banding can be added to lots of curtain styles, including flat panel, tab, or rod-pocket as well as pleated draperies. Since the heading (or top) of the treatment is usually finished last, simply follow the directions for the banding and complete the treatment following the directions for the style you choose.

Banding is suitable for treatments made from medium-weight, lightweight, or even sheer **fabrics**, offering stability to the edges as well as a decorative effect. For best results, the banding fabric should be a stable, opaque fabric. Whenever possible, cut the banding strips on the lengthwise grain of the fabric, eliminating or minimizing the need for distracting seams in the banding.

Follow the guidelines for **mounting** the treatment that are included with the style you choose.

Cutting directions

• To determine the *cut length*, follow the cutting directions for the curtain or drapery style you choose, but allow only ½" (1.3 cm) for a lower seam allowance instead of the usual lower hem allowance.

• To determine the *cut width*, follow the cutting directions for the curtain or drapery style you

Materials

• Decorative curtain rod or traverse rod
• Tools and hardware for installation
• Clip-on or sew-on rings for flat panel curtains
• Decorator fabric
• Contrasting fabric for the band
• Lining fabric for lined curtains
• Other materials as needed for specific styles

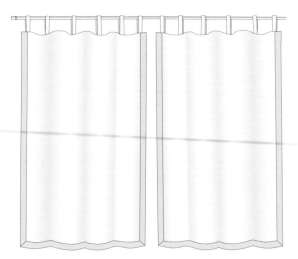

choose, but allow only ½" (1.3 cm) for a side seam allowances instead of the usual side hem allowances.

• Cut banding strips ½" (1.3 cm) longer than the cut length or cut width of each edge to be banded and 1" (2.5 cm) wider than the desired finished width of the band.

• If lining is desired, cut the lining pieces to the same size as the curtain or drapery pieces.

Making unlined banded treatments

1 Seam the fabric widths together as necessary for each curtain panel, adding any half widths at the *return* ends of the panels. Finish the seam allowances together, and press them toward the side of the panel.

2 Press under ½" (1.3 cm) along one long edge of each banding strip. Mark a point ½" (1.3 cm) from the end of the strip, ½" (1.3 cm) from the unpressed edge. Repeat for all the strips.

3 Pin the ends of adjoining strips right sides together, matching the pressed edges and raw edges. Draw a line from the marked point to the pressed edge at a 45-degree angle.

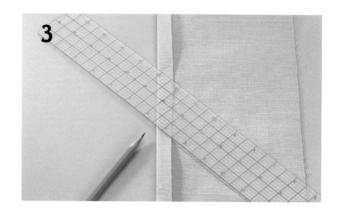

4 Stitch along the line through the marked point to the outer corner. Trim the seam allowance to ¼" (6 mm). Press the seam allowances open. Repeat for each set of adjoining strips to miter the corners.

5 Pin the banding strip, right side out, to the right side of the curtain, matching raw edges. Pin the band facing over the band, right sides together, matching raw edges and mitered seams.

6 Stitch ½" (1.3 cm) from the raw edges through all layers. Pivot the stitching at the mitered seams.

7 Trim the seam allowances diagonally across the corners. Fold out the facing strip, and press the seam open between the band and facing, getting as close as possible to the corners.

8 Turn the facing to the back of the curtain. Press along the seam. Glue-baste or pin the banding and facing strips in place along the inner pressed edges.

9 Topstitch along the inner edge of the band, catching the inner edge of the facing on the back of the treatment.

10 Finish the top of the curtain or drapery following the directions for the desired style. Treat the band and fabric as one.

Making lined banded treatments

1 Follow step 1, opposite, for the curtain or drapery panels and for the lining panels. Pin or baste the pieces wrong sides together.

2 Finish the treatment as in steps 2 to 10, treating the decorator fabric and lining as one.

Interlined Treatments

THE SECRET to an opulent look in curtains or draperies is a flannel interlining. It is a must with decorator silks, which would look limp and skimpy otherwise, but it also gives other fabrics a body-building boost. The insulating quality of the interlining also helps protect the fabric from sunlight. Once available only to the professional workroom, drapery interlining is now sold in fabric stores.

Pinstripes and tassels (opposite)
Salmon pinstripe silk, sewn into a relaxed rod-pocket curtain, is given extra body and volume with invisible flannel interlining. Trimmed with tassel fringe and flipped casually behind a metal holdback, this is a lush window treatment.

Lavish layers (top)
Muted earth tones and a lavishly layered window treatment are soothing and cozy in this bedroom. The interlined rod-pocket curtain, trimmed with tassel fringe, is pulled back to reveal the contrasting lining.

Crumpled silk (right)
Interlining exaggerates the wonderfully scrunched look of these silk draperies. Installed just under the molding and wall-to-wall across a bay of windows, the draperies soften the room corners and emphasize the high ceiling. To make it easier to manipulate the extra bulk, these pinch pleats have two folds instead of three.

What you need to know

The directions that follow are for any style of pleated draperies, though interlining can also be used to boost the volume of other treatments, including relaxed rod-pocket curtains and styling tape curtains. **Design** your treatment using the guidelines and worksheets for pinch-pleated draperies (pages 197 to 200). To emphasize the beefed-up look, draperies are often made extra long to brush the floor, puddle on the floor, or billow over tiebacks.

Use interlining with any **fabric** when you want to make it appear more billowy. Lightweight fabrics, especially decorator silks, really benefit from the use of interlining.

When choosing hardware and **mounting** it on the wall, follow the guidelines for the treatment style. Because the interlining will add more weight to your draperies, be sure to use enough brackets for the rod and install them into wall studs or use molly bolts (page 294).

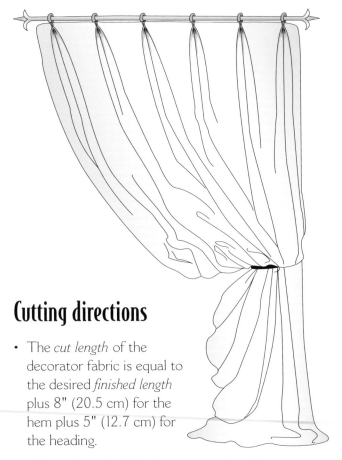

Cutting directions

- The *cut length* of the decorator fabric is equal to the desired *finished length* plus 8" (20.5 cm) for the hem plus 5" (12.7 cm) for the heading.

- The cut length of the lining is equal to the cut length of the drapery minus 6" (15.2 cm).

- The cut length of the interlining is equal to the cut length of the drapery minus 9" (22.9 cm).

- Follow the same guidelines for width as for pleated draperies.

Making interlined draperies

1 Follow steps 1 to 3 for pinch-pleated draperies on page 197. Repeat for the lining panels, making 2" (5 cm) double-fold lower hems and omitting weights. Repeat for the interlining, making 1" (2.5 cm) double-fold lower hems and omitting weights.

2 Place the lining right side up on a large flat surface. Place the drapery panel, right side down over the lining, aligning the tops of the hems. Place the interlining over the drapery panel, right side up, aligning the tops of the hems. The lining will be

2" (5.1 cm) shorter than the drapery, and the inter-lining will be 3" (7.5 cm) shorter than the drapery.

3 Measure from the bottom of the drapery panel a length equal to the finished length plus the width of the buckram plus ½" (1.3 cm), and mark a line. Cut off excess fabric of all three layers evenly on the marked line.

4 Pin the buckram over the three layers, even with the upper edge. Stitch through the buck-ram and all three layers ¼" (6 mm) from the lower edge of the buckram.

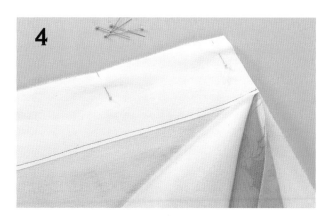

5 Turn the drapery right side out. At the top back, ¼" (6 mm) of decorator fabric will show above the lining. Press the heading over a padded surface to avoid imprinting the seam allowances onto the front. At the bottom, the lining hem will be slightly lower than in step 2.

6 Press under 3" (7.5 cm) on one side, treating all three layers as one. Then unfold the pressed edge and turn the cut edge back, aligning it to the pressed fold line. Press the outer fold. To reduce bulk at the bottom hem, cut away the interlining up to the inner fold; cut away the lining up to the outer fold. Insert a drapery weight between the layers of the decorator fabric hem, and tack it in place.

7 Refold the edge, forming a 1½" (3.8 cm) dou-ble-fold side hem. Repeat for each side of each curtain panel. Blindstitch the side hems from the base of the heading to the top of the bottom hem, leaving long tails of thread at the beginning and end. Using the thread tails, finish stitching the hems by hand.

8 Pleat the heading as desired, beginning with step 6 on page 198 for pinch-pleated draperies, or following the directions for one of the pleat variations on page 203, or following the direc-tions for inverted box pleats on page 210.

Treatments with Attached Valances

GET THE LAYERED LOOK with a curtain and valance all in one. This stationary treatment is perfect as side panels over another treatment like pleated shades or blinds, when you don't want to build an additional layer with a valance on another rod. Vary the look with the heading style of your choice.

Formal gathering (opposite)
Full rod-pocket side panels frame the window behind the sofa in this formal living room. Mounted at ceiling height and drawn back very low, these curtains with attached valances are very elegant and sophisticated.

Buttoned goblets (top)
Goblet pleats accented with covered buttons top off the attached valance on side panel draperies. Contrast banding and glass bead fringe define the angled lower edge of the valance, transforming a minimal treatment into a dynamic statement.

Flat-panel plus (left)
Beefed up with interlining and topped with a jaunty plaid attached valance, this flat-panel silk curtain is anything but flat. Bullion fringe at the bottom of the valance adds even more elegance.

What you need to know

Attached valances can be **designed** as two separate curtain panels, each with its own valance, hanging at the sides of the window. Two pulled-back panels can meet in the center of the window and share one attached valance. The top can be pleated in one of the pleat styles on pages 203 to 211. It can also be pleated or gathered, using styling tape as on page 157, or it can have a *rod pocket* with or without a *heading*. Banding, fringe, or decorator trim along the lower edge of the valance will help separate it visually from the curtain or drapery.

Lightweight **fabrics** work well because of the multiple layers. Lining adds body and support to the side hems and heading.

Mount the hardware before you cut to ensure accurate measurements. The curtains can be installed on standard or decorative curtain rods or on pole sets with rings. To hang panels from flat curtain rods, use drapery pins.

Materials

- Conventional curtain rod or pole or decorator rod and rings
- Tools and hardware for installation
- Decorator fabric
- Drapery lining for lined curtains
- Drapery weights for floor-length curtains
- *Buckram*, 4" (10 cm) wide, for pleated draperies
- Drapery hooks

Cutting directions

- The *cut length* of the fabric is equal to the desired *finished length* of the curtain plus the bottom hem allowance (see chart on page 127).

- The *cut width* of the fabric is determined by the length of the curtain rod, including the *returns*, multiplied by the amount of *fullness* desired in the curtain.

- The cut length of the lining is 5" (12.7 cm) shorter than the decorator fabric; the cut width of the lining is the same as the decorator fabric.

- For rod-pocket curtains, the cut length of the valance fabric is equal to the desired finished length from the top of the heading to the lower edge plus the depth of the rod pocket and heading, plus ½" (1.3 cm) for turn-under at the upper edge plus 4" (10 cm) for the hem.

- For styling tape draperies, the cut length of the valance fabric is equal to the desired finished length from the top of the heading to the lower edge plus 5" (12.7 cm).

- For pleated draperies with a 4" (10 cm) heading, the cut length of the valance fabric is equal to the desired finished length from the top of the heading to the lower edge plus 9" (23 cm).

• The cut width of the valance for any style is equal to the *finished width* of the curtain plus 6" (15 cm) for the side hems. If two curtain panels are to be attached to the same valance, base the cut width of the valance on the combined finished width of the panels.

Making unlined rod-pocket curtains with attached valances

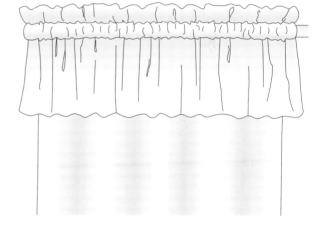

1 Seam the fabric widths together, if necessary, for each curtain panel. If half widths are needed, add them at the sides of the panels. Finish the seam allowances together, and press them toward the side of the panel.

2 Press under the lower edge 8" (20.5 cm) for the hem. Then unfold the pressed edge and turn the cut edge back, aligning it to the pressed fold line. Press the outer fold. If the panel has more than one fabric width, tack a drapery weight to the upper layer of fabric at the base of each seam, with the bottom of the weight near the inner fold.

3 Refold the lower edge, forming a 4" (10 cm) double-fold hem, encasing the weights at the seams. Pin. Stitch, using a blindstitch for an invisible hem or a straight stitch for a visible hem.

4 Press under 3" (7.5 cm) on one side. Then unfold the pressed edge and turn the cut edge back, aligning it to the pressed fold line. Press the outer fold. Insert a drapery weight between the layers of the lower hem, and tack it in place. Refold the edge, forming a 1½" (3.8 cm) double-fold side hem. Stitch, using a blindstitch. Repeat for each side of each curtain panel.

(continued)

5 Repeat steps 1 to 4 for the valance, omitting weights.

6 Press under ½" (1.3 cm) on the upper edge of the valance. Then press under an amount equal to the rod-pocket depth plus the heading depth.

7 Place the valance right side down on a flat surface, and open out the upper fold. Place the curtain panel(s) over the valance, right side down, aligning the upper edge of the curtain to the fold line of the valance. Refold the upper edge of the valance, encasing the upper edge of the curtain. Pin in place.

8 Stitch close to the lower fold through all layers. Stitch again at the depth of the heading, using tape on the bed of the sewing machine as a stitching guide.

9 Insert the rod into the rod pocket and hang the curtains.

Making lined rod-pocket curtains with attached valances

1 Follow steps 1 to 3 for unlined rod-pocket curtains on page 161. Repeat for the lining, but make a 2" (5 cm) double-fold hem in the lining and omit drapery weights.

2 Place the curtain panel and lining panel wrong sides together, matching the raw edges at the sides and upper edge; pin. At the bottom, the lining panel will be 1" (2.5 cm) shorter than the curtain panel. Hem the sides as in step 4, page 223.

3 Complete the curtain following steps 5 to 9, above, handling the decorator fabric and lining as one fabric.

Making styling tape draperies with attached valances

1 Prepare the curtain panels and valance as for the lined or unlined curtains through step 5. Press under 1" (2.5 cm) on the upper edge of the valance. Pin the valance to the drapery panels, as in step 7.

2 Attach styling tape and finish the drapery as in steps 5 to 9 on pages 223 and 224.

Making pleated draperies with attached valances

1 Prepare the curtain panels and valance as for the lined or unlined curtains through step 5. Press under 1" (2.5 cm) on the upper edge of the valance. Then press under 4" (10 cm).

2 Cut buckram 1" (2.5 cm) shorter than the finished width of the drapery. Tuck the buckram into the upper folds of the valance. Pin the valance and drapery panels together as in step 7 on page 224.

3 Pleat the draperies, using the desired pleat style, following the directions on page 197 or 202 to 207.

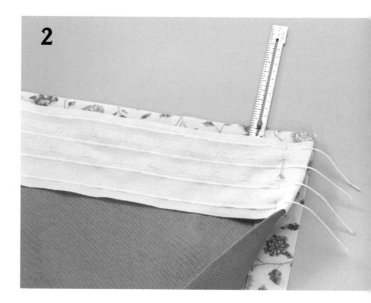

Tiebacks

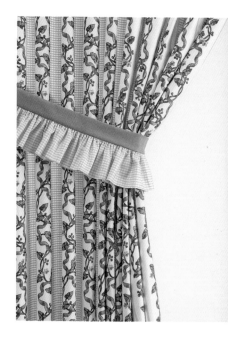

GRACEFULLY SWEEPING curves and lavish billows of fabric—features of many impressive window treatments—are held neatly and securely in place by tiebacks. More than a clever mechanism, the tieback is also an integral part of the design and can be made in matching or complementary fabric. Tiebacks can be tailored straight bands of fabric, shallow crescent shapes with welted edges, or even narrow bands with romantic ruffles. They give character and shape to a variety of curtain and drapery styles, from rod pockets to pinch pleats.

Tailored (opposite)

Less is sometimes more. In this window treatment, pleated drapery panels in uniform folds are harnessed with simple tailored tiebacks. Just breaking at the floor, these panels are stationary—only the sheer curtains behind them traverse the rod.

Ruffled (top)

When a little frill won't hurt, a ruffled tieback can be just enough to bring out the feminine side of your curtain. This one is done in contrasting fabrics that stand out against the busy printed fabric of the curtain.

Shaped and welted (left)

Welted, shaped tiebacks hold these large-scale floral panels in perfect proportion to the expansive bay window. The welting repeats the banding fabric, and the rounding off of the tiebacks at the back is a soft touch. The tieback placement is perfectly orchestrated, with slightly higher ones in the back drawing you into the depth of the bay.

What you need to know

Choose a tieback **design** that fits the size and character of your curtain or drapery. Tailored tiebacks can be 2" to 4" (5 to 10 cm) wide. Shaped tiebacks are widest at the center and taper at the rounded ends. For ruffled tiebacks, the band should be in proportion to the ruffle width, usually less than half as wide. The best way to judge the length of the tieback is to wait until you have installed the curtain or drapery and then experiment with a strip of fabric so you know how far you want to pull the treatment back.

Use the same **fabric** as the curtain if you want the tieback to be less noticeable or use a companion fabric to make it more prominent. Stiff interfacing helps the tieback hold its shape against the weight of the curtain. For shaped tiebacks, use a contrasting fabric for the welting to define the graceful curved edge.

Use tieback holders (page 296) and **mount** them at the side of the treatment directly under the *return* of the curtain or drapery. One end of the tieback attaches to the outside of the holder; the other end attaches to the inside. The holder keeps the return edge of the treatment from collapsing against the wall. The general rule for the tieback height is never to cut the window treatment in half. Rather, place the tieback about one-third the distance from the top or bottom of the treatment; often this will be near the sill.

Materials

- Tieback holders
- Tools and hardware for installation
- Paper and pencil for pattern
- Flexible curve or a curved ruler
- Heavyweight fusible interfacing for tailored or shaped tieback
- Decorator fabric
- Fusible web strip for tailored tieback
- Medium-weight fusible interfacing for ruffled tiebacks
- Heavy thread or cord, such as crochet cord, for ruffled tiebacks
- Fusible fleece or interfacing for shaped tiebacks
- Cording for welted, shaped tieback
- Brass or plastic rings or tieback pins, two for each tieback

Cutting directions

- For tailored tiebacks, cut a piece of heavyweight fusible interfacing the finished length and width of the tieback. Cut the fabric 1" (2.5 cm) longer than the finished size. The cut width is twice the finished width plus 1" (2.5 cm).

- For ruffled tiebacks, cut a straight tieback and interfacing as above. Cut fabric for the ruffle the desired width plus 1" (2.5 cm) and two to two-and-one-half times the finished length of the tieback.

- For shaped tiebacks, make the pattern as in steps 1 to 3 on page 230. For each tieback, cut two pieces of decorator fabric and one piece of fusible fleece or interfacing, using the pattern. Cut *bias* strips for welting (page 299) 2" to 3" (5 to 7.5 cm) longer than the circumference of the tieback.

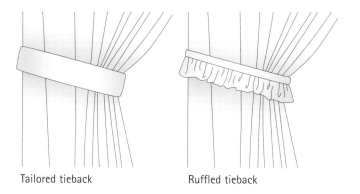

Tailored tieback   Ruffled tieback

Making tailored tiebacks

1 Press the short ends of the tieback strip under
½" (1.3 cm); unfold. Fold the tieback in half
lengthwise, right sides together. Stitch a ½" (1.3 cm)
seam, leaving the ends open. Press the seam open
without creasing the outer folds.

2 Turn the tieback right side out. Center the
seam on the back and press.

3 Slide the interfacing into the tieback, fusible
side toward the back. Turn the pressed ends
inside, encasing the ends of the interfacing. Fuse
the interfacing in place.

4 Insert a strip of fusible web into each end and
fuse the ends closed.

5 Attach a ring or tieback pin to the seam on
the back at each end of the tieback. Secure
the tiebacks to the holder (page 296).

Making ruffled tiebacks

1 Fuse the interfacing to the wrong side of the
tieback in the center. Press under ½" (1.3 cm)
on one long edge and both ends.

2 Seam the ruffle strips, as necessary. Stitch a
¼" (6 mm) double-fold hem on one long edge
and both short ends of the ruffle strips.

(continued)

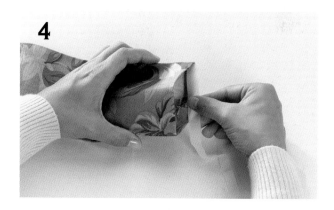

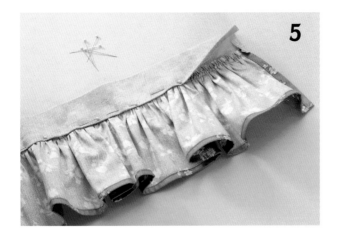

3 Zigzag over a cord within the ½" (1.3 cm) seam allowance on the remaining long edge of the ruffle strip, stitching from the right side.

4 Divide the ruffle strip and tieback into fourths and mark. Pin the ruffle, right side up, to the right side of the tieback, matching marks. Pull up the gathering cord, distributing the fullness evenly. Stitch the ruffle to the tieback ½" (1.3 cm) from the edge.

5 Fold the tieback in half lengthwise, wrong sides together, encasing the raw edges. Pin the folded edge over the ruffle seam.

6 Edgestitch across the ends and along the lower edge if the band. Attach rings to the wrong side of the tieback at the ends. Secure the tiebacks to the holder (page 296).

Making shaped tiebacks

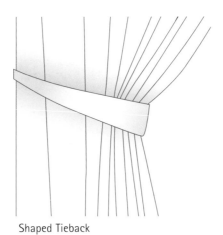

Shaped Tieback

1 Draw a rectangle on paper, with the short sides 5" (12.7 cm) and the long sides equal to half the finished length of the tieback. Mark a point on the right short side 3" (7.5 cm) from the lower corner. Mark another point on the bottom line 3" (7.5 cm) from the same corner. Draw a 3" (7.5 cm) line from the first point parallel to the bottom line. Mark a third point on the left short side 2" (5 cm) down from the upper corner.

2 Use a flexible curve or a curved ruler to mark a gradual curve for the upper edge of the tieback, connecting the end of the 3" (7.5 cm) line to the upper left corner. For the lower edge of the tieback, draw a curved line from the third point to the second point.

3 Mark the center fold line for the tieback on the right side. Round the corners on the left end of the pattern. Add ½" (1.3 cm) seam

allowances on the upper and lower edges and around the curved end.

4 Cut the fabric and interfacing (page 229). Trim ½" (1.3 cm) from the outer edge of the interfacing. Center the interfacing on the back of the tieback, and fuse it in place.

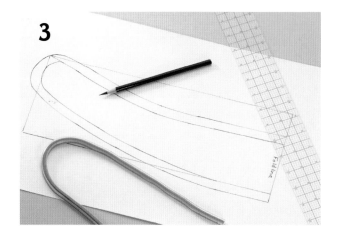

5 Seam the bias fabric strips together in ¼" (6 mm) seams. Fold the fabric strip over the cording, right side out, matching the raw edges. Using a zipper foot, machine-baste close to the cording.

6 Stitch the welting to the right side of the tieback, matching the raw edges. Start 2" (5 cm) from the end of the welting in an area of the tieback that will be concealed behind the curtain. To ease the welting at the rounded corners, clip into the seam allowances.

7 Stop stitching 2" (5 cm) from the point where the ends of the welting will meet. Cut off one end of the welting so it overlaps the other end by 1" (2.5 cm)

8 Remove the stitching from one end of the welting, and trim the ends of the cording so they just meet.

9 Fold under ½" (1.3 cm) of fabric on the overlapping end. Lap it around the other end, and finish stitching the welting to the tieback.

10 Pin the outer tieback and lining pieces right sides together. Stitch ½" (1.3 cm) from the raw edges, crowding the cording. Leave an opening for turning. Trim the seam allowances. Clip the curved edges; notch the curved of the return end.

11 Turn the tieback right side out and press. Slipstitch the opening closed.

12 Attach a ring or tieback pin to the back at each end of the tieback. Secure the tiebacks to the holder (page 296).

Shades

Flat Roman Shades

A FLAT ROMAN shade is a tailored, economical window treatment that controls light and provides privacy. Completely flat when lowered, this style is a good choice layered under tied-back curtains, drapery side panels, or swags.

Tailored solution (opposite)
A busy landing with an imposing bay window becomes an attractive focal point with the addition of flat Roman shades under an architectural cornice. With their large-scale pattern and warm, earthy colors, these tailored shades are the perfect solution for this challenging window.

Tasteful in toile (top)
Roman shades on French doors—how European! Mounted high on the doors, flat shades sit close to the glass but clear most of it when raised. Shaped hems with tassels complement the interesting toile design. The ingenious designer showcased different areas of the design on each shade, rather than make them identical.

Inset stripes (left)
Flanked with goblet-pleated side panels, this flat Roman shade was mounted inside the plaster frame flush with the walls. Combined, they offer maximum light control, ease of operation, and easy access to the casement window.

What you need to know

This shade **design** is minimal and uncomplicated, but it doesn't have to be boring. *Lining* provides added body, prevents fabric fading, and creates a uniform appearance from the outside. A system of evenly spaced rings through which cords are run on the back of the shade makes it possible to raise and lower the shade. The rings are spaced in even columns and rows so the shade will fold neatly at regular intervals when raised.

Choose a sturdy, firm decorator **fabric** to give the shade a crisp look. Because the shade is absolutely flat when lowered, it is a great way to show off a large all-over print. These directions are suitable for a shade that is at least 2" (5.1 cm) narrower than the fabric width. If the window is wider, use one full width of fabric for a center panel and add equal, narrow pieces to the sides.

Mounted on a board, the shade can be installed as an inside mount, secured inside the upper window frame, flush with the front of the frame. For an outside mount, the shade is installed on the wall at least 1" (2.5 cm) above the frame. Use a very narrow *projection* because the shade does not wrap over the ends of the board. To find the finished length of the shade for an outside mount, measure from the top of the mounting board to the sill or ¹/₂" (1.3 cm) below the apron; for an inside mount, measure the inside frame to the sill. The finished width of the shade is equal to the length of the mounting board plus ¹/₄" (6 mm).

Materials

- Mounting board
- Decorator fabric
- 1" (2.5 cm) angle irons with screws for outside mount
- Tools for installation
- Paper-backed fusible adhesive strip, ³/₄" (1.9 cm) wide
- Drapery lining
- Graph paper
- Plastic rings, ³/₈" or ¹/₂" (1 or 1.3 cm)
- Flat metal weight bar, ¹/₂" (1.3 cm) wide, cut ¹/₂" (1.3 cm) shorter than finished width of shade
- Staple gun and staples
- Screw eyes
- Shade cord
- White glue
- Drapery pull, optional
- Awning cleat

Cutting directions

- Cut a mounting board 2" (5.1 cm) longer than the outside measurement of the window frame for an outside mount or ½" (1.3 cm) shorter than the inside measurement for an inside mount. Cut a strip of fabric for covering the board ½" (1.3 cm) wider than the board circumference and 2" (5.1 cm) longer than the board length.

- The *cut width* of the decorator fabric is equal to the *finished width* plus 2" (5.1 cm). The *cut length* is equal to the finished length plus 7" (17.8 cm). This includes allowance for length that may be lost in stitching; the exact length is cut after the panel has been sewn. Do not use a selvage as an edge. Cut the lining fabric with the width equal to the finished width and the length equal to the finished length plus 3½" (8.9 cm).

Making a flat Roman shade

1 Cut the mounting board and cover it with fabric. If the shade will be mounted outside the window frame, secure angle irons to the bottom of the board, near the ends and at 45" (114.3 cm) intervals, using pan-head screws. Mount the board (page 296), centered above the window frame. Measure for the finished size of the shade. Remove the screws that hold the mounting board to the angle irons, leaving the angle irons on the wall.

2 Press under 1" (2.5 cm) on the sides of the shade. Cut strips of ¾" (1.9 cm) paper-backed fusible adhesive the length of each side. Turn back the hem and place the strips near the cut edge. Press over the strips to fuse them to the hem allowance, following the manufacturer's directions.

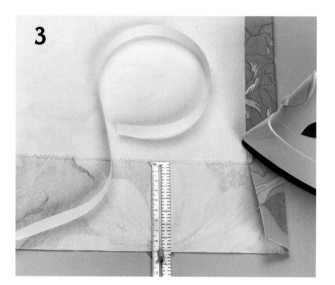

3 Place the lining over the shade fabric, wrong sides together, with the lower edge of the lining 3½" (8.9 cm) above the lower edge of the shade fabric; tuck the lining under the side hems. Remove the paper backing from the fusible adhesive, and press to fuse the hems in place.

4 Press under ½" (1.3 cm) at the lower edge; then press under 3" (7.6 cm) to form the hem pocket. The lower edge of the lining should now be even with the bottom fold of the shade. Pin the hem in place. Edgestitch along the top fold of the hem through all layers.

(continued)

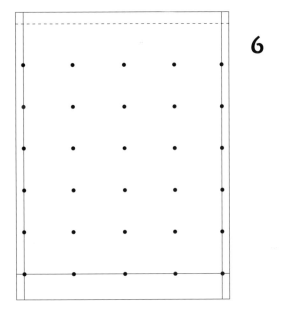

6

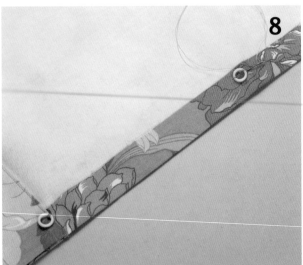

8

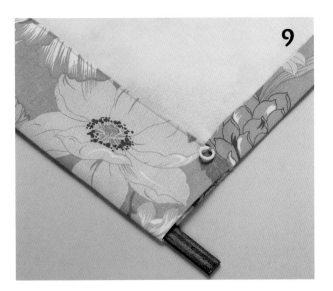

9

5 On the lining side, draw a line across the top of the shade at the finished length. Draw a second line 1½" (3.8 cm) above it (equal to the board projection). Cut off excess fabric along the top line. Pin the layers together, and finish the upper edges together by serging or using wide zigzag stitches.

6 Diagram the back of the shade on paper, indicating the finished length and width. Mark the hem 3" (7.6 cm) from the lower edge. Plan the locations of rings in columns spaced 8" to 12" (20.3 to 30.5 cm) apart, with the outer columns ¾" (1.9 cm) from the edges of the shade. Space them in even horizontal rows 5" to 8" (12.7 to 20.3 cm) apart with the bottom row at the top of the hem and the top row on the marked line.

Here's how to do the math: Subtract 1½" (3.8 cm) from the finished width of the shade. Divide this adjusted width by 12" (30.5 cm) and round up to the nearest whole number to find the number of spaces between columns—there will be one more column than spaces. Divide the adjusted width by the number of spaces to find the distance between columns.

Measure the length of the shade from the top of the hem to the upper marked line. Divide this distance by 8" (20.3 cm) and round up to the nearest whole number to find the number of spaces between rows. Divide the distance by the number of spaces to find the distance between rows.

7 Mark the placement for the rings on the lining side of the shade, following your diagram. The bottom row of rings is at the upper edge of the hem; the top row is the determined distance below the top marked line. (There are no rings on the top line.) Pin horizontally through both layers of fabric at each mark.

8 Stitch a ring at each mark through both layers of fabric, stitching either by machine or by hand. Reinforce the rings in the bottom row with extra stitches because they carry the weight of the shade.

9 Insert the flat weight bar into the hem pocket. Slipstitch the side openings closed.

10 Staple the shade to the top of the mounting board, aligning the marked line to the top front edge of the board.

11 Drill pilot holes and insert screw eyes, centered on the underside of the mounting board, aligning them to the columns of rings.

12 On the side where you want the cords to hang, run cord through the first column of rings, through the top screw eye, and at least halfway down the side. The extra length needed depends on the location of the window and whether or not you want it to be accessible to children. Cut the cord and tie a nonslip knot at the bottom ring. Repeat for each column in order, running the cords also through the previous screw eyes. Apply glue to the knots for security.

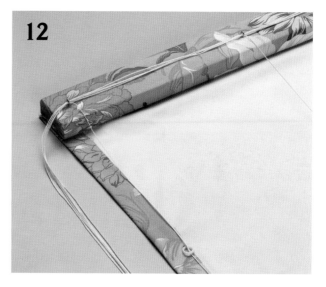

13 Reattach the mounting board to the angle irons for an outside mount or install the mounting board directly to the underside of the window frame, inserting screws through pilot holes, for an inside mount.

14 Adjust the cords with the shade down so the tension on all cords is equal. Tie the cords in a knot just below the first screw eye. Braid the cords, insert them through a drapery pull, if desired, and knot and trim the ends.

15 Secure an awning cleat to the edge of the window frame or on the wall. Pull gently on the cords to raise the shade, forming soft folds. Wind the cord around the cleat to hold the shade in its raised position. Train the shade by raising it and pulling the excess fabric forward to form gentle rolls. Leave the shade in the raised position for a few days to set the folds.

Banded Roman Shades

FOR AN eye-catching accent, bands of contrasting fabric are sewn around the outer edges of a Roman shade. Banding emphasizes the rigid geometric shape of the shade when it is down and the rhythmic folds of the shade when it is raised.

Golden band (opposite)
Wide gold banding around a white shade makes a crisp statement. The colors are timeless and twice as effective because they echo the banded shower curtain.

Seaside simplicity (top)
With colors that draw the outdoors in, this simple shade with narrow banding really enhances the ocean view. A mere swish of a scarf swag is suspended from starfish finials—a fitting accent.

Divide and conquer (bottom)
Large banks of windows can easily overpower a room. By making a separate, identical shade for each window, the massive space is broken up yet unified. Even the designs on the banding and tabs are perfectly aligned.

What you need to know

Banding is a **design** accent that can be applied to various styles of shades, including the flat shade taught in the directions that follow. Banding also works well for relaxed, hobbled, tucked, and coach shades. A band width of 3" to 4" (7.6 to 10.2 cm) works well in proportion to the folds of the shade. Corners of the banding are *mitered* to reduce bulk and produce a clean, professional look. Outer seam allowances are hidden between the layers of the band and shade, leaving only lining to show from the back.

Choose firmly woven decorator **fabrics** of equal weights for the shade and band. Use a print for the shade and a solid for the band, or vice versa. Using a large print for the shade and a coordinating smaller print for the band produces a subtle but effective contrast. The shades are lined for added body and light control.

Mounted on a board, the shade can be installed as an inside mount, secured up inside the window frame, flush with the front of the frame. For an outside mount, install the shade on the wall at least 1" (2.5 cm) above the frame. Use a very narrow *projection* because the shade does not wrap over the ends of the board. To find the finished length of the shade for an outside mount, measure from the top of the mounting board to the sill or 1/2" (1.3 cm) below the apron; for an inside mount, measure the inside frame to the sill. The finished width of the shade is equal to the length of the mounting board plus 1/4" (6 mm).

Materials

- Mounting board
- Decorator fabric
- 1" (2.5 cm) angle irons with screws for outside mount
- Tools for installation
- Drapery lining
- Contrasting fabric for banding
- Graph paper
- Plastic rings, 3/8" or 1/2" (1 or 1.3 cm)
- Flat metal weight bar, 1/2" (1.3 cm) wide, cut 1/2" (1.3 cm) shorter than finished width of shade
- Staple gun and staples
- Screw eyes
- Shade cord
- White glue
- Drapery pull, optional
- Awning cleat

Cutting directions

- Cut a mounting board 2" (5.1 cm) longer than the outside measurement of the window frame for an outside mount or ½" (1.3 cm) shorter than the inside measurement for an inside mount. Cut a strip of fabric for covering the board ½" (1.3 cm) wider than the board circumference and 2" (5.1 cm) longer than the board length.

- The *cut width* of the decorator fabric is equal to the *finished width* plus 1" (2.5) cm. The *cut length* is equal to the *finished length* plus 3" (7.6 cm). This includes allowance for length that may be lost in stitching; the exact length is cut after the panel has been sewn. If more than one width of fabric is required for the shade, use one full width for a center panel and add equal, narrow pieces to the sides. Do not use a selvage as an edge. Cut the *lining* the same size as the decorator fabric.

- Cut fabric strips for the banded edges 1" (2.5 cm) wider than the desired finished width of the band. For the side bands, the cut length of the fabric strips is equal to the cut length of the shade. For the lower band, the cut length of the fabric strip is equal to the cut width of the shade.

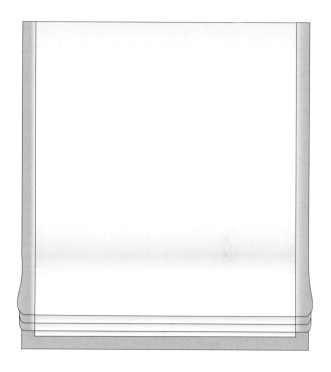

Making a banded shade

1 Cut the mounting board and cover it with fabric. If the shade will be mounted outside the window frame, secure angle irons to the bottom of the board, near the ends and at 45" (114.3 cm) intervals, using pan-head screws. Mount the board (page 296), centered above the window frame. Measure for the finished size of the shade. Remove the screws that hold the mounting board to the angle irons, leaving the angle irons on the wall.

2 Seam the fabric widths together, if necessary. Pin the lining to the shade fabric, wrong sides together, matching the raw edges. Machine-baste ⅜" (1 cm) from the edges.

(continued)

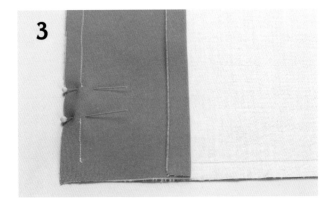

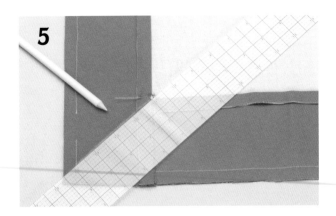

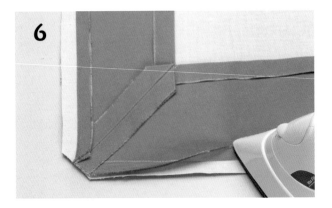

3 Press under ½" (1.3 cm) on one long edge of each banding strip. Pin one side band to the shade panel, with the right side of the band to the wrong side of the panel, aligning raw edges. Stitch a ½" (1.3 cm) seam, starting and stopping ½" (1.3 cm) from the ends. Repeat for the opposite side, leaving a 1" (2.5 cm) opening 1" (2.5 cm) above the end of the stitching line.

4 Pin the lower band to the lower edge of the shade. Stitch a ½" (1.3 cm) seam, starting and stopping ½" (1.3 cm) from the sides.

5 Mark the band for mitering, placing pins at the inner corner as shown. Draw lines from the inner corners of the banding to the stitched corners at a 45 degree angle. Stitch the miter on the marked line from the inner corner to the end of the stitching at the outer corner. Take care not to catch the shade panel in the stitching.

6 Trim the mitered seam allowances to ½" (1.3 cm), and press them open. Trim the corners diagonally. Press the seam allowance of the band toward the band, using the tip of the iron.

7 Turn the band to the right side of the shade so the seam is on the outer edge of the shade; press. Pin the band in place. Topstitch around the band, close to the inner edge.

8 On the lining side, draw a line across the top of the shade at the finished length. Draw a second line 1½" (3.8 cm) above it (equal to the board projection). Cut off excess fabric along the top line. Pin the layers together, and finish the upper edges together by serging or using wide zigzag stitches.

9 Diagram the back of the shade on paper, indicating the finished length and width and the width of the band. Plan the locations of rings in

columns spaced 8" to 12" (20.3 to 30.5 cm) apart, with the outer columns of rings 1" (2.5 cm) from the edges of the shade. Space them in even horizontal rows 5" to 8" (12.7 to 20.3 cm) apart, with the bottom row at the top stitching line of the band and the top row on the marked line.

Here's how to do the math: Subtract 2" (5.1 cm) from the finished width of the shade. Divide this adjusted width by 12" (30.5 cm) and round up to the nearest whole number to find the number of spaces between columns—there will be one more column than spaces. Divide the adjusted width by the number of spaces to find the distance between columns.

Measure the length of the shade from the top stitching line of the lower band to the upper marked line. Divide this distance by 8" (20.3 cm) and round up to the nearest whole number to find the number of spaces between rows. Divide the distance by the number of spaces to find the distance between rows.

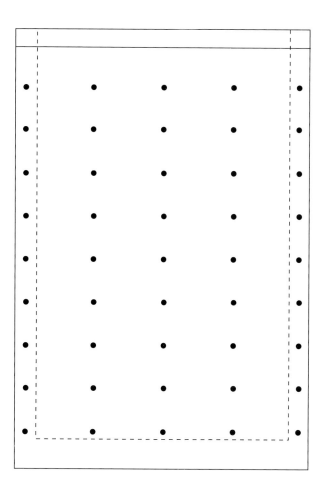

9

10 Mark the placement for the rings on the lining side of the shade, following your diagram. The bottom row of rings is at the upper stitching line of the band; the top row is the determined distance below the top marked line. (There are no rings on the top line.) Pin horizontally through both layers of fabric at each mark.

11 Stitch a ring at each mark through both layers of fabric, stitching either by machine or by hand. Reinforce the rings in the bottom row with extra stitches because they carry the weight of the shade.

12 Insert the flat weight bar into the opening near the lower corner. Slipstitch the opening closed.

13 Complete the shade as in steps 10 to 15 on page 239.

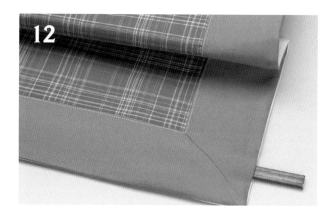

Butterfly Shades

A BUTTERFLY SHADE has the sleek smoothness of a flat Roman shade, with draped softness at the lower edge. As the shade is drawn up, the folds stack in the center and flare at the sides, creating a butterfly effect.

Alcove retreat (opposite)

The beauty of this room lies in all the subtle details, from the wispy dragonflies to the lasso band trim that accents the gentle swag at the bottom of the shade. This shade appears to be interlined for extra body, light control, and warmth.

Beads on plaid (left)

When the view's not so great, a well-dressed window is especially pleasing to the eye. This plaid butterfly shade is mounted inside the deep frame, showing off the woodwork. Bead trim along the lower edge draws attention to the dramatic curve.

Bold color (top)

Bold, warm color against a buttery wall makes this butterfly shade the center of attention. Notice how the sides wrap to the wall for a cozy fit and conceal the underlying mechanism.

What you need to know

This Roman shade **design** works best if the finished width does not exceed 49½" (126.3 cm). A shade of this width can be made from 54" (137 cm) fabric, with no seaming necessary. A dowel, inserted into a pocket in the *lining*, keeps the sides from falling inward as the shade is raised.

For best results, choose firmly woven, light- to medium-weight decorator **fabric**. Plain colors, small all-over prints, stripes, plaids, and large prints are all good options. The shade is lined to give it extra body and protect the fabric from sunlight.

Mount the shade above the window frame, so the finished length from the top of the mounting board to the highest point of the hem is evenly divisible by six. The swagged fabric at the bottom of the shade hangs below the sill.

Materials

- Mounting board
- Decorator fabric
- 1" (2.5 cm) angle irons with screws for outside mount
- Tools for installation
- Drapery lining
- $^3/_8$" (1 cm) wooden dowel, with length equal to two-thirds the finished shade width minus $^1/_2$" (1.3 cm)
- Plastic rings, $^3/_8$" or $^1/_2$" (1 or 1.3 cm)
- Staple gun and staples
- Three screw eyes
- Shade cord
- White glue
- Drapery pull, optional
- Awning cleat

Cutting directions

- Cut the decorator fabric so the *cut length* is equal to the desired *finished length* of the shade to the sill plus 24" (61 cm) for the bottom swag plus 2" (5.1 cm) for the hem allowance plus the *projection* of the mounting board. The *cut width* of the decorator fabric is equal to the desired *finished width* of the shade plus 3" (7.6 cm) for side hems plus twice the projection of the mounting board.

- Cut a strip of fabric for covering the board ½" (1.3 cm) wider than the board circumference and 2" (5.1 cm) longer than the board length.

- Cut the lining fabric with the length equal to the cut length of the decorator fabric plus 1¼" (3.2 cm) and the width 3" (7.6 cm) narrower than the cut width of the decorator fabric.

Making a butterfly shade

1 Cut the mounting board and cover it with fabric. Secure angle irons to the bottom of the board, near the ends and in the center, if necessary, using pan-head screws. Mount the board (page 296), centered above the window frame. Measure for the finished size of the shade. Remove the screws that hold the mounting board to the angle irons, leaving the angle irons on the wall.

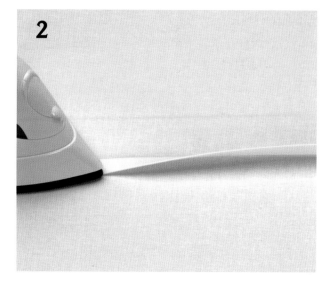

2 Mark a line across the wrong side of the lining 26⅝" (67.6 cm) from the bottom. Fold the lining, right sides together, along the marked line; pin. Stitch ⅝" (1.6 cm) from the fold, forming the dowel pocket. Press the pocket toward the bottom.

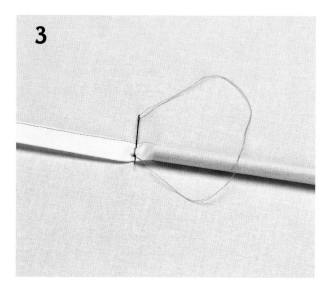

3 Insert the dowel into the pocket and slide it to the center of the lining. At the ends of the dowel, tack through the dowel pocket to hold the dowel in place.

(continued)

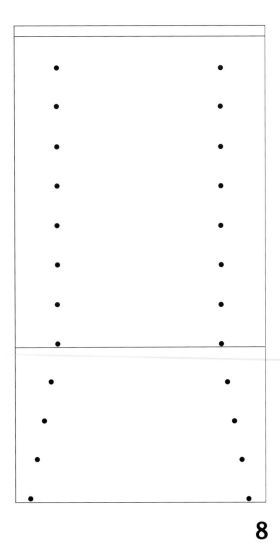

8

4 Press under ¾" (1.9 cm) twice on the sides of the shade fabric. Place the lining over the shade fabric, wrong sides together, matching the upper and lower edges. At the sides, place the lining under the hems, up to the second fold line; pin. Blindstitch the side hems.

5 Press under 1" (2.5 cm) of the lining and shade fabric twice at the lower edge; pin. Stitch in place.

6 Finish the upper edge of the shade and lining together, using overlock or zigzag stitches.

7 Place the shade facedown on a flat surface. Mark a line a distance from the upper edge equal to the projection of the mounting board. Mark the placement for two columns of rings, each positioned one-sixth of the shade width from the hemmed sides. Space the rings 6" (15.2 cm) apart vertically, with the bottom rings at the ends of the dowel and the top rings 6" (15.2 cm) below the upper marked line.

8 Mark the placement for two rings in the center of the lower hem, at the edge of the side hems. Mark the placement for the remaining three rings in each column spaced evenly along a diagonal line between the dowel pocket ring and the bottom ring.

9 Pin horizontally through both layers of fabric at each mark. Stitch a ring at each mark through both layers of fabric, stitching either by machine or by hand. Reinforce the rings on the dowel pocket because they carry the weight of the shade.

10 Center the shade on top of the mounting board, aligning the marked line to the top front edge of the board; the sides will extend beyond the board. Staple the shade to the mounting board; wrap the sides over the ends of the board, and staple in place, forming squared corners.

11 Drill pilot holes and insert screw eyes, centered on the underside of the mounting board, aligning them to the columns of rings. Install a third screw eye 1" (2.5 cm) from end of the board on the draw side.

12 On the side where you want the cords to hang, run cord through the rings from bottom to top and across the shade through three screw eyes; extend the cord about halfway down the draw side of the shade.

13 String the remaining row of rings, running the cord through two screw eyes and extending the cord about halfway down the draw side. Tie the lower five rings of each row together securely. Apply glue to the knots and ends of the cords to prevent them from slipping.

14 Reattach the mounting board to the angle irons. Complete the shade as in steps 13 to 15 on page 239. Arrange the lower folds neatly.

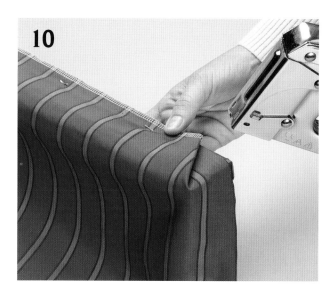

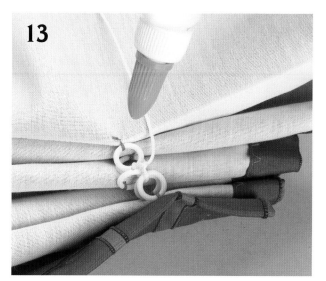

Tucked Roman Shades

N ARROW, HORIZONTAL stitched tucks "remind" this shade where to fold each time it is raised. With its trim, clean-lined appearance, a tucked shade allows as much of the window to be exposed as desired and provides complete coverage when needed.

Tall order (opposite)
Tucked shade triplets operate independently of each other on a tall bank of windows. Widespread tucks break up their height, while the striped soft cornice unites them.

Sunny view (top)
A wall of glass opens through French doors onto a sunny patio. Tucked shades fold up compactly at the top of the windows and doors to reveal a beautiful backyard. They can be lowered to any level for blocking out mid-day heat and protecting the dining room furnishings.

A different angle (right)
The angled hem, edged in blue and punctuated with a medallion and tassel, adds an interesting perspective to a kitchen window. The shade has tucks only on the back folds, so the large print is minimally disrupted.

What you need to know

Design this shade with narrow tucks that alternate from front to back or with tucks in the back only. The rings are attached to the back tucks. When the shade is raised, the fabric folds along the tucks accordion-style, starting from the bottom, and taking up minimal space. To help the shade hang smoothly, a weight bar is inserted into the hem at the lower edge.

Use firmly woven decorator **fabric** for crisp, straight tucks. The tucks break up the surface, so this style works best for small all-over prints, solids, and stripes. If you choose a large print, you may want to stitch only back tucks to avoid breaking up the design too much. *Lining* provides added body and light control while helping support the tucks.

This shade is attached to a **mounting** board and may be installed as either an out-side mount or an inside mount. For an outside mount, the board is installed above the win-dow and the shade extends to either the sill or ½" (1.3 cm) below the apron. The sides should extend at least 1" (2.5 cm) beyond the window frame. Use a very narrow *projection*

because the shade does not wrap over the ends of the board. For an inside mount, measure across the window inside the frame. The finished width should be ⅛" (3 mm) less than this measurement.

For an outside-mounted shade, if the esti-mated finished length of the shade is not evenly divisible by the desired space between the tucks, the length can be increased until it is, if there is the necessary wall space above the window. For example, if you would like 4" (10.2 cm) spaces between the tucks and the estimated finished length is 45" (114.3 cm), you can make the shade 48" (122 cm) long, which is divisible by 4.

Sometimes the length of the shade cannot be adjusted, as for an inside-mounted shade. In this case, the spacing between the tucks can be adjusted. For example, if the estimated space between the tucks is 4" (10.2 cm) and the finished length of the shade is 45" (114.3 cm), you can have ten 4½" (11.4 cm) spaces or nine 5" (12.7 cm) spaces, including the top space and the hem depth.

Cutting directions

- Cut a mounting board 2" (5.1 cm) longer than the outside measurement of the window frame for an outside mount or ½" (1.3 cm) shorter than the inside measurement for an inside mount. Cut a strip of fabric for covering the board ½" (1.3 cm) wider than the board circumference and 2" (5.1 cm) longer than the board length.

- Cut the decorator fabric to the desired *finished length* of the shade plus twice the hem depth plus the pro-jection of the mounting board plus ¾" (1.9 cm) for each tuck. Also add 2" (5.1 cm) to allow for any reduction in the length that results from multiple rows of stitching. After the shade is sewn, excess length is trimmed off at the top.

- The *cut width* of the shade fabric is 3" (7.6 cm) wider than the *finished width* of the shade. If more than one fabric width is needed, use one full width for a center panel and add equal partial widths on each side.

- Cut the lining to the same length as the decorator fabric minus twice the depth of the hem. The cut width of the lining is equal to the finished width of the shade; if necessary, piece the lining.

Making a tucked Roman shade

1 Before you cut the fabric, diagram the shade on paper, indicating the finished length and width, the number of tucks and spaces, and the columns of rings. Decide on the distance between tucks; a spac-

Materials

- Graph paper
- Decorator fabric
- Liquid fray preventer, optional
- Paper-backed fusible adhesive strip, $^3/_4$" (1.9 cm) wide
- Drapery lining
- Plastic rings, $^3/_8$" or $^1/_2$" (1 or 1.3 cm)
- Mounting board
- 1" (2.5 cm) angle irons with screws for outside mount
- Tools for installation
- Flat metal weight bar, $^1/_2$" (1.3 cm) wide, cut $^1/_2$" (1.3 cm) shorter than finished width of shade
- Staple gun and staples
- Screw eyes
- Shade cord
- White glue
- Drapery pull, optional
- Awning cleat

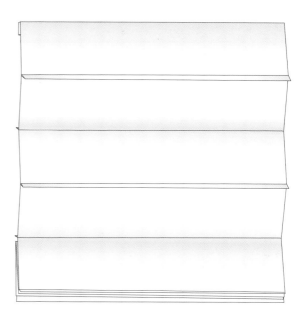

number of spaces between columns—there will be one more column than spaces. Divide the adjusted width by the number of spaces to find the distance between columns.

(continued)

ing of about 4" (10.2 cm) between the tucks is attractive. The bottom tuck is a back tuck and is located just above the hem. Position the rings along the back tucks, starting 1" (2.5 cm) from the sides and spacing the columns evenly 8" to 12" (20.3 to 30.5 cm) apart.

Here's how to do the math: Divide the desired space between tucks into the finished length of the shade; round up or down to the nearest whole number. This is the number of spaces, including the space at the top of the shade and the hem depth at the bottom. Then divide the number of spaces into the finished length of the shade to find the exact space between tucks and the hem depth. There is one less tuck in the shade than there are spaces.

Subtract 2" (5.1 cm) from the finished width of the shade. Divide this adjusted width by 12" (30.5 cm) and round up to the nearest whole number to find the

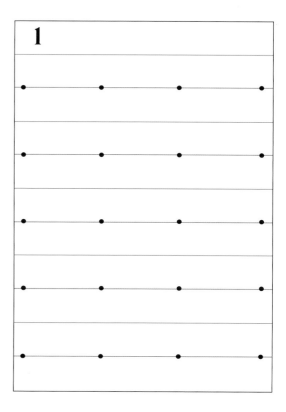

2 Cut the fabric. Seam fabric widths together, if necessary. Stabilize the side edges by applying liquid fray preventer, or finish the edges, using overlock or zigzag stitches.

3 Press under 1½" (3.8 cm) on each side for the hems. Cut strips of paper-backed fusible adhesive the length of each side. Turn back the hem and place the strips near the cut edge. Press over the strips to fuse them to the hem allowance, following the manufacturer's directions.

4 Place the lining over the shade fabric, wrong sides together, with the upper edges matching; tuck the lining under the side hems. Remove the paper backing from the fusible adhesive, and press to fuse the hems in place.

5 Press under an amount equal to the hem depth at the lower edge of the shade fabric; then press under again to make a double-fold hem. Pin in place. Stitch along the upper fold.

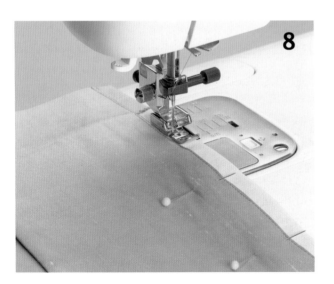

6

6 Place the shade facedown on a flat surface. On the lining, mark a line for the first back tuck ⅜" (1 cm) above the stitched upper fold of the hem.

7 Mark lines on the lining for the remaining back tucks. To determine the distance between the marked lines, multiply the space between tucks by 2, and add 1½" (3.8 cm) if you will be making both front and back tucks; if you only want back tucks, add only ¾" (1.9 cm). For example, mark the lines 9½" (24.1 cm) apart for a shade with 4" (10.2 cm) spaces between the front and back tucks. Mark the lines 8¾" (22.2 cm) apart if you only want back tucks. Each tuck takes up ¾" (1.9 cm).

8

8 Pin the lining to the shade fabric along the marked lines. Press the shade along the first marked line, right sides together. Stitch ⅜" (1 cm) from the fold. Repeat for the remaining back tucks. For the bottom tuck, it may be helpful to use a zipper foot, because the stitching line is even with the top fold of the hem.

9   Fold the shade, lining sides together, aligning the
    first two back tucks. From the right side, press
the fold for the first front tuck. Pin along the fold.
Fold, press, and pin the remaining front tucks.
Stitch all the front tucks ³⁄₈" (1 cm) from the folds.

10 Fold the shade, stacking the front tucks and
    back tucks. Mark the placement for the
rings on the back tucks, beginning 1" (2.5 cm) from
the sides and spacing the remaining columns of
rings, following your diagram.

11 Attach a ring at each mark through both
    layers of fabric, stitching either by machine
or by hand. Reinforce the rings in the bottom row
with extra stitches because they carry the weight
of the shade.

12 Cut the mounting board and cover it with
    fabric. If the shade will be mounted outside
the window frame, secure angle irons to the bottom
of the board, near the ends and at 45" (114.3 cm)
intervals, using pan-head screws. Mount the board
(page 296), centered above the window frame.
Measure for the finished size of the shade. Remove
the screws that hold the mounting board to the
angle irons, leaving the angle irons on the wall.

13 Place the shade facedown on a flat surface.
    Pulling the fabric taut, measure from the
lower edge of the shade to the desired finished
length; mark a line on the lining fabric. This may
change the upper space of the shade somewhat but
ensures that the shade is the correct length. Mark
a second line a distance away equal to the projection of the mounting board. Cut off excess fabric
along the top line. Pin the layers together, and finish
the upper edges together by serging or using wide
zigzag stitches. Complete the shade as in steps 9 to
15 on page 239.

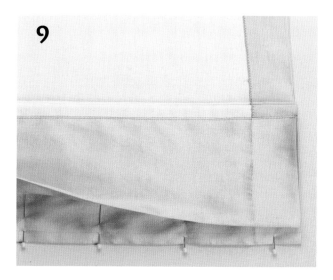

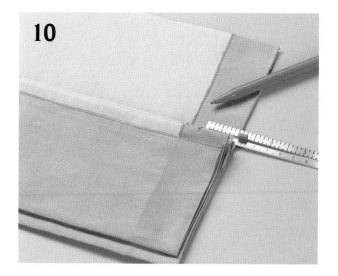

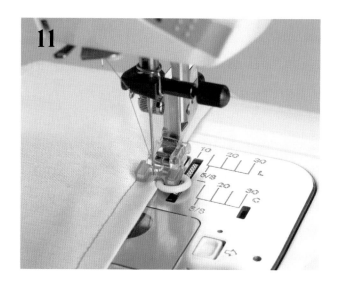

Hobbled Roman Shades

HOBBLED ROMAN shades have rolling horizontal folds that lap over each other in a gentle cascade down the length of the window. When the shades are raised, the excess fabric folds up from the bottom into soft accordion folds.

Masculine appeal (opposite)
Hobbled shades work well for a home office or den. This shade is simple and elegant with clean lines, a natural color, and a no-frills attitude.

Seclusion (above)
These hobbled shades are mounted on boards that are cut to fit the window arches perfectly. They offer complete privacy while bringing a feminine softness to the area around the bathtub.

Harmony (above right)
The subtle tweed texture of these hobbled shades echoes the granite countertop in this kitchen and dining area. When the shade is raised completely, the folds tuck up out of sight under the deep pleated valance.

$\mathcal{W}$hat you need to know

For this **design**, rings are stitched to the back of the shade through columns of twill tape. These points of attachment to the twill tape also hold the folds in place and fix the length of the shade. The distance between rings can vary, depending on the look you want. A distance of 4" to 6" (10.2 to 15.2 cm) between rings is attractive for most windows. A longer distance between folds creates a more casual appearance. The length of the fabric in each fold is equal to twice the distance between the rings. Mock up a sample on your window to help you decide.

Because the shade surface is interrupted by repeated folds, plain **fabrics** or small, all-over prints work best. Firmly woven, crisp fabric will hold the shape of the folds without collapsing between ring columns. *Lining* supports the folds and keeps light from casting shadows through the shade.

This shade is attached to a **mounting** board and may be installed as either an outside mount or an inside mount. For an outside mount, the mounting board is installed above the window and extends to either the sill or $1/2$" (1.3 cm) below the apron. The shade should extend at least 1" (2.5 cm) beyond the window frame on each side. Use a very narrow *projection* because the shade does not wrap over the ends of the board.

For an inside mount, measure across the window inside the frame. To allow for any variance in the width of the frame, measure it across the top, middle, and bottom. The finished width should be $1/8$" (3 mm) less than the shortest of these three measurements.

For an outside-mounted shade, if the estimated finished length of the shade is not evenly divisible by the desired space between the rings, the length can be increased until it is if there is the necessary wall space above the window. For example, if you would like 4" (10.2 cm) spaces between the rings and the estimated finished length is 45" (114.3 cm), you can round up the measurement to a 48" (122 cm) finished length, which is divisible by 4. This allows for a 4" (10.2 cm) hem depth, ten 4" (10.2 cm) spaces between the rings, and 4" (10.2 cm) between the top ring and the top of the mounting board.

If the length cannot be adjusted, as for an inside-mounted shade, the spacing between the rings can be adjusted. For example, a shade 45" (114.3 cm) long can have a $4\frac{1}{2}$" (11.4 cm) hem and nine $4\frac{1}{2}$" (11.4 cm) spaces, including the space between the top ring and the top of the shade. Another option is a 5" (12.7 cm) hem depth and eight 5" (12.7 cm) spaces.

Cutting directions

- Cut a mounting board 2" (5.1 cm) longer than the outside measurement of the window frame for an outside mount or $1/2$" (1.3 cm) shorter than the inside measurement for an inside mount. Cut a strip of fabric for covering the board $1/2$" (1.3 cm) wider than the board circumference and 2" (5.1 cm) longer than the board length.

- The *cut length* of the decorator fabric is equal to twice the *finished length* of the shade plus the hem depth plus the projection of the mounting board. The *cut width* of the decorator fabric is equal to the *finished width* of the shade plus 3" (7.6 cm). If more than one fabric width is required for the shade, use a full width for a center panel and seam equal partial widths to each side.

Materials

- Graph paper
- Decorator fabric
- Liquid fray preventer, optional
- Paper-backed fusible adhesive strip, $^3/_4$" (1.9 cm) wide
- Drapery lining
- Polyester twill tape, $^1/_2$" (1.3 cm) wide; to find length needed, multiply the number of columns by the finished shade length
- Plastic rings, $^3/_8$" or $^1/_2$" (1 or 1.3 cm)
- Mounting board
- Tools for installation
- 1" (2.5 cm) angle irons with screws for outside mount
- Flat metal weight bar, $^1/_2$" (1.3 cm) wide, cut $^1/_2$" (1.3 cm) shorter than finished width of shade
- Staple gun and staples
- Screw eyes
- Shade cord
- White glue
- Drapery pull, optional
- Awning cleat

- Cut the lining to the cut length of the decorator fabric minus twice the hem depth. The cut width of the lining is equal to the finished width of the shade.

- Cut the number of twill tape lengths needed as determined in step 1, cutting each tape to the length of the finished shade.

Making a hobbled shade

1 On paper, diagram the back of the shade, including the hem, the correct number of spaces between rings, and the length of fabric in the folds. Label the finished length of the shade, the distance between rings, and the hem depth. The hem depth and the distance between the top ring and the top of the board should be equal to the distance between rings. Draw the columns of twill tape and rings. Place one column 1" (2.5 cm) from each side, and evenly space the remaining columns 8" to 12" (20.3 to 30.5 cm) apart across the shade.

Here's how to do the math: Divide the desired space between the rings into the finished length of the shade; if necessary, round the number up or down to the nearest whole number. This is the number of spaces, including the space at the top of the shade and the hem depth at the bottom. Then divide the number of spaces into the finished length of the shade to find the exact space between the rings and the hem depth.

(continued)

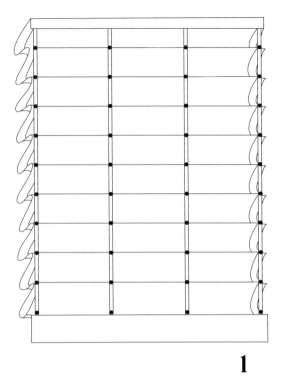

1

Subtract 2" (5.1 cm) from the finished width of the shade. Divide this adjusted width by 12" (30.5 cm) and round up to the nearest whole number to find the number of spaces between columns—there will be one more column than there are spaces. Divide the adjusted width by the number of spaces to find the distance between columns.

2 Cut the fabric. Seam fabric widths together, if necessary. Stabilize the side edges by applying liquid fray preventer, or finish the edges by serging or using wide zigzag stitches.

3 Press under 1½" (3.8 cm) on each side for the hems. Cut strips of paper-backed fusible adhesive the length of each side. Turn back the hem and place the strips near the cut edge. Press over the strips to fuse them to the hem allowance, following the manufacturer's directions.

4 Place the lining over the shade fabric, wrong sides together, with the upper edges matching; tuck the lining under the side hems. Remove the protective paper backing from the fusible web, and press to fuse the hems in place.

5 Press under an amount equal to the hem depth at the lower edge of the shade fabric; then press under again to make a double-fold hem. Pin in place.

6 Mark a line on the lining side of the shade a distance from the top equal to the projection of the mounting board. Mark the placement for the rings, following your diagram. The bottom row of rings is at the upper edge of the hem; the top row is the determined distance below the top marked line. Space the other marks a distance apart equal to twice the distance between rings, following your diagram. (There are no rings on the top line.) Pin horizontally through both layers of fabric at each mark.

7 Place the lengths of twill tape side by side on an ironing surface. Steam-press the tapes to preshrink them. When they are dry, tape or pin them taut. Mark a line across the tapes ½" (1.3 cm) from one end. Mark additional lines across the tapes at the distance between the rings.

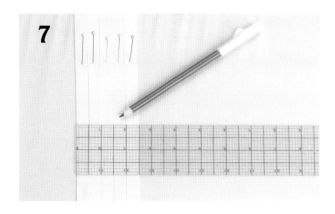

8 Insert the ends of the tapes under the top edge of the hem up to the ½" (1.3 cm) line, centering a tape at each ring placement mark; pin in place. Stitch the hem in place, catching the tapes in the stitching.

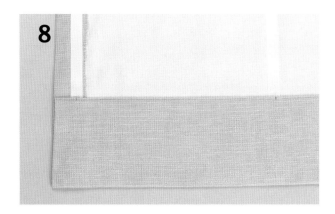

9 Pin the twill tapes to the ring marks, beginning at the bottom of the shade, centering the tapes on the ring marks, and pinning through all the layers.

10 Stitch a ring at each mark through the twill tape and both layers of fabric, stitching either by machine or by hand.

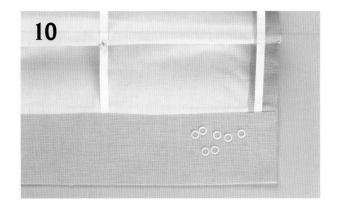

11 Tack the tapes in place at the top of the shade, matching the last marks on the tapes to the marked lines on the shade; do not stitch rings at the top marks. Trim excess tapes even with the upper edge of the shade, and pin the ends to the shade. Finish the upper edge of the shade by serging or using zigzag stitches; catch the ends of the tapes in the stitching.

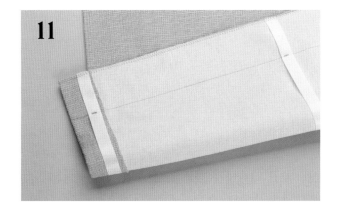

12 Cut the mounting board and cover it with fabric. If the shade will be mounted outside the window frame, secure angle irons to the bottom of the board, near the ends and at 45" (114.3 cm) intervals, using pan-head screws. Mount the board (page 296), centered above the window frame. Measure for the finished size of the shade. Remove the screws that hold the mounting board to the angle irons, leaving the angle irons on the wall.

13 Complete the shade as in steps 9 to 15 on page 239.

Cloud Shades

A CLOUD SHADE is gathered across the top and hangs as a softly shirred panel when lowered full length. When raised, the bottom of the shade forms soft cloudlike poufs. Because of the decorative heading and billowy appearance, cloud shades are usually used alone.

Sensuous curves (opposite)
Circles and curves abound in this Victorian bedroom, from the carpet motifs to the wallpaper swoops and the design of the massive bed frame. Continuing the curvy effect is a cloud shade with deep, full poufs edged in tassel fringe.

Relaxing mood (left)
The softly gathered, casual appearance of this cloud shade and the tone-on-tone color scheme make for a quiet, relaxing living area.

Lively stripes (top)
Green stripes in a billowy cloud shade enliven this little bedroom. A wooden cornice hides the mechanism at the top of the shade and adds an architectural element.

What you need to know

For this **design**, the *heading* of the shade is gathered or softly pleated using a styling tape. There are several styles of sew-in and fusible tapes, including pencil pleat, multi-cord shirring tape, or smocking tape. The tape style you select determines the amount of *fullness* required for the shade. Most tapes require two to two-and-one-half-times fullness. The shade is made extra long so the lower edge forms soft poufs when the shade is down. The poufs can be evenly spaced or you can create a larger pouf in the center with a smaller one on each side. If you space the billows evenly, an odd number is more appealing than an even number.

Choose lightweight, soft **fabric** for a cloud shade. Lace, semisheer, or silky fabrics all work well. *Lining* is usually not necessary.

Because they are puffy, cloud shades are best **mounted** outside the window frame on a mounting board with a 3½" (8.9 cm) *projection*. The outer edges of the heading (called *returns*) wrap around the ends of the mounting board, closing the side view. In its raised position, a cloud shade takes up more stacking space than a flat, tucked, or hobbled shade does, so you may want to mount it higher above the window.

A thin metal rod or wooden dowel works well for the weight bar. When you raise the shade, gently pull the weight rod out from the window a few inches; then pull the draw cord to raise the shade as you release the rod. Air trapped behind the shade makes it puff out as it gathers up from the bottom.

Materials

- Mounting board
- Decorator fabric
- 2" (5.1 cm) angle irons with screws for outside mount
- Tools for installation
- Self-styling tape
- Plastic rings, ³⁄₈" or ¹⁄₂" (1 or 1.3 cm)
- Thin piece of cardboard, optional
- Round metal or wood weight bar, such as a ³⁄₈" (1 cm) dowel, cut ¹⁄₂" (1.3 cm) shorter than finished width of shade
- Adhesive-backed hook and loop tape
- Staple gun and staples
- Screw eyes
- Shade cord
- White glue
- Drapery pull, optional
- Awning cleat

Cutting directions

- Cut a mounting board 2" (5.1 cm) longer than the outside measurement of the window frame. Cut a strip of fabric for covering the board ½" (1.3 cm) wider than the board circumference and 2" (5.1 cm) longer than the board length.

- The *cut length* of the shade fabric is equal to the *finished length* plus 15" (38.1 cm). Measure for the *finished width* of the shade and add twice the projection of the mounting board for returns. Multiply this measurement by the amount of fullness required by the styling tape; then add 4" (10.2 cm) for side hems to find the *cut width*. Seam fabric widths together as necessary, using French seams.

- Cut a strip of fabric for covering the weight rod 1" (2.5 cm) longer than the finished width of the shade and 1" (2.5 cm) wider than the rod circumference.

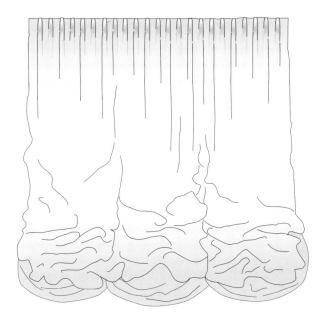

Making a cloud shade

1 Cut the mounting board and cover it with fabric. Secure angle irons to the bottom of the board, near the ends and at 45" (114.3 cm) intervals, using pan-head screws. Mount the board (page 296), centered above the window frame. Measure for the finished size of the shade. Remove the screws that hold the mounting board to the angle irons, leaving the angle irons on the wall.

2 Cut the fabric. Press under 1" (2.5 cm) twice on the sides of the panel, and stitch the hems.

3 Press under a 1" (2.5 cm) double-fold hem pocket at the lower edge. Stitch along the upper edge.

(continued)

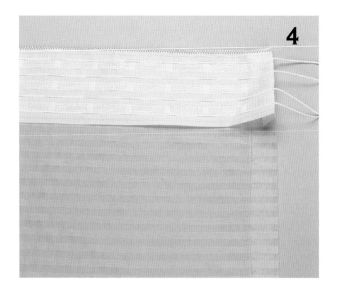

4 Cut styling tape to the width of the hemmed panel plus 2" (5.1 cm). Turn under 1" (2.5 cm) on the ends of the tape, keeping the cords free. Place the tape right side up on the right side of the panel, aligning the lower edge of the tape to the upper edge of the panel. Finish the edges together using overcast stitches.

5 Fold the tape and panel to the wrong side, forming a ¼" (6 mm) fold above the upper edge of the tape. Press the fold. Pin the tape in place. Stitch the tape to the panel, stitching next to the cords. Stitch all stitching lines in the same directions to avoid ripples.

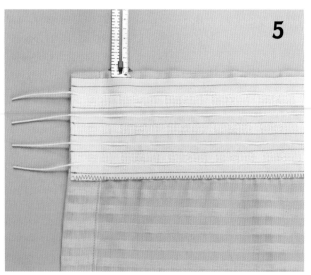

6 Mark the placement for the rings in evenly spaced rows 6" to 10" (15.2 to 25.4 cm) apart. Mark them in evenly spaced columns 18" to 36" (45.7 to 91.4 cm) apart (the ring columns will be closer together after the styling tape is gathered).

Here's how to do the math: Measure the width of the hemmed panel and subtract 2" (5.1 cm). Divide the remainder by the number of poufs you want to find the distance between ring columns.

Measure the length of the shade from the top of the hem to the bottom of the styling tape. Divide this distance by 8" (20.3 cm) and round up to the nearest whole number to find the number of spaces between rows. Divide the distance by the number of spaces to find the distance between rows.

7 Stitch a ring at each mark through both layers of fabric, stitching either by machine or by hand. Do not stitch rings at the base of the styling tape. Reinforce the rings in the bottom row with extra stitches because they carry the weight of the shade.

8 Knot the cords together or in pairs at each end of the styling tape. At one end, pull evenly on the cords to gather the fabric, adjusting the width of the heading to the desired finished width of the shade including returns. Knot the cords together close to the shade. Cut off excess cords or wrap them in a circle and safety-pin them behind the heading. If the cords are not cut, the heading can be smoothed flat for laundering.

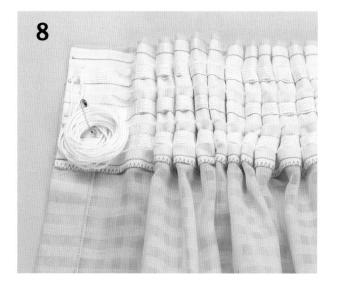

9 Fold the weight rod cover strip in half lengthwise, wrong sides together. Stitch a ⅜" (1 cm) seam on one end and the long side; turn the tube right side out. Insert the weight rod, and stitch the end closed. Insert the covered rod into the hem pocket, distributing the fullness of the pocket evenly along the rod. Slipstitch the hem ends closed. Tack the hem to the rod cover at the ends and near each ring to hold the spacing.

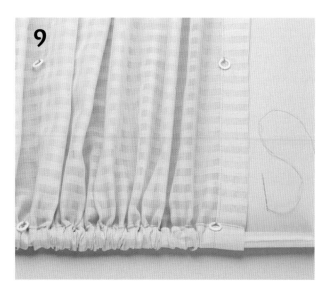

10 Cut hook and loop tape to the finished width of the shade. Adhere the hook side of the tape to the front edge and ends of the mounting board; reinforce with staples. Adhere the loop side to the styling tape at the upper edge of the shade. Attach the shade to the covered mounting board, aligning the strips of hook and loop tape.

11 Follow steps 11 and 12 on page 239. In step 11, insert the end eye screws 1" (2.5 cm) from the ends of the mounting board. In step 12, leave a long tail at each bottom knot. Using the tails, tie together the bottom three rings of each column to secure the bottom poufs.

12 Finish the shade as in steps 13 to 15 on page 239.

Balloon Shades

TAILORED BOX pleats meld with luxurious poufs to create the ever-popular balloon shade. With its split personality, a balloon shade can be equally at home in a living room, a breakfast nook, or a child's bedroom. Your choice of fabric helps determine the degree of formality.

Colorful serenade (opposite)
The gentle swags that form at the bottom of this balloon shade as it is raised echo the formidable archway that divides these rooms. The mirrored pocket doors double the impact of the colorful, graceful shade.

Luxurious color (top right)
The deep raspberry hue of these luxurious balloon shades is a striking contrast to the white woodwork. Simply, yet elegant, they allow the room's accessories and spectacular architectural lines shine through.

Strong focus (bottom right)
Adjoining balloon shades on corner windows leave no doubt where the center of attraction is for this bathroom. When the shades are lowered, they offer warmth and complete privacy.

What you need to know

A series of box pleats gives this shade **design** controlled *fullness* when lowered and a billowy, soft effect when raised. Evenly spaced pleats should be about 12" (30.5 cm) apart. With careful planning, vertical seams, which are usually necessary in a shade with so much fullness, can be hidden in the folds of the pleats.

Lightweight, soft **fabrics** work best for gentle, relaxed gathers. Medium-weight, tightly woven fabrics with more body tend to retain wrinkles, which are unavoidable with this shade style. *Lining* is optional. Though it protects the fabric from sun fading, it may also provide more body than you want.

Because of its depth, it is best to **mount** a balloon shade outside and above the window frame. An inside mount will work on a window with a deep frame. When attaching the shade to the mounting board, extend the sides of the shade around the ends of the board to hide the side view.

Materials

- Mounting board
- Decorator fabric
- Angle irons with screws for outside mount
- Tools for installation
- Adding machine paper
- Drapery lining, optional
- Plastic rings, $3/8$" or $1/2$" (1 or 1.3 cm)
- Flat metal weight bar, $1/2$" (1.3 cm) wide, cut $1/2$" (1.3 cm) shorter than finished width of shade
- Staple gun and staples
- Screw eyes
- Shade cord
- White glue
- Drapery pull, optional
- Awning cleat

Cutting directions

- Cut a mounting board 2" (5.1 cm) longer than the outside measurement of the window frame. Cut a strip of fabric for covering the board $1/2$" (1.3 cm) wider than the board circumference and 2" (5.1 cm) longer than the board length.

- Cut the fabric with the *cut length* equal to the *finished length* of the shade plus 12" (30.5 cm) plus the *projection* of the mounting board. The *cut width* is equal to two times the *finished width* plus 4" (10.2 cm) for side hems. Don't cut the fabric to the final width until step 3.

- Cut a facing strip 2" (5.1 cm) wide and 1" (2.5 cm) longer than the finished width of the shade.

Making a balloon shade

1 Cut the mounting board and cover it with fabric. Secure angle irons to the bottom of the board, near the ends and at 45" (114.3 cm) intervals, using pan-head screws. Mount the board (page 296), centered above the window frame. Measure for the finished size of the shade. Remove the screws that hold the mounting board to the angle irons, leaving the angle irons on the wall.

2 Cut a strip of adding machine paper the same length as the cut width of the shade to make a pattern for the pleats. Mark a 2" (5.1 cm) hem allowance at each end of the pattern. Mark pleat fold lines in the pattern about 12" (30.5 cm) apart and about 6" (15.2 cm) deep. Mark a half pleat at each end.

Here's how to do the math: Divide the length of the mounting board by 12" (30.5 cm) and round the number up or down to find the number of poufs (and pleats) there will be. Subtract the length of the mounting board from the width of the pattern between side hem marks. Divide the remainder by the number of pleats to find how much excess fabric must be folded out in each pleat. Fold the pattern into pleats and measure to check for accuracy.

3 Seam fabric widths together. Trim the seam allowances to ¼" (6 mm), finish them together, and press them to one side. Place the pattern on the fabric, aligning the seams to points in the pattern where they will be hidden in pleats, and mark the fabric at the pattern ends. Cut the fabric to the width of the pattern.

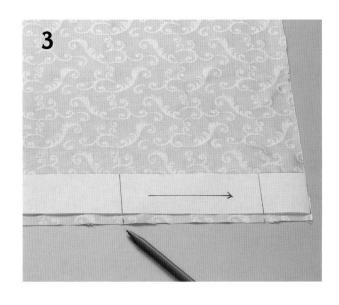

4 Press under 1" (2.5 cm) twice on the sides of the panel, and stitch the hems.

5 Place the pattern on the shade at the lower edge. Mark the pleat fold lines. Repeat at the upper edge.

(continued)

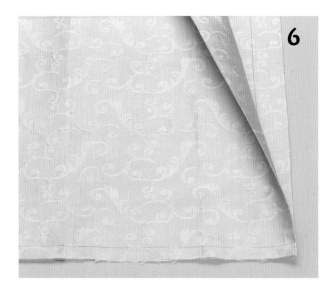

6 Pin the pleats in place along the lower edge; the side hems will be hidden under the half-pleats at the sides of the shade. Stitch ½" (1.3 cm) from the lower edge to secure the pleats.

7 Pin the pleats in place along the upper edge. Extend the hemmed edges away from the pleat fold a distance equal to the projection of the mounting board. Stitch a distance from the upper edge equal to the projection of the mounting board. Finish the upper edges together.

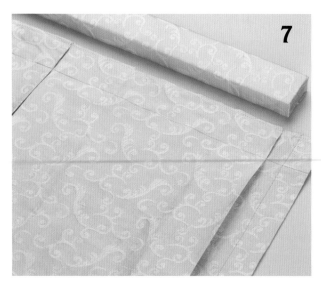

8 Place the shade faceup on a large flat surface and pin the pleats in place from top to bottom. The shade will be slightly wider at the top. Press the pleats.

9 Press under ½" (1.3 cm) on one long edge of the facing strip. Pin the other side to the bottom of the shade, right sides together, with the ends of the strip extending equally. Stitch a ½" (1.3 cm) seam.

10 Press the seam toward the facing. Turn the ends in over the seam allowance; then turn the facing to the wrong side. Edgestitch along the fold, forming a weight rod pocket.

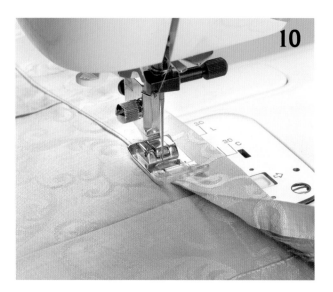

11 Mark the placement for the rings in columns at the side hems and at the center of each pleat. Mark the bottom row at the upper edge of the pocket, and space the rows evenly, about 6" (15.2 cm) apart.

Here's how to do the math: Measure the length of the shade from the top of the pocket to the stitching line at the top of the shade. Divide this distance by 6" (15.2 cm) and round up to the nearest whole number to find the number of spaces between rows. Divide the distance by the number of spaces to find the distance between rows.

12 Stitch rings to the shade at the marks, taking care not to catch the pleat fabric in the stitches.

13 Insert the weight bar into the pocket. Slipstitch the ends closed.

14 Center the shade on top of the mounting board, aligning the stitched line to the top front edge of the board; the sides will extend beyond the board. Staple the shade to the mounting board; wrap the sides over the ends of the board, and staple in place, forming squared corners.

15 Follow steps 11 and 12 on page 239. In step 11, insert the end eye screws 1" (2.5 cm) from the ends of the mounting board. In step 12, leave a long tail at each bottom knot. Using the tails, tie together the bottom three rings of each column to secure the bottom poufs.

16 Finish the shade as in steps 13 to 15 on page 239.

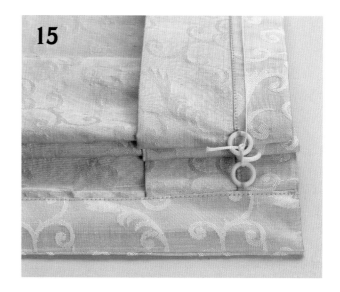

Austrian Shades

SOFT, LAVISH gathers, with fullness in both directions, give Austrian shades a formal, romantic air. They are classic in plain sheer curtain fabric, but they're also magical in lightweight silk or an all-over miniprint.

Sheer romance (opposite)
Everything luxurious and romantic about this bedroom is tied up into the wall-to-wall Austrian shades. The gathers and draping of the sheer fabric are utterly soothing.

Accented curves (top)
Austrian shades were the perfect choice for accenting the impressive curves of these side-by-side arched windows. Contrast edging on the draperies and tiebacks ties the window treatment nicely to the rest of the room.

Star treatment (left)
Tasteful accessories and dramatic draperies give this stately room its character. With its star-splashed sheer fabric and gentle shirring, the Austrian shade glows with filtered sunlight.

What you need to know

This **design** has *fullness* in both directions. Double to triple fullness vertically one-and-one-half times fullness horizontally makes the fabric droop in gathered columns between lines of special shirring tape. Austrian shade tape has gathering cords along the sides and plastic rings at regular intervals for stringing the shade cord. Manufacturer's directions for using the tape may vary and should be available at the point of purchase.

Use only lightweight **fabric** with a soft drape. An Austrian shade made of sheer fabric will filter sunlight but will not provide total privacy at night. It's impossible to press an Austrian shade, so choose fabric that does not wrinkle. Austrian shades often have fringe along the lower edge. Be sure to take the length of the fringe into account when you plan the finished length of the shade.

In these directions, the shade is stapled to a **mounting** board and mounted inside the window frame, flush with the front of the frame. You could create a *rod pocket* at the top and hang the shade from a curtain rod, but you still have to mount a board with screw eyes to carry the cord for raising and lowering the shade or insert the screws directly into the window frame. Austrian shades do not stack tightly when raised, so if you intend to raise the shade often, you may want to mount the shade outside the frame and higher than usual to clear more glass.

Materials

- Mounting board
- Decorator fabric
- 1" (2.5 cm) angle irons with screws for outside mount
- Tools for installation
- Austrian shade tape
- Decorative trim, such as fringe, optional
- Twill tape, 1" (2.5 cm) wide
- Staple gun and staples
- Wood weight bar, such as a $^3/_8$" (1 cm) dowel, cut $^1/_2$" (1.3 cm) shorter than finished width of shade
- Screw eyes
- Shade cord
- White glue
- Drapery pull, optional
- Awning cleat

Cutting directions

- Cut a mounting board $^1/_4$" (6 mm) shorter than the inside measurement of the window frame. Cut a strip of fabric for covering the board $^1/_2$" (1.3 cm) wider than the board circumference and 2" (5.1 cm) longer than the board length.

- Cut the shade fabric 2 to 3 times longer than the *finished length* of the shade. The *cut width* is equal to the *finished width* plus 3" (7.6 cm) for side hems plus 4" (10.2 cm) for each swag column (determined in step 2). If you must seam fabric widths together, don't cut the fabric width until you have determined the spacing for the shirring tapes.

- Cut a strip of fabric for covering the weight rod 1" (2.5 cm) longer than the finished width of the shade and 1" (2.5 cm) wider than the rod circumference.

Making an Austrian shade

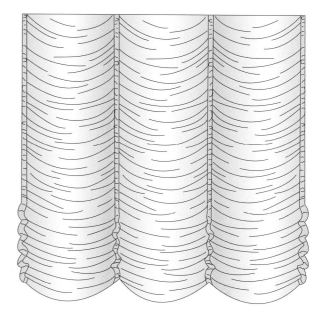

1 Cut the mounting board and cover it with fabric. If the shade will be mounted outside the window frame, secure angle irons to the bottom of the board, near the ends and at 45" (114.3 cm) intervals, using pan-head screws. Mount the board (page 296), centered above the window frame. Measure for the finished size of the shade. Remove the screws that hold the mounting board to the angle irons, leaving the angle irons on the wall.

2 Plan the number of swag columns there will be, making them 8" to 12" (20.3 to 30.5 cm) wide, with the first tapes positioned 1" (2.5 cm) from the sides.
   Here's how to do the math: Subtract 2" (5.1 cm) from the finished width of the shade. Divide this number by 10" (25.4 cm), and round off to find the number of swag columns.

3 Seam fabric widths together, if necessary, planning the seams to fall where there will be a line of shirring tape.
   Here's how to do the math: Subtract 2" (5.1 cm) from the finished width of the shade. Divide this measurement by the number of swag columns to find the finished width of each column. Add 4" (10.2 cm) of fullness to each swag column to plan the space between tapes.

(continued)

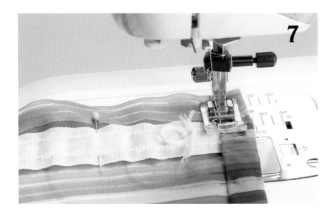

4 Press under 1½" (3.8 cm) on the sides of the panel. The raw edges will be covered later by the shade tape. If the fabric frays easily, finish the upper edge using zigzag stitches or by overcasting.

5 Turn under a double-fold ½" (1.3 cm) hem at the lower edge, and press but don't stitch yet. Mark the upper edge of the hem at each tape placement line, as determined in step 3. The outer tapes will be 1" (2.5 cm) from the sides, straddling the raw edges of the side hems. There will be one more tape than the number of swag columns.

6 Cut lengths of Austrian shade tape the same length as the hemmed panel, cutting each tape so the bottom cut is 1" (2.5 cm) below a ring.

7 On each tape, pick out the gathering cords below the bottom ring and tie them together securely. Insert the ends of the tapes and the knots under the top edge of the hem, centering a tape at each placement mark; pin in place. Stitch the hem in place, catching the tapes in the stitching.

8 Pick out the gathering cords at the top of each tape and tie them together securely. Pin the tapes in place to the top of the shade. Stitch along both sides of each tape, always stitching from the same direction.

9 If you want fringe along the lower edge, stitch the fringe in place with the heading just covering the hem stitching line. Turn under the ends of the fringe to keep them from raveling.

10 Pull up on the gathering cords of each tape to gather the shade to the finished length. Make sure the fullness is distributed equally on all tapes and the rings line up horizontally. Tie the cords securely to keep the shade length. If you don't cut the cords, you can release the gathers for laundering the shade.

11 On the right side of the shade, at the upper edge, fold a 2" (5.1 cm) tuck of fabric over the gathered fabric on each side of each swag column, abutting the tuck folds of adjoining columns. Pin in place. Check the finished width of the edge and adjust the size of the tucks, if necessary.

12 Cut twill tape 1" (2.5 cm) longer than the finished width of the shade. Turn under the ends of the tape ½" (1.3 cm) and stitch the tape over the upper raw edge on the right side of the shade.

13 Align the free edge of the twill tape to the top back of the mounting board, and staple the shade in place.

14 Fold the weight rod cover strip in half lengthwise, wrong sides together. Stitch a ⅜" (1 cm) seam on one end and the long side; turn the tube right side out. Insert the weight rod, and stitch the end closed. Tack the covered rod to the lower edge of the shade just below the bottom rings to hold the spacing.

15 Follow steps 11 to 15 on page 239.

Coach Shades

THESE SHADES recall the window coverings on stage coaches of the Wild West. Fabric rolls up from the bottom and is controlled with loops of cord. Pair the shade with a top treatment to hide the mechanism, or make a shade and valance all in one as in the directions that follow.

Bright, bold pattern (opposite)
The tropical print of these coach shades plays well against the vast expanse of the ocean view beyond the windows. Straps cut from striped fabric repeated in the sofa cushion hold the rolled shades at the desired height.

Center tie (left)
The blue stripes of this coach shade really pop against the lemon yellow bedroom walls. Tied only in the center, the shade imparts a relaxing, casual mood.

Reversed rolls (top)
These coach shades roll toward the back. Their cords are barely visible behind the soft white swag valances. Made in a companion print to the chairs, the shades are an eye-catching complement to the yellow walls.

What you need to know

This is a simple **design**, suitable for a window that is narrower than one fabric width. Two fabrics fused together roll up around a wooden pole at the bottom and flip over the mounting board to form a valance at the top. One fabric shows on the face of the shade; the other fabric shows on the valance and the bottom roll. Two cords, strung through screw eyes on the underside of the mounting board, raise and lower the shade and wrap around an awning cleat to hold the shade at the desired level. Because the cords form a continuous loop, don't use this shade where it can be reached by small children and potentially cause harm.

Use firmly woven, lightweight to medium-weight **fabric**. Avoid glazed fabrics, such as chintz, because these fabrics do not bond well to the fusible adhesive. Also, some fabrics with stain-resistant and water-repellent finishes may not bond well. Before using these fabrics, make a test sample to check the bond. If the window receives strong light, avoid dark or bold colors that will fade noticeably. If show-through is a concern, use a print fabric on the front and a solid fabric on the back to prevent shadowing of the fabric designs.

Mounting directions are for an outside mount. The shade will hug the window frame closely for optimal light control. To install the shade and valance inside the frame, omit the angle irons and finials and simply screw the mounting board directly up into the window frame.

Materials

- Mounting board
- Two coordinating decorator fabrics
- 1" (2.5 cm) angle irons with screws for outside mount
- Nuts and bolts for mounting the board to the angle irons
- Tools for installation
- Paper-backed fusible adhesive in a wide sheet
- Iron and large flat pressing surface
- Carpenter's square
- Liquid fray preventer or fabric glue and a small paintbrush
- Decorative trim
- Fabric glue
- Three screw eyes
- Staple gun and staples
- Awl
- Wooden dowel, $1/2$" to $3/4$" (1.3 to 1.9 cm) diameter
- Two round ball finials or drawer pulls
- Paint and paintbrush, optional
- Shade cord
- Two small drapery pulls, optional
- Awning cleat

Cutting directions

- Cut a mounting board 2" (5.1 cm) longer than the outside measurement of the window frame. Cut a strip of fabric for covering the board ½" (1.3 cm) wider than the board circumference and 2" (5.1 cm) longer than the board length.

- Cut both fabrics 1" (2.5 cm) wider than the *finished width* of the shade and 20" (50.8 cm) longer than the *finished length* of the shade. The extra length will allow for the valance and the amount rolled onto the pole. Cut the fusible adhesive to the same width and length. Long strips can be fused next to each other in step 1 to obtain the full width needed.

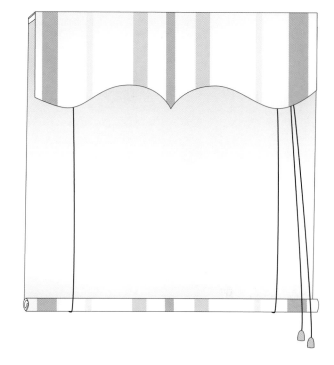

Making a coach shade

1 Cut the mounting board and cover it with fabric. Secure angle irons to the back top of the board, using nuts and bolts. Mount the board (page 296), centered above the window frame. Measure for the finished size of the shade. Remove the nuts and bolts that hold the mounting board to the angle irons, leaving the angle irons on the wall.

2 Fuse the adhesive to the wrong side of one of the fabrics, following the manufacturer's directions. If more than one long strip is needed, fuse the strips so the edges just meet.

3 Remove the paper backing. Fuse the second fabric to the first, wrong sides together. Allow the fabric to cool completely.

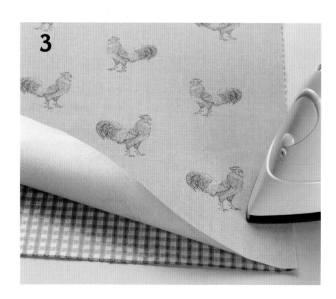

(continued)

4 Mark the finished width on the shade. Square off the upper and lower edges, using a carpenter's square for accuracy. Draw a symmetrically shaped upper edge (this will become the bottom of the self valance). Cut along the marked lines. Apply liquid fray preventer or diluted fabric glue along the cut edges, using a small paintbrush.

5 Glue decorative trim to the valance edge. Make sure you apply it to the side that will face the room.

6 Drill pilot holes and insert three screw eyes, centered on the underside of the mounting board. Insert one screw eye 1" (2.5 cm) from the end on the side of the shade where you want the cords to hang. Insert the other two screw eyes 3" (7.6 cm) from each end.

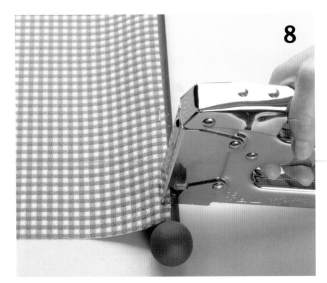

7 Staple the shade over the top of the mounting board, allowing the desired length to hang forward for the valance. Pierce the fabric with an awl over the mounting holes.

8 Cut the dowel to the shade width. Paint the dowel and knobs, if desired, and allow them to dry. Staple the shade bottom to the dowel, with the back of the shade facing up. Roll the shade around the dowel until the shade is the desired finished length. Staple along the back of the dowel.

9 Cut a length of shade cord equal to three times the finished length of the shade plus the width of the shade. Cut a second length of cord equal to three times the finished length of the shade. Tie a small loop in one end of each cord, leaving 6" (15.2 cm) tails. Staple the cords to the top of the mounting board with the loops over the bolt holes.

10 Mount the shade on the angle irons, making sure the bolts go through the cord loops. Just before tightening the bolts, secure the loops with two or three knots.

11 Wrap the cords under the rolled dowel, up over the shade front, and through the screw eyes. String the longer cord also through the opposite screw eye and both cords through the end screw eye on the draw side. Knot the cords together just outside the last screw eye. Attach a small drapery pull to the end of each cord. For child safety, do not tie the cords together at the ends.

12 Secure an awning cleat to the edge of the window frame or on the wall. Pull gently on the cords to raise the shade, causing the fabric to roll around the dowel. Wind the cord around the cleat to hold the shade in its raised position.

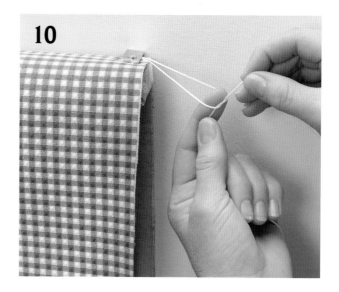

Fabric Roller Shades

HE HUMBLE roller shade still has a lot going for it—total privacy, light control, affordability, ease of operation—and it can be decorative as well. Simply fuse the fabric of your choice to a special backing, add designer details, like a shaped bottom edge or decorator trim, and tape it to a roller. No need to sew a stitch!

Floral fantasy (opposite)
Roller shades made in fabric that matches the wallpaper turn this bedroom into a floral fantasy. The solid cream valances and bedspread keep the pattern from overpowering the room.

Cute as a bug (top right)
A parade of adorable bugs marching across the cornices and roller shades in this room send the cute meter soaring. Bold stripes taken from the drapery fabric strike a bold chord across the bottoms of the shades.

Layered to perfection (right)
Each layer of this window treatment was carefully planned and beautifully executed. The roller shade blocks harmful sunlight while highlighting the couch upholstery. Long side panels add drama and block light at the sides of the window. The valance hides the mechanics of the underlayers, adds height, and unifies the treatment.

What you need to know

Roller shade kits make it easy to **design** these beautiful and functional window treatments. The kits include the roller, mounting hardware, hem stick, fusible adhesive strips, and fusible backing. Some have a pulley system with a cord for raising and lowering the shade; others operate by means of a spring inside the roller. Depending on the brand of the kit, the shade fabric is attached either to an adjustable metal roller or to a cardboard roller that is cut to size. The kits are sold in fabric stores and on Internet web sites.

Use firmly woven, lightweight to medium-weight **fabric**. Avoid glazed fabrics, such as chintz, because these fabrics do not bond well to the fusible backing. Also, some fabrics with stain-resistant and water-repellent finishes may not bond well. Before using these fabrics, make a test sample to check the bond.

Roller shades are rarely used alone; they are at least topped with a valance that hides the hardware. Then the shade can be installed so it rolls off the back of the roller with the wrong side of the shade facing out as it wraps around the roller. This allows you to install the shade closer to the window for better energy efficiency and light control. If the roller will be visible when the shade is **mounted**, install the shade so it rolls off the front of the roller with the right side of the shade facing out as it wraps around the roller. For an inside-mounted shade, the window frame must be deep enough to accommodate the installed roller with the entire shade wrapped around it. If this is not the case, the shade can be installed as an outside mount, either to the front of the window frame or on the wall just above the frame. Follow the manufacturer's instructions to determine the size of the roller and install the shade.

Shade rolls off the front of the roller.

Materials

- Roller shade kit that includes adjustable roller, mounting brackets, fusible backing, and hem stick
- Tools for installation
- Decorator fabric
- Carpenter's square
- Fusible adhesive strip, if not included in shade kit
- Liquid fray preventer or fabric glue and small brush
- Decorative trim
- Fabric glue
- Vinyl tape

Shade rolls off the back of the roller.

Making a roller shade

1 Install the mounting brackets and roller, and measure the roller to determine the finished width of the shade.

2 Steam-press the fabric thoroughly to prevent shrinkage during fusing. Cut the fabric 2" (5.1 cm) wider and 14" (35.6 cm) longer than the desired finished size. Cut the fusible backing 1" (2.5 cm) wider and 12" (30.5 cm) longer than the desired finished size. Use a carpenter's square to ensure square corners.

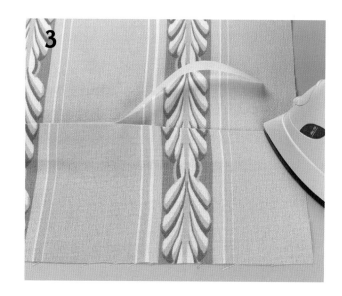

3 Turn up the lower edge of the fabric 6" (15.2 cm) from the bottom, wrong sides together, and press a crease. Turn the lower edge back down, right sides together, 1½" (3.8 cm) from the first crease, forming a pocket. Using a ⅜" (1 cm) wide strip of fusible adhesive, fuse the upper edge of the pocket closed.

(continued)

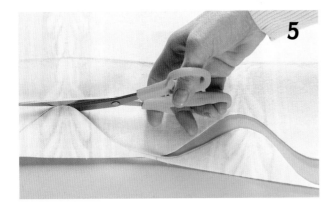

4 Fuse the backing to the wrong side of the fabric, centering it on the width of the fabric. Use a press cloth and follow the manufacturer's directions.

5 Mark the finished width on the shade backing. Square off the upper and lower edges, using a carpenter's square. Draw a symmetrically shaped hem. Cut along the marked lines.

6 Apply liquid fray preventer or diluted fabric glue along the cut edges, using a small paintbrush.

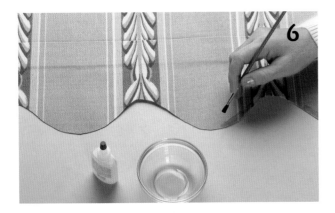

7 Apply a decorative trim along the cut edge of the shaped hem, using fabric glue.

8 Attach the shade to the roller, using tape. For the shade to roll up properly, the upper edge must be square with the center of the roller. Attach the shade with the backing facing up if you want the shade to roll off the back of the roller as shown; attach it with the fabric facing up if you want it to roll off the front of the roller.

9 Trim the hem stick to fit the pocket. Slide the stick into the pocket. Mount the roller on the shade brackets.

Window Treatment Basics

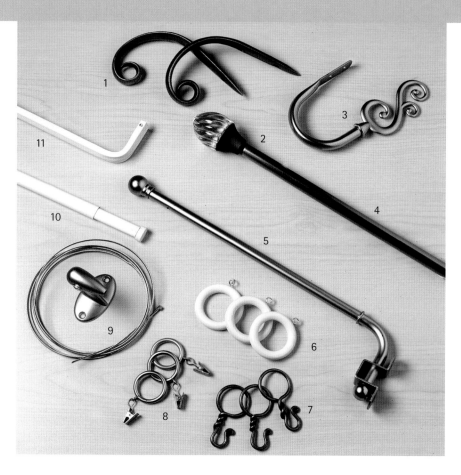

THIS SECTION will help you plan, sew, and install your window treatments. On page 300, you will find definitions of words that are printed in italics.

Choosing and installing hardware

There are lots of choices for window hardware, including multi-component systems with parts that are sold separately and can be combined to suit any purpose and style. Some items have multiple uses, such as rod brackets (1) that can also be used as holdbacks. Ornate finials (2) can be attached to holdbacks (3) or poles (4). Crane rods (5) are designed to swing away from the window. Wooden and metal rings can be slipped onto a rod and sewn (6) to the curtain, hooked through a buttonhole or grommet (7), or clipped in place (8). A steel cable system (9), used instead of a rod, gives the window treatment a sleek, modern look. When the entire rod will be covered by the treatment, inexpensive utility rods, such as spring pressure rods (10) or oval curtain rods (11) can be used. It is important to install the hardware before measuring for the cut length and width of the treatment.

Where do you mount the hardware? Most curtains and draperies are mounted outside the window frame far enough above and to the sides so the treatment covers the glass and wood. For traversing draperies, the rod should extend far enough to the sides of the window to accommodate the *stacking space* of the pleats. Some styles, like hourglass and stretched curtains that lie close to the glass, are mounted inside the frame on spring pressure rods or onto the frame with sash rods. When the curtains or draperies are layered over another treatment, leave at least 2" (5 cm) of *clearance* between the curtain and the *undertreatment* at the front and sides. If the outer treatment must open and close, leave 3" (7.5 cm) between the layers.

The correct height for mounting curtains and draperies varies with the style, ceiling height, window size, and overall treatment. It should be high enough to cover the top of the window frame or any undertreatments. If you want to create the illusion that the window is taller than it is, the treatment can be mounted higher.

Window treatment hardware comes with mounting brackets, screws or nails, and installation instructions. Use screws alone if installing through drywall or plaster directly into wall studs. When brackets are between wall studs, support the screws for lightweight treatments with plastic anchors in the correct size for the screws. If the brackets must support a heavy treatment, use plastic toggle anchors or molly bolts in the correct size for the wallboard depth. Nails supplied with hardware should be used only for very light-weight treatments installed directly into wood.

Plastic anchors

1. Mark screw locations on the wall. Drill holes for plastic anchors, using a drill bit slightly smaller than the diameter of the anchor. Tap the anchors into the holes, using a hammer.

2. Insert a screw through the hole in the bracket and into the installed anchor until it is flush with the wall. Continue to tighten the screw several more turns; the anchor expands in the drywall, preventing it from being pulled out of the wall.

Toggle anchors

1. Mark screw locations on the wall. Drill holes for toggle anchors, using a drill bit slightly smaller than the diameter of the toggle anchor shank.
2. Squeeze the wings of the toggle anchor flat, and push the toggle anchor into the hole; tap it in with a hammer until it is flush with the wall.

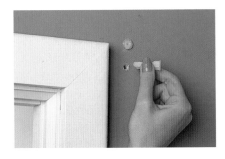

3. Insert a screw through the hole in the bracket and into the installed anchor; tighten the screw until it is flush with the wall. The wings spread out and flatten against the back of the drywall.

Molly bolts

1. Mark the screw locations on the wall. Drill holes for the molly bolts, using a drill bit slightly smaller than the diameter of the molly bolt.
2. Tap the molly bolt into the drilled hole, using a hammer; tighten the screw several turns after it is flush with the wall. The molly bolt expands and flattens against the back of the drywall.

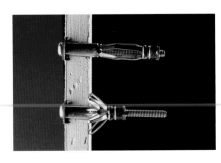

3. Remove the screw from the molly bolt; insert the screw through the hole in the bracket and into the installed molly bolt. Screw the bracket securely in place.

Installing a traverse rod

1. Mount the end rod brackets with the U-shaped socket facing upward.

2. Hook the lipped support clip of the center bracket over the center of the rod; position the rod, fitting the ends of the rod into the end brackets. Mark the screw holes for the center bracket.

3. Take the rod down, and mount the center bracket. Lift the rod into position again; snap the center support clip over the rod, hooking it into the groove at the front of the rod. Using a screwdriver, turn the metal cam on the underside of the support clip counterclockwise, locking the clip in place.

4. Push the overlap and underlap master slides to the opposite ends of the rod. At the left side, reach behind the underlap slide for the cord. Pull the cord slightly to form a small loop; hook the loop securely over the plastic finger that projects from the back of the master slide (next page).

5. Separate the stem from the pulley base; hold the base against the wall near the floor, directly below a point 2" (5 cm) in from the right end bracket of the rod. Mark screw locations; mount the bracket.

6. Attach the stem to the pulley base. Pull up on the cord housing, exposing the hole on the inner stem. Insert a small nail through the hole so the stem remains extended. Attach the cord to the pulley, slipping the loop end of the cord through the slot in the cord housing.

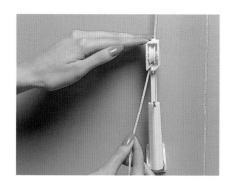

7. Reach behind the overlap master slide at the right end of the rod; locate the two knots at the back of the slide.

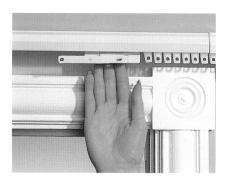

8. Pull the knot nearest the glides until the cord hanging at the side of the rod is taut against the pulley wheel. Tie a new knot in the cord at the back of the slide, with excess cord hanging down. Remove the nail from the inner stem of the pulley. Cut off the excess cord; tighten the knot securely.

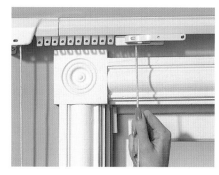

Tieback holders

Short, lightweight curtains with tiebacks can be held in place with cup hooks, small metal tieback hooks, or tenter hooks installed in the side of the window frame or the wall. For curtains and draperies that have more body, however, use plastic tieback holders with a deep projection. These concealed tieback holders are mounted inside the returns at the sides of the treatment to keep the tiebacks from crushing the folds in the fabric.

Mounting boards

Some curtains, such as tent flaps (page 190), are mounted on boards instead of window hardware. The mounting board is covered with extra curtain fabric, much as you would wrap a gift box, but secured with staples instead of tape. Then the curtain is stapled to the board.

The size of the mounting board depends on whether the curtain will be mounted inside or outside the window frame. Stock pine lumber is often the best choice because it is inexpensive, lightweight, and only needs to be cut to the right length. Keep in mind that the actual measurement of stock lumber differs from the nominal measurement. A 1 × 2 board is really ¾" × 1½" (2 × 3.8 cm), a 1 × 4 board is ¾" × 3½" (2 × 9 cm), a 1 × 6 board is ¾" × 5½" (2 × 14 cm), and a 1 × 8 board is ¾" × 7¼" (2 × 18.7 cm).

For an inside-mounted curtain, the depth of the window frame must be at least 1½" (3.8 cm) to accommodate a 1 × 2 mounting board. Cut the board ½" (1.3 cm) shorter than the inside measurement of the frame so it will still fit after being covered with fabric.

Choose the mounting board width for outside-mounted curtains following the general guidelines for clearance on page 294. Install the board to the wall outside and above the window frame using angle irons that are more than one-half the projection of the board. You will need one at each end and others spaced about 36" (91.5 cm) apart.

Measuring the window

For accurate measurements, mount the hardware or mounting board first—don't just estimate where it will be. Use a steel tape measure, not a cloth or plastic one. Measure and record the measurements for each window in the room separately, even if they appear to be the same size.

You'll need to determine the finished length and width of the window treatment before you can figure out how long and wide to cut the fabric. Cutting directions for each project help you do this. If a patterned fabric is used, you will also need to allow extra fabric for matching the pattern (page 298). To find the finished length of the treatment, measure from the rod or mounting board to where you want the lower edge of the window treatment. The measurement is taken from the top of a utility rod or mounting board.

When decorative rods are used, the measurement is taken from the pin hole in one of the rings or glides. Depending on the style of the treatment, you may need to add to this measurement an amount for a heading or clearance above the rod. To find the finished width of the treatment, measure the length of the rod or mounting board. For many treatments it is also necessary to measure the depth of the return. For traversing draperies, you also have to consider stacking space and the center *overlap*. These terms are defined on page 300.

Here are some more tips for measuring:
• Allow ½" (1.3 cm) clearance between the bottom of the curtain or drapery and the floor when measuring for floor-length treatments. If the fabric is loosely woven, allow 1" (2.5 cm) clearance because the weight of the treatment will probably stretch the fabric.
• Add 2" to 4" (5 to 10 cm) to the measurement for a floor-length treatment that breaks/brushes on the floor.
• Add 12" to 20" (30.5 to 51 cm) to the measurement for a floor-length treatment that puddles on the floor.
• Allow 4" to 6" (10 to 15 cm) clearance above electric baseboard heaters for safety.
• Short, outside-mounted curtains should fall to ½" (1.3 cm) below the window frame or apron. Treatments mounted inside the frame can stop at the sill.
• If the windows in the room are different heights, measure all treatments in the room to the same height from the floor for a uniform look. Use the highest

window in the room as the standard for measuring the others.
• For layered treatments, make underdraperies ½" (1.3 cm) shorter than the overdraperies at the top and bottom, so they will not show.

Working with decorator fabric

Decorator fabrics intended for window treatments have characteristics not found in fashion fabrics. They are more durable and often have been treated to resist stains. When cleaning is necessary, most decorator fabrics must be dry-cleaned to avoid shrinkage. Care information is given on the fabric identification label, found on the bolt or tube.

Decorator fabrics should be preshrunk to ensure they won't shrink during construction or the first time they are cleaned. To do this, roll out the fabric and slowly hover a steam iron back and forth just above the surface. If the treatment is short curtains that you intend to launder, wash and press the fabric before cutting.

To make sure the treatment will hang correctly, the fabric lengths must be cut *on-grain*. Tightly woven fabrics that do not need to be matched at the seams can be cut perpendicular to the *selvages*, using a carpenter's square as a guide for marking the cutting line. For lightweight and loosely woven fabrics, it is better to pull a thread along the *crosswise grain* and cut along the pulled thread.

Seams

Sew your curtain and drapery panels together with ½ (1.3 cm) seam allowances. Straight-stitch seams, sewn on a conventional machine, are suitable for most decorator fabrics that are tightly woven. Seam allowances are usually *finished* together with zigzag stitching or serging and pressed toward the *return* side of the panel. You can also use a 4-thread or 5-thread overlock seam stitched on a serger. Use a very narrow, medium-length zigzag stitch on lace and other loosely woven fabrics to prevent puckering along the seamline. The fabric will stretch slightly as it hangs, and the zigzag stitches can "relax" without breaking.

Before seaming tightly woven fabric, trim away the selvages evenly to prevent the seam from puckering after the treatment is installed. For loosely woven fabrics that would fray easily, don't trim the selvages but clip into them every 2" (5 cm) to allow them to relax.

For sheer treatments that will be seen from both sides, such as stretched and hourglass curtains, join panels with French seams, following these steps:

1. Trim away the selvages evenly.
2. Pin the raw edges wrong sides together. Stitch a scant ¼" (6 mm) seam. Trim the seam allowance edges to remove any fraying ends. Press the seam allowances to one side.
3. Turn the fabric panels right sides together, enclosing the seam allowances. The stitching line should be exactly on the fold. Stitch ¼" (6 mm) from the folded edge, enclosing the seam allowances. Press the seam to one side.

Matching patterns
Patterned decorator fabrics are designed to match at the seams.

Cuts are made across the fabric, from selvage to selvage, following the *pattern repeat* rather than the fabric grain, so it is very important to purchase fabric that is printed on-grain. The pattern repeat is the lengthwise distance from one distinctive point in the design, such as the tip of a petal in a floral pattern, to the same point in the next repeat of the design. Some patterned fabrics have pattern repeat markings printed on the selvages.

Extra yardage is usually needed so you can match the pattern. After finding the cut length for the main pieces of a curtain or drapery, round this measurement up to the next number divisible by the size of the pattern repeat to determine the revised cut length. To have the design match from one panel to the next, each panel must be cut at exactly the same point of the pattern repeat.

1. Cut the fabric pieces to the revised cut length, allowing extra for matching the print. Place two fabric pieces right sides together, aligning the selvages. Fold back the upper selvage until the pattern matches. Adjust the top layer slightly up or down so the pattern lines up exactly. Press the fold line.

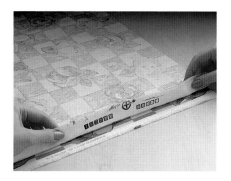

2. Unfold the pressed selvage and pin the layers together, in the

fold line. Turn the fabric over and check the match from the right side. Make any necessary adjustments.

3. Re-pin the fabric so the pins are perpendicular to the fold line; stitch on the fold line. Trim away the selvages, cutting the seam allowances to ½" (1.3 cm). Finish the seam allowances, if necessary.
4. Repeat steps 2 to 4 for all the pieces in the panel. Trim the entire panel to the necessary cut length.

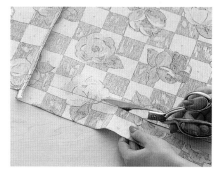

Hems
If you have measured, figured, and cut accurately, your curtains should fit windows perfectly once they are hemmed. For the neatest and easiest hems, follow the procedure used in professional workrooms: sew the lower hems first, the side hems next, and rod pockets and headings last.

Side and lower hems of curtains

are always double to provide strength, weight, and stability. The most accurate way to make a double-fold hem is to press the full hem depth under first, and then turn the cut edge under up to the foldline. Cut off the selvages evenly before pressing the side hems.

Curtains hang better when hems are weighted or anchored. Sew drapery weights into the hems at the lower corners and bottoms of seams to keep the curtain from pulling or puckering. Use heavier weights for full-length curtains, lighter weights for lightweight fabrics and shorter curtains. Do not use weights for sheer curtains. They are not necessary for treatments that puddle on the floor.

There are three ways to finish curtain and drapery hems. Test the methods first on your fabric to see which one you prefer.

a. Straight stitch. The stitching will be visible from the right side but is often inconspicuous. This is the best method to use for sheer and semisheer fabrics. Straight stitch on the folded hem edge, using 8 to 10 stitches per inch. Use thread to match a solid color fabric or blend with multicolor fabric. Stitch slowly through the multiple layers.
b. Blindstitch. This is less visible from the right side. Adjust a conventional sewing machine to the blindstitch setting and attach a blindstitch foot. Fold the hem under, leaving the inner fold extending 1/8" (3 mm). Align the guide in the foot to the soft fold. Adjust the stitch width to take a tiny bite into the soft fold.

c. Fusing. This method is quick and easy; recommended for medium-weight, firmly woven fabrics. Fuse paper-backed fusible adhesive strip to the underside of the hem close to the upper edge. Remove the paper backing, and fuse the hem in place. Follow the manufacturer's instructions for fusing. Press from both sides.

Lining

Lining gives curtains and draperies extra body and also protects the fabric from sun fading, supports the side hems and heading, and gives a uniform appearance to the windows from the outside. Lining also reduces light filtration through the treatment, making seams and hems less visible.

Select drapery lining fabric in the same width as the decorator fabric for your project, so that seams will fall in the same location and the finished panels will be the same width. You can choose white or ivory. The best lining is treated for stain and water resistance. For bedrooms, when total darkness is preferred, select blackout lining.

Decorative trims

Welting, fringes, and other decorative accents dramatically change the appearance of window treatments. They give rich style and grace to curtains and draperies by accenting design lines and adding color and textural interest.

Fabric-covered welting

Welting adds an attractive emphasis to seam lines and edges. In a rod-pocket curtain with an extended heading (page 167), for instance, welting defines the upper edge and stiffens it for better shaping. Welting can also be used to accent the outline of shaped tiebacks. Ready-to-sew fabric-covered cording is available in a limited selection of decorator colors and thicknesses.

You can cover filler cord with the fabric of your choice for a perfect match to your window treatment. To make fabric-covered welting, fabric strips are cut on the *bias* so the welting will be more flexible around curves and corners. Cut bias strips as wide as the circumference of the filler cord plus 1" (2.5 cm).

1. Fold the fabric diagonally so the selvage is parallel to the crosswise grain; cut on the fold. Measuring from this cut edge, cut bias strips of the necessary width, cutting the ends at 45-degree angles on the straight grain.
2. Seam the strips together as necessary; press the seam allowances open. Cut the end of the strip straight across. Center the filler cord on the wrong side of the strip, with the end of the cord 1" (2.5 cm) from the end of the strip. Fold the end of the strip over the cording.
3. Fold the fabric strip around the cording, wrong sides together, matching the raw edges and encasing the cording.
4. Machine-baste close to the cording, using a zipper foot.
5. Stitch the welting to the right side of the curtain, as indicated in the project instructions, matching raw edges and stitching over the basting stitches. Stop stitching 5" (12.7 cm) from where you want the welting to stop.

6. Cut the welting 1" (2.5 cm) beyond the desired end point. Remove the basting stitches from the end of the welting, and cut the cord even with the desired end point.

7. Fold the end of the bias strip over the cord, encasing the cut end. Finish stitching the welting to the curtain fabric.

Twisted cord welting

Twisted cord welting, a stylish alternative to fabric-covered welting, is available in a variety of styles and colors. A welt tape, or lip, is attached to decorative cord for sewing into a seam. From the right side of the welting, the inner edge of the tape in not visible. Be sure to attach the welting with the right side facing out.

1. Pin the welting to the curtain fabric, right sides together, with the cord ½" (1.3 cm) from the raw edge of the fabric and the ends extending 1" (2.5 cm) beyond the starting and stopping points.

2. Remove the stitching from the welting tape for about 1½" (3.8 cm) at the ends.

3. Turn the welting tape into the seam allowance and pin or tape it in place. Turn the untwisted cords into the seam allowance, following the pattern of the twist and flattening them as much as possible.

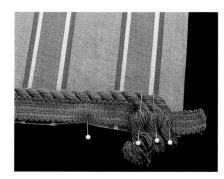

4. Stitch the welting to the fabric ½" (1.3 cm) from the raw edge, using a zipper foot and crowding the cord. Trim the ends of the cord.

Decorator fringes

Fringes that have a decorative heading should be sewn, glued, or fused onto the right side of the curtain. Those that have a plain heading should be sewn into a seam, encasing the heading so only the fringe is exposed.

In the photograph, numbers identify the following types of fringe:

Brush fringe (1) is a dense row of threads all cut to the same length. When you buy it in the store, the cut ends of the threads are secured with a chain stitch, which should be left in until you complete the

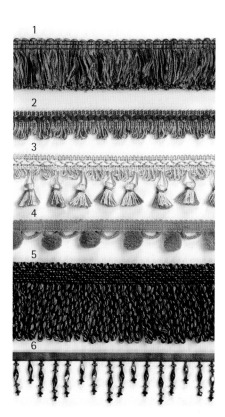

project. After pulling out the chain stitch, fluff out the fringe by steaming and gentle brushing. Cut fringe has a decorative heading and is similar to brush fringe but not usually as dense. The threads are often multicolored.

Loop fringe (2) is made with a decorative heading. The fringe is a series of overlapping looped threads that can be the same or different lengths.

Tassel fringe (3) is a continuous row of miniature tassels attached to a decorative heading.

Ball fringe (4) is a continuous row of pom-poms hanging from a plain heading. Similar to the popular craft trim, decorator ball fringe is more ornate.

Bullion fringe (5) is a row of twisted cords attached to a decorative heading. Styles vary in length and weight with single-color or multi-colored cords. Cotton bullion fringe is casual, while rayon or acetate bullion fringes are very elegant.

Beaded fringes (6) are very chic. They are available in many styles; some resemble cut, loop, or ball fringes but are made with hundreds of beads in all sorts of shapes, sizes, and colors.

Terms to Know

Bias. Any diagonal line intersecting the lengthwise and crosswise grains of fabric. While woven fabric is very stable on the lengthwise and crosswise grains, it has stretch on the bias.

Buckram. Stiffened fabric that gives support to the headings of pleated draperies. Available in the decorating department of fabric stores, it comes on a roll in a standard width of 4" (10 cm). It is also available, though sometimes harder to find, in 5" and 6" (12.7 and 15 cm) widths for making draperies with deeper headings. You can purchase the length you need. Because cut edges of buckram will not fray, it is also useful for making templates for marking the pleats and spaces.

Clearance. The distance between the back of the rod or treatment and the wall or under-treatment, measured at the front and sides. There must be enough clearance so the layers of the window treatment do not interfere with each other.

Crosswise grain. On woven fabrics, the crosswise grain is perpendicular to the selvages. Fabric has slight "give" in the crosswise grain.

Cut length. The total length at which fabric pieces should be cut for the treatment. It includes allowances for any hems, headings, rod pockets, and ease.

Cut width. The total width the fabric should be cut. If more than one width of fabric is needed, the cut width refers to the entire panel after seams are sewn, including allowances for any side hems.

Finish. To improve the durability of a seam, the raw edges are secured with stitches that prevent them from fraying. This can be done with zigzag stitches that wrap over the edge or with serging.

Finished length. The total length of a treatment after it is sewn.

Finished width. The total width of the treatment after it is sewn, including the depth of the returns.

Flounce. An extra-long heading sewn at the top of a rod-pocket curtain that falls forward over the rod pocket.

Fullness. The finished width of a treatment compared to the length of the rod or mounting board. For example, two times fullness means that the width of the fabric is two times the length of the rod.

Heading. The portion at the top of a rod-pocket treatment that forms a ruffle when the treatment is on the rod. The depth of the heading is the distance from the finished upper edge to the top stitching line for the rod pocket.

Interlining. A layer of fabric encased between the top fabric and the lining to prevent light from shining through or to add body to the treatment.

Lengthwise grain. On woven fabrics, the lengthwise grain runs parallel to the selvages. Fabrics are generally stronger along the lengthwise grain.

Lining. A fabric backing sewn to the face fabric to provide extra body, protection from sunlight, and support for side hems.

Miter. A square corner is made by joining two pieces with a seam at a 45-degree angle.

On-grain. When the lengthwise and crosswise yarns in woven fabric are perfectly perpendicular to each other. If the fabric is not on-grain as it is printed, it will be impossible to match up the pattern or to have a treatment that hangs evenly with straight-cut lower edges.

Overlap. On traversing draperies, the panels lap over each other at the center. The standard overlap distance is 3½" (9 cm).

Pattern repeat. The lengthwise distance from one distinctive point in the fabric pattern to the same point in the next pattern design.

Projection. The distance a rod or mounting board stands out from a wall.

Railroading. Normally the lengthwise grain of the fabric runs vertically in a window treatment. Since decorator fabric is usually 54" (137 cm) wide, treatments that are wider than this must have vertical seams joining additional widths of fabric. Railroading means the fabric is turned sideways, so the lengthwise grain runs horizontally. The full width can then be cut in one piece, eliminating the need for any seams.

Return. The portion of the treatment that extends from the end of the rod or mounting board to the wall, blocking the side light and view.

Rod pocket. The fabric tunnel where the curtain rod or pole is inserted. Stitching lines at top and bottom of pocket keep the rod or pole in place.

Self-lined. A fabric panel lined to the edge with the same fabric. Rather than cutting two pieces and sewing them together, one double-length piece is cut, folded right sides together, and stitched on the remaining three sides. When turned right side out, one edge will have a fold instead of a seam.

Selvage. The narrow, tightly woven edges of the fabric that do not ravel or fray. These should be cut away on firmly woven fabrics before seaming to prevent puckering of long seams. On loosely woven fabrics, the selvages should not be trimmed off because they are needed for support.

Stacking space. The distance from the sides of the window to the end brackets of the hardware that allows traversing draperies to clear or partially clear the window when draperies are open; sometimes referred to as *stackback*. About one-third of the total treatment width, this distance must be figured into the finished width of the treatment so you know what size rod to buy.

Undertreatment. A window treatment—curtains, draperies, blinds, or a shade—installed under the top treatment, either inside or outside the window frame. The undertreatment is mounted on its own hardware, independent of the top treatment.

Index